TAPE

A Radio News Handbook

by F. Gifford

MP
Morton Publishing Company
925 W. Kenyon Ave., Unit 4
Englewood, Colorado 80110

© 1987 by Morton Publishing Company

All rights reserved. No part of this publication may be reproduced, stored in a retrieval system, or transmitted, in any form or by any means, electronic, mechanical, photocopying, recording, or otherwise, without the prior written permission of the publisher.

Printed in the United States of America.

ISBN: 0-89582-163-X

—Chris Durney

One of America's most listened-to broadcasters, F. Gifford ("Frank Gentry") anchors morning-drive newscasts for the Mutual Broadcasting System in Washington, D.C. His 20-year background in radio news includes positions as News Director, anchor and reporter in Dallas, Detroit, Houston, Indianapolis, Raleigh, San Antonio and Toronto. He belongs to AFTRA and RTNDA.

For Franklin, Monique, and Sean.

Contents

Preface		v
1	**History and Philosophy of Tape**	1
	• German Technology	2
	• Magnetic Ribbon and Convenient Tape	3
	• Tape and Live Reporting on Radio	4
	• TV: A New Competitor	5
	• All-News	6
	• The Rise of FM	6
	• Deregulation	7
	• Philosophy of Tape	7
2	**Fundamentals**	9
	• How a Radio Station is Set Up	9
	• How a Board Works	10
	• Patching and Switching	11
	• Feedback	12
	• How Tape Works	12
	• Recording Basics	13
	• Tape Speeds	16
	• Tape Tracks	16
	• Cleaning and Maintenance	19
3	**Splicing Step-By-Step**	21
	• Erasing Tape	21
	• Splicing Overview	23
	• Using a Reel-to-Reel Recorder and Control Board	24
	• The 12 Steps of Splicing	25
	• Splicing Tips and Shortcuts	30
	• Marking Tape	33

- Internal Editing 35
- Splicing Speeds and Angles 36
- Tape Thicknesses and Materials 36
- Splicing Devices 37
- Splicing Materials 38
- The Ethics of Splicing 39

4 Dubbing Step-By-Step 41
- The 7 Steps of Dubbing 41
- Quality Control 44
- Generations of Dubs 47
- Electronic Splicing 47
- Carts 48
- Cart Splice-Finding 50

5 Broadcast Tape Forms and Content 51
- The Six Basic Tape Forms 51
- Actualities 52
- Q&A 54
- Voicers 54
- Voicer Variety 57
- Past Tense 58
- Present Tense 58
- Future Tense 59
- Feeding Voicers 59
- Wraparounds 61
- Amputated Wraparounds 62
- Compound Wraparounds 63
- Voice-alities 63
- Sound 65
- Montages 65
- No Tape 66

6 Telephone Newsgathering 67
- Life after Ma Bell 67
- Phone vs. On-Scene 68
- Legalities 70
- To Tape or Not to Tape? 71
- Equipment for Gathering 72
- Equalizing Tape 73
- General Phone-Gathering Tips 76
- Spot News via Phone 77
- News Conferences via Phone 78
- Overseas Calling 79
- Callbacks 79
- News Hotlines and Tipsters 80
- Opinion Lines 81

7 Telephone Feeding 83
- Equalizing Revisited 83
- How Phone Feeding is Done 84
- Building the Octopus Kit 85
- Modular Handset Feeds 87
- Modular Line Cord Feeds 87
- Alligator Clip Feeds 88
- Pay Phone Feeds 90
- Problem Phones 92
- Party Line Phones 92
- Other Useful Phone Equipment 92
- Talk-Through 93
- Mixing Without a Mixer 94
- Action Central in Your Basement 95
- Voice-Act 96
- Other Improvement Devices 97
- Frequency Extenders 98
- Feeding the Networks 99

8 Portable Recorders and Equipment 103
- Human Equipment 103
- Audio Connectors 104
- Equipment Kits 107
- Choosing a Cassette Recorder 110
- Cassettes 112
- Cassette Repairs 113
- Microcassette Recorders 114
- Microcassettes 116
- Care and Feeding of Outside Recorders 117
- Microphone Types 117
- Mike Impedance 118
- Line Level Mikes 119
- Mike Patterns 119
- Mike Systems 121
- Wind and Other Problems 121
- Batteries 122
- Mixers 123

9 Live Broadcasting and Equipment 125
- Mobile Equipment 126
- Two-Way Radios 126
- Mobile Telephones 127
- Cellular Telephones 128
- Remote Pickups 129
- Portable Equipment 130
- Walkie-Talkies 130
- Hand-Held Mobile Telephones 131

- Hand-Held Cellular Phones 131
- Hand-Held RPUs 132
- Cordless Telephones and Wireless Microphones 133
- Live Reporting Problems 133
- Live or Tape? 135
- Monitoring on Live Broadcasts 135
- Format Considerations 136
- Satellites and the Future 137

10 Reporting Situations 139
- Public Relations 139
- Free Tape 140
- News Conferences 142
- Speeches 143
- Quick Tape 145
- Late Tape 145
- Personal Interviews 146
- Tough Tape 148
- Tape-on-the-Run 149
- Legalities of On-Scene Tape 150
- Tape in Court 151
- Tape from Other Sources 152
- Canned Tape 153

11 Writing for Tape 155
- Actuality Leads 157
- Voicer and Wraparound Leads 160
- Q&A and Voice-ality Leads 161
- Sound Leads 162
- Different Leads and Dangers 163
- Hard and Throwaway Leads 163
- Multiple Cuts 164
- Tags 164
- Tape Quality 166

12 Tape Labelling, Handling and Morgue Systems 169
- Numbered Labels 169
- Informational Labels 170
- Handling Systems 171
- Elements of a Tape Morgue 175

Appendix 177
- List of equipment manufacturers

Glossary of Terms 179

Index 205

Preface

TAPE was written to fill a void. The best broadcast news textbooks deal with live and recorded audio material only superficially. We've been passing along the essence of radio news by individual instruction, much like medieval craftsmen.

TAPE starts at ground zero. It presumes no knowledge of news and no experience with any broadcast equipment. It is designed as a newsroom reference tool and college text for the U.S. and Canada. It can also be a "teach-yourself" manual if you have access to the typical equipment at a small radio station.

TAPE shows the real world of commercial radio, a world of ratings and deadlines . . . deregulation and chronic under-staffing. It explains the latest expensive state-of-the art gear *and* shows how to do news without it.

Most chapters concentrate on reporting and editing techniques, others go into journalistic content and style. TAPE shows the wide range of reporting and writing techniques that can be used for live or taped news and sports reports, depending on the story and the station's format.

Important terms are introduced in quotation marks the first time they appear. Most are in an extensive glossary after Chapter 12.

An appendix lists addresses of major equipment manufacturers. In addition the text includes Radio Shack parts numbers for minor items such as patch cords.

For generous help with this edition, I'm indebted to Sharon M. Adams, Peter Burns, Howard Dicus, Bill Groody, Peter Maer, Rosemary McCarthy Peacock, Robert Rappleye II, Craig Roberts, Mike Rogers, Joseph Slife, Oliver Smith and Bill Torrey.

I appreciate the support of Robert G. Allen, Warren Beck, Eliot Frankel and Chuck Wolf who helped make this third edition a reality.

The Library of Congress and FCC Library provided valued research help. Additional material came from the Canadian Radio-television and

Telecommunications Commission, the National Association of Broadcasters, the National Radio Broadcasters Association and the Radio-Television News Directors Association.

Many people both in and out of the profession helped with two earlier editions which form the basis for this one. Thanks again to: Bill Blanchard, Alex Burton, Bernard Cousino, Dan Cutrer, Mike Dellinger, Paul Dudeck, Lois Goldthwaite, Joe Graham, E. R. Hanson, Jack Hines, the late John Nagy, Robert Nowac, Greg Ogonowski, Nancy Perdue, Nancy Reynolds, Bill Ridenour, Joe Salvador, Robert Schuman, W. R. Sims, Jess Smith, Dick Smyth, Jack Swanson, Kris Van Cleave, Dick Wheeler, Bob Wieland and Lynn Woolley.

Thanks also to stations, nets and colleges that answered survey questions about their likes, dislikes, equipment and news practices. Hundreds of U.S., Canadian and Mexican stations contributed, indirectly, by allowing me to tour their operations over the years.

Opinions and value judgments are solely my own. They do not necessarily represent the policies or standards of any news organization.

F. Gifford
Washington DC, 1987

1 | History and Philosophy Of Tape

(Edward R. Murrow) believed, and always would believe that radio was a more useful and serious means of communication (than television), and he frequently said that a commentator had no need to be seen, only to be heard.
—Alexander Kendrick, in *Prime Time*

Magnetic recording began in 1893. A Danish telephone engineer-turned-inventor, named Valdemar Poulsen, began work on a wire recording cylinder. By 1900, he had taken out the first patent on his "Telegraphone" and was trying to market it in the U.S. That cumbersome device used steel piano wire wound around a brass drum. Maximum recording time was one minute.

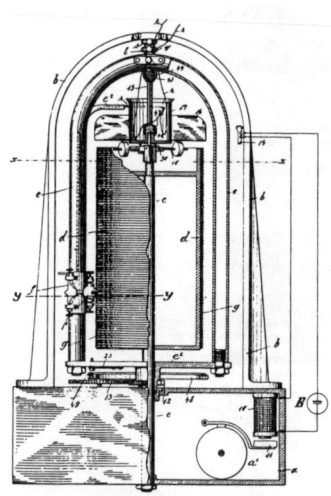

The original "Telegraphone" as disclosed in patent information. The recording head (figure "Y") moved up and down the cylinder . . . putting magnetic impulses on the piano wire.

But also by 1900, Thomas Edison had been working on his phonograph for 25 years. It cost less, and played longer. And commercially-recorded discs, or records, were already available for it. So the "Telegraphone" fizzled.

German Technology

Magnetic recording didn't really attract much interest until the early 1930s. Then, the Nazis discovered military uses for it. By 1932, the German firm BASF had plastic recording tape available. As early as 1934, the Germans had a steel-tape machine in use, in a radio station. By 1935, the Nazis had a plastic tape containing magnetic particles, allowing longer playing time and far superior quality. And by 1941, several German-built "Magnetophone" tape recorders were being used in German-controlled radio stations.

This is the machine that started the American tape-recording industry. Ampex Project Engineer Harold Lindsay (shown here) developed the Model 200 in the late 1940s, based on the Nazi "Magnetophone." —*Courtesy Ampex*

Magnetic Ribbon and Convenient Tape

Recorders didn't start appearing in American radio stations until after World War Two. The first broadcast-quality American machines were Ampexes, modeled after the German-built Magnetophones. Several of the Nazi machines were shipped back when the Allies liberated Germany. American recorder technology today can be traced to them.

Improved wire recorders were produced for a few years, but faded out soon after 3M Company (the "Scotch Tape" people) began producing what was then known as "magnetic ribbon."

Entertainer Bing Crosby is responsible for bringing the tape recorder into American radio. It was through his efforts that ABC bought 12 Ampex machines in 1947 (at $5,200. each) to start the tape revolution in this country. In a few months, all the Crosby shows were recorded and edited on tape, rather than by cumbersome discs.

The first "splicing block," used to edit tape, dates from 1949.

Portable recorders have been around since the late 1940s. Some early ones were wind-up models, others used batteries. By 1954, the technology was good enough that a "pocket" tape recorder was on the market.

—*Courtesy Cousino Corporation*

The first self-contained, continuous loops of tape resembled typewriter ribbons, with a dangling loop that had to be threaded. Work on the original tape cartridge (the "Fidelipac") began in 1953, and this revolutionary unit was on the market four years later. It made taped inserts in newscasts not only possible, but practical.

News took another quantum jump in the mid-1960s, when Norelco/Philips introduced miniature cassettes and portable cassette recorders for outside news coverage.

Since then, we've had several improvements in electronic communication, allowing us to feed "broadcast quality" tape, live, from remote places. And new improvements in existing equipment promise to improve tape quality, and to make our life easier, as well.

Tape and Live Reporting on Radio

At the very beginning, radio was a news medium. Some say the first newscast dates to 1909 when an experimental station (that later became KCBS) started in San Jose, California. Canada's first station, CFCF/Montreal, signed on in 1919 and one of its first regular programs was "the weather."

In 1920, station 8MK in Detroit (later WWJ) signed on, with election returns. And, in Pittsburgh, Westinghouse engineers rigged a low-powered transmitter to broadcast the 1920 Presidential election. That station has since grown into 50,000 watt KDKA.

At first, radio relied on newspapers for coverage. All three wire services in existence at that time refused to sell their product to radio. To counteract this, radio pioneers began to use the unique potential of their infant

This is what a live report involved in 1939. The reporter is relaying sound from his microphone through the back-pack to the "mobile unit" in the background. From there, it was beamed to the studios. Portable recording equipment available at the time was primitive. —*Courtesy WWJ/Detroit*

By the late '50s, many stations, like WXLW/Indianapolis, had reporters "cruising" for news. They could do live reports through the "two-way" radios in their cars. And portable recorders were also available.

medium—sound. They began doing sporadic reports from the scene of news events. This "live" reporting has since grown into the practice of using taped inserts, or "tape," in newscasts.

As radio grew, chains of stations were organized. NBC was established in 1926, and eventually had two networks—the Red and Blue. In 1927, CBS went on the air. The forerunner of MBS, or Mutual, started in 1934. ABC was established in 1944 from the old NBC Blue Network.

Before the war, American radio started to make large use of live "on-scene" coverage of feature stories. Things like tulip festivals, gypsy singers, and even a "Singing Mouse Convention" (on NBC) were broadcast from overseas. In those days, when the great bulk of programming was provided by the networks, recording the material was strictly forbidden. Even reports from across the ocean were done "live" through complicated, unreliable telephone and short-wave hookups.

Edward R. Murrow and other World War Two-era correspondents made on-scene reports into a radio institution. Their stories from Europe before and during the Second World War brought radio into the forefront as a swift, serious news medium, rather than one that merely scalped newspapers and wire-service stories. Many people still vividly remember listening to the live reports from overseas—complete with technical difficulties—that brought the war into their living rooms.

The ridiculous "no-recording rules" were relaxed in the final years of the war . . . then discarded entirely.

TV: A New Competitor

In the early 1950s, television created giant shock waves that are still being felt. Nearly all the shows that had made radio popular began moving to TV.

Until this era, most radio stations were "block programmed" as most television stations are today. They had a soap opera, followed by a variety show, followed by something else. When television grabbed the big-name entertainment, a few stations resorted to playing hit rock-and-roll records, interspersed with an upbeat host or "disc jockey."

To fit this format, known as "Top-40" the news was often flamboyant. In 1959, KBOX/Dallas opened its newscast this way:

"From every point in the universe, instant news coverage!"

There were other "formats"—or station sounds—developed. But to this day most still offer the same elements (in varying proportions). They are: music; a host; and capsulized news that is supposed to fit the station's overall sound.

All-News

By the early 1960s, specialization in news had begun. North America's first "all-news" station was actually licensed to Tijuana, Mexico—but put its signal over Southern California. XETRA, operated by the late Gordon McLendon, was a "rip-and-read" operation. News came straight from the "wire services"—AP and UPI. There were no outside reporters.

Group-W, Westinghouse Broadcasting, greatly expanded and improved the concept when it launched its first all-news station, WINS/New York, in 1965. WINS had reporters in the field and some in radio-equipped news vehicles.

In 1975 NBC launched an all-news network. NIS—the "News and Information Service"—failed within two years because of high costs and few affiliates.

In the 1980s, Ted Turner launched the second all-news network, "CNN Radio," based largely on his already-operating service for cable TV.

The Rise of FM

Throughout the 1950s and even until the late-60s, the FM band languished with very little except background music and classical music stations. Some AM stations would "simulcast" their programming on FM to maintain the FM license, but there were virtually no listeners.

By 1970 or so, "underground" or "progressive rock" stations brought a new audience to FM. Then, other formats based on the same music-host-news mix took hold. With better fidelity, stereo sound, and a lack of commercials—FM gradually became dominant.

But FM grew up without a news tradition. Very few FM stations had any use for information—and most prospered with just a token effort to satisfy the U.S. government's regulators, the "Federal Communications Commission" or "FCC."

Additional FM competition, and changing tastes in society, led to increased specialization throughout the 70s and 80s. In some markets, FM growth doubled the number of stations competing for a mass-audience in the "ratings." Many AM stations, their ratings and profits under pressure, cut back on outside news reporting and shortened newscasts.

Deregulation

U.S. government regulation kept many radio stations marginally in the news business until the early 1980s. To get and keep their FCC license—they had to commit themselves to airing some news. But frequently this was done from midnight to 5 AM, while the station played nearly-solid music (and commercials) during the day.

Beginning in the 1980s the process of "deregulation" eased requirements on stations. Some dropped their token news operations entirely. Many cut back.

The bottom line now is that radio news must pay its own way—in ratings and revenue. It must fit within the overall station sound. It must interest and relate to an audience which may be listening for music or entertainment. Of course, on an *all*-news station the product must be good enough to stand alone.

Philosophy of Tape

Get a dozen newspeople together and you may get a dozen ideas of "news" and what is or is not "newsworthy." But here's a broad definition most could endorse:

> "News is information. It's anything interesting, important and previously unknown to your audience."

Tape adds impact to news. Frequently, tape *is* the news—it goes beyond illustration and forms the story itself. Tape can be a dramatic contrast to the sound of prepared copy written by newspeople. If you get people *themselves* talking on the air or get a reporter to the scene, you can make the story more interesting and relevant to your audience.

You gather *news* and *tape* at the same time and in the same way—by asking questions with a tape recorder on, or by simply being somewhere with a cassette machine running.

"The Magic of Radio" —*Courtesy RCA*

The premise of this book is: All good radio news operations produce tape. Just as all successful TV news operations get pictures, and all successful newspapers get quotes, we get the voices, words, sounds and emotions.

Nothing seems to happen through the "Magic of Radio" any more. The old Atwater-Kent or Crosley set in the living room has been replaced by a color television.

But we still have some advantages over other media. One is speed— we're still faster. Another is brevity—because we deal only in sound, stories have to be reduced to interesting essentials. Perhaps the biggest advantage of all is tape.

Because of the relative ease of gathering, feeding, and using tape cuts on the air, we're able to do far more with on-scene reports than any other medium. Our possibilities for *live* reports are immense.

The "Magic of Radio" is still available for use.

Although the first part of this book will deal with the technical and mechanical processes of *recorded* news, the reporting techniques outlined later are equally valid for *live* news.

The best operations do a lot of both.

2 | Fundamentals

> ... no one has a higher calling in an increasingly complex free society bent on self-government than he who informs and moves the people. ...
> —Former FCC Commissioner Nicholas Johnson
> in *How to Talk Back to Your Television Set.*

How a Radio Station is Set Up

All radio stations use much the same equipment, and most are arranged similar to this:

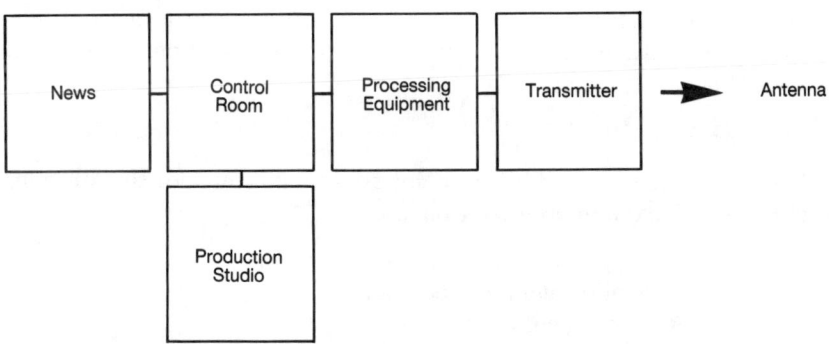

Nearly all stations have a "control board" which is used to mix sound (known to us as "audio") from different sources. In a conventional music-and-news station, for example, there may be two or more boards. One would be operated by the air personality and the other would be in the "news studio." This typical arrangement is shown above. It is possible to have several more boards wired in. A larger station might have half-a-dozen studios. A station with a large news operation might have boards in the newsroom that are wired in to the news studio.

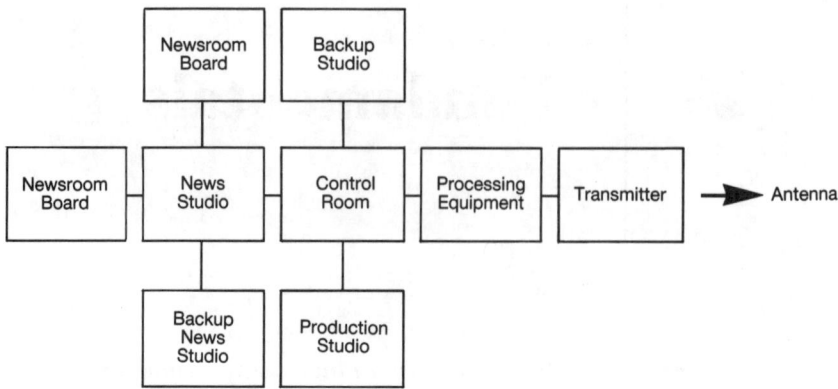

Typically, the air personality (or an engineer in union operations) will control which board is "hot" and thus "on-the-air."

The signal goes from the main board to processing equipment. The simplest processors merely keep high levels from overloading the "transmitter." More sophisticated processing equipment will clean-up and condition the sound.

At the transmitter, sound is combined with a carrier signal that puts it on the station's authorized frequency or "dial position." Both are then fed into the antenna system. Ironically, "frequency response" is pretty comparable on AM and FM transmitters. There are several reasons why AM doesn't sound as good—the main one is low quality in typical AM radios.

How a Board Works

A typical news studio board might contain controls for the following audio sources (explained in later chapters):

- News studio microphone
- Reel-to-reel tape recorder
- Cart machine(s)
- Network
- Auxiliary

All routinely-used audio sources are wired into the board and each appears on a separate volume control device. Some are rotary controls known as a "potentiometer," "pot" or "gain control." Other boards include straight-line controls commonly called "faders" or "slide pots." Both do the same thing equally well.

Fundamentals

Volume is raised or lowered to produce appropriate "modulation" levels. For our purposes—this is the same as "loudness." Modulation will be indicated either on a "VU meter" (short for Volume Units) or on a series of lights known as "LEDs" (short for Light-Emitting Diodes). With either, the aim is to keep your loudest material, known as "peaks," between 80 and 100%. There's no problem if the volume *occasionally* shoots beyond 100%.

But modulation that is consistently above 100% ("over-modulation") may sound muffled and unnatural. We call this "distortion."

Modulation that is too low ("under-modulation") may be lost in noise, and difficult for listeners to hear. Or processing equipment may try to raise the level, typically also raising noise.

No matter whether the station is AM or FM, rock or Bach, you want to deliver a consistently clean, properly modulated product to the transmitter.

Patching and Switching

While boards contain wired audio sources that are used frequently, most stations have provisions for *temporary* electronic connections. These are known as "patch panels" or electronic "routing switchers." They can be used at several places in the "audio chain" from studio to transmitter.

In news, for example, they allow infrequently used audio sources to be "patched" into an auxiliary pot or fader on the board. The switchers create an electronic patch through push-button or "thumbwheel" controls.

Learning operation of this equipment is simple. Make sure you understand the labels that may be heavily-abbreviated on patch panels.

Eight-channel board in news studio. Note remote starts for carts, etc., located below board. A well-marked patch panel is at the upper left. Control room is through glass. —*Courtesy KSL/Salt Lake City*

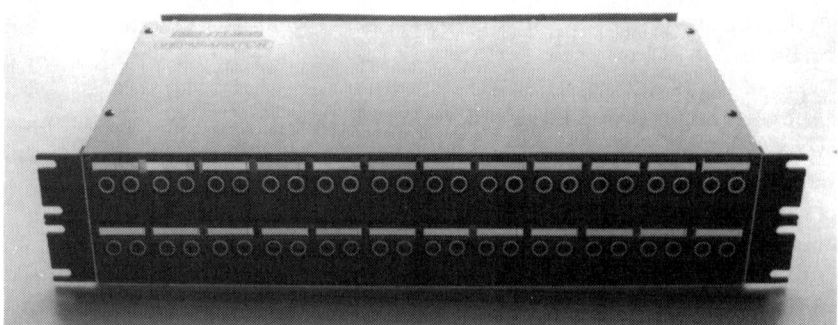

A typical patch panel with two jacks per circuit. Some use only one.
—Courtesy Gentner Engineering

Feedback

Now is a good time to go over the phenomenon called "feedback" . . . before you have a chance to cause it. It's a loud high-pitched howling noise or strange reverberation produced when sound circulates rapidly through a tape recorder, board, microphone, or even over the station's air signal.

Feedback can damage speakers, VU meters and transmitters and must be stopped immediately!

If you get it in a recording situation, chances are the tape recorder's pot on the board has been left "on." Thus, the original sound source is immediately fed through the recorder back into the board, and then to the recorder where the process is repeated again.

To kill feedback—turn off all pots on the board (not just the speaker control). Then start over and figure out what you did wrong. Chances are, the reel-to-reel recorder was playing through the board—creating your feedback.

How Tape Works

All magnetic tape consists of rust, or metal particles, glued to a strip of plastic. As crude as that sounds, it's the basis for modern recording technology. The rust is actually a highly-developed product known as "oxide." It's produced under exacting quality-control conditions. The tiny needle-shaped oxide particles act like tiny magnets. When a strong magnetic charge is brushed against them, they line up in a certain order. They remember the magnetic charge, and stay in that position for replaying.

Tape comes in different forms, and it contains different ingredients. But all tape does the same job—storing magnetic impulses for later use. The device that rearranges the oxide particles is called a "tape recorder." It simply converts sound energy to electrical energy, and then to magnetic energy. If you've ever looked inside a tape recorder, you realize that's not as easy as it sounds.

Basically all recorders use electricity to produce a magnetic charge in the "heads." The heads brush against the moving tape, forcing the oxide or metal particles into line. Then, later, the recorder uses another head to translate or "playback" the tape's magnetic impulses. The process is just the opposite. The magnetic energy is converted into electrical energy, then back into sound energy.

It's important to remember that *all* recorders and *all* forms of tape do the very same thing. The different types available enable us to use the best one for a particular job.

Highly-magnified oxide particles show up like little needles. —*Courtesy Maxell*

Recording Basics

There are three types of recording tape. Each has an advantage and a use in radio news. The first is "reel-to-reel tape," which is wound on plastic or metal reels. Tape passes from the "supply" (or "feed") reel, over the recording and playback mechanism of a tape recorder, and onto the "take-up" reel. In this form the tape is very accessible.

The second type of tape is called a "cassette." It's a miniature reel-to-reel system, completely enclosed in plastic. With this type, there's no need to thread the tape over the recording and playback mechanism. You simply pop a cassette into a recorder, press a button or two and begin recording. The cassette is the most convenient tape for use in outside-the-station news coverage. Its simplicity eliminates most chances for human error. (A smaller version, the "Microcassette," operates the same way and works with a smaller recorder.)

A Typical Reel-to-Reel Recorder

1 — Supply (Feed) Reel
2 — Take-up Reel
3 — Idler Wheel ("Lollypop")
4 — Head Cover
5 — Typical Erase Head location
6 — Typical Record Head location
7 — Typical Playback Head location
8 — Capstan
9 — Pinch Roller ("Pressure Roller" or "Puck")
10 — Machine Controls

—Courtesy LJ Scully

Fundamentals

The third type of tape operates on a different principle. It's called a "cartridge" or a "cart" for short. It's a continuous loop of tape, that uses only one reel. Tape is drawn from the center, passed over the record and playback mechanism, then fed onto the outside of the reel. Standard-sized carts can be wound with different lengths of tape, good for ten seconds to more than ten minutes worth of recording. After a cart is played, it will automatically continue running until the same portion of tape is in position over the playback mechanism. It then shuts off, ready to play again.

A cart uses only one reel of tape. It is spliced (joined together) at one point to form a continuous loop. —*Courtesy Fidelipac*

Nearly all tape used in radio news today is transferred to cart for actual use on the air. Reason is, the tape is ready to go at the touch of a button. It does not need to be re-wound after use.

All forms of recording tape (whether reel-to-reel, cassette, or cartridge) store magnetic impulses. They're imprinted by the recording head of a tape machine, and played back, appropriately enough, on the playback head.

During recording on reel and cassette machines, *both* the erase and record heads are in use.

Some reel recorders only have two heads. In this case, the one on the *left* will be the erase head. The one on the *right* will serve for both record and playback. Most professional broadcast recorders, however, have three heads.

Reel-to-reel tape is wound with the recording (or oxide) side facing inward. It used to be that the oxide side was always "dull" and the other side "shiny." But with some of today's newer tapes, both sides look "dull".

Tape Speeds

Most reel-to-reel recording for radio is done at 7½ inches per second. This means 7½ inches of tape pass over the record and playback mechanism every second. Slower speeds (3¾ and 1⅞ ips) mean lowered sound quality, and more difficulty in splicing.

Recording high-frequency sounds on tape is what's difficult, and this requires lots of tape passing by the heads. In other words—a faster speed. And, also, for splicing you don't want the words all scrunched together.

If somebody said the title of this book, and you recorded it at 1⅞ ips, here's how it would look and how much space it would occupy:

> koobdnaH sweN oidaR A :EPAT

(Of course you can't actually *see* the words, but they are backward compared to our written language.) At 3¾ ips the title will occupy a space *twice* as long. And at 7½ ips (the speed we commonly use for splicing) it will be *four-times* as long. Some machines are equipped with an even faster speed of 15 ips. This makes for very easy splicing because the title would stretch across two feet of tape!

Cassettes operate at one standard speed, 1⅞ inches per second (some machines have an additional speed, either ¹⁵⁄₁₆ ips or 3¾ ips). The standard speed for carts is 7½ ips.

A basic newsroom edit station for recording telephone interviews, dubbing cassette interviews and network material onto cart. A wall-phone is immediately left of the board-mounted VU meter. On the desk below is a typewriter. —*Courtesy WGAR/Cleveland*

Tape Tracks

Many reel-to-reel recorders used in radio news have a "full track," also known as a "single track." They record over the full width of the tape, and only one thing can be recorded at any one point on the tape.

Fundamentals

Some machines operate on the "two-track" (or "half track") system. This means that when you're finished recording on one side of the tape, you can reverse reels and record on the other side.

Cassette recorders use the two-track system. When the cassette has run out of tape on the first side, it can be flipped over and reinserted for more recording time.

Cartridges used in radio news have two tracks. One contains the "sound" you hear. The other track is used for the tones that tell the cart machine when to shut-off, and so on.

To make things "perfectly clear":

Tape type	Speed	Track(s)	Use in Radio
Reel	various 1⅞ to 15 ips	generally one	studio recording and splicing for air-use
Cassette	1⅞ ips	two	outside coverage
Cartridge	7½ ips	one-audio one-machine cues	on-air

Tape Tracks:

Full Track (Single Track).
Uses entire width in single recording. Found on many professional reel-to-reel machines.

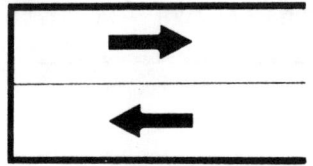

Two Track (Half Track).
Uses half of tape, recording in each direction. Found on cassette recorders, some reel-to-reel machines.

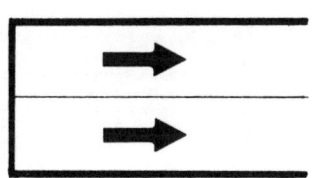

Two Track (Half Track).
Both record in same direction at same time. One contains audio, other has tones for machine functions. Found *only* on cart machines.

Table of Recording Times for Reel-to-Reel:

Reel	Tape Thickness	Tape Length	Name	Playing time per side at: 15 ips	7½ ips	3¾ ips
10½"	1½ mil	2400 ft.	Standard	30 min	60 min	120 min
10½"	1 mil	3600 ft.	Extra Play	45 min	90 min	180 min
10½"	less than 1 mil	4800 ft.	Double Play	60 min	120 min	240 min
7"	1½ mil	1200 ft.	Standard	15 min	30 min	60 min
7"	1 mil	1800 ft.	Extra Play	22½ min	45 min	90 min
7"	more than ½ mil	2400 ft.	Double Play	30 min	60 min	120 min
7"	½ mil	3600 ft.	Triple Play	45 min	90 min	180 min
5"	1½ mil	600 ft.	Standard	7½ min	15 min	30 min
5"	1 mil	900 ft.	Extra Play	11¼ min	22½ min	45 min
5"	more than ½ mil	1200 ft.	Double Play	15 min	30 min	60 min
5"	½ mil	1800 ft.	Triple Play	22½ min	45 min	90 min

For Cassettes:

Divide label designation (such as C-60) in half.
Result is minutes-per-side.

For Carts:

Frequently stamped on side.
Otherwise, look directly down at cart thorugh clear top, and compare amount of tape in center, with cart of known length.

Fundamentals

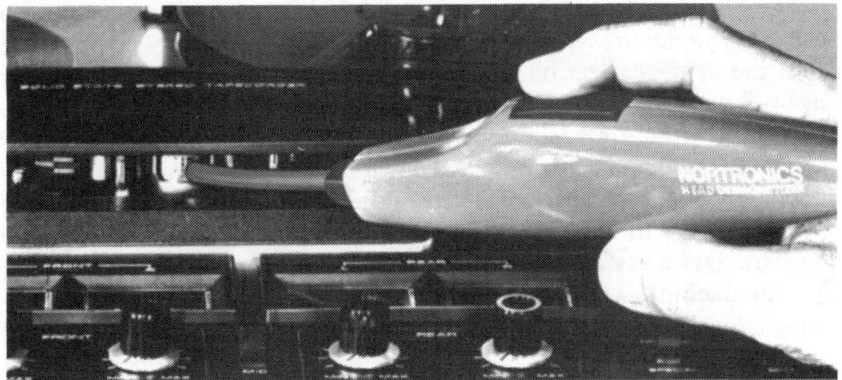

Demagnetizing the heads of a tape recorder.   —*Courtesy Nortronics*

Cleaning and Maintenance

Several routine maintenance chores are common to all types of tape recorders. Regular maintenance not only preserves the machine, it helps it function at peak efficiency.

All recorders need to have the heads, guides, pinch roller, and capstan cleaned every day when they're in constant use. If you thoroughly clean a recorder each day before it's used, that's generally all that's needed. But keep an especially close watch on the playback head of a reel machine being used for splicing. If marking material coagulates on the head, clean it *immediately!* The crud can be transferred to the tape, and foul other parts of the machine.

There are several commercially-concocted cleaning preparations on the market now. But regular old drug store alcohol does a good job, at far less cost. The "denatured" alcohol works best, and can be used on any metal or rubber part. A chemical called "Xylene" (pronounced: ZY-lene) also does a good job. But it cannot be used on rubber parts, such as the pinch roller. The key factor isn't the chemical you use, it's how often and how thoroughly you use it. Cotton swabs are the easiest way to apply the cleaning agent. You can use sterilized "Q-Tips" available at any drug store, or buy some cotton swabs, that aren't sterilized, from an electronics shop.

The other maintenance chore that can be performed by newspeople is demagnetization. Ideally, this should also be done once a week, but generally isn't. Heads build up what is known as "residual magnetism" when they're in regular use. This can mean some loss in quality, because of extraneous magnetic forces in the head, and on metal parts.

Small demagnetizers, made for the purpose, simply plug into the wall. *Always demagnetize with the recorder's AC or battery power OFF!* Turn the demagnetizer on a couple of feet away, then gradually bring it in, over the heads, and other metal parts. Come as close as you can to the metal, without actually touching it. You'll feel the magnetic force.

Move the demagnetizer up and down the heads, several times, before moving on to another part. Clean even the stainless steel parts that come into contact with the tape. When you've finished, gradually bring the demagnetizer away from the machine—before turning it off.

All machines—reel, cart, and cassette—should get this same maintenance. Cassette machines should also receive regular checks of their battery condition.

Any other work on your machine falls under the category of "repairs" rather than "maintenance." Unless you're experienced enough to make the repairs, they're best left to a qualified engineer.

3 | Splicing Step-By-Step

One of the more imprecise things in the world is the printed word. There is no comparison between language spoken versus language printed. Listen to language and see how words are being used and what a difference emphasis makes. . . . There are no adequate compensations, no matter how many italics you use.

—Frank Zappa, interview with
Dallas Times-Herald, 1975

This chapter explains the mechanics of tape editing through your recording of a 10-word sentence. It also introduces the operation of a control board and related equipment—and how they work.

You'll need a 7" reel of tape (it can be only partially full), and we'll start the process by getting this tape ready for recording.

Erasing Tape

One of the beauties of magnetic tape is that it can be used and re-used, countless times. Erasing (or "demagnetizing") is a simple process. It's not possible to *over*erase tape.

Bulk-erasers differ radically in design and strength. There are three main types.

Typically, *heavy-duty* erasers include a conveyor belt that moves tape over the magnetic field. After the first pass, turn the tape over and run it down the belt again. Grab it before it falls off—and *gradually* pull it three-feet away from the bulk-eraser before turning off the power. (Erasers generate a magnetic field, and keeping the tape on the unit could leave some noise.)

A razor blade will be pulled to a magnetically "active" area of the medium duty bulk-eraser when it is turned on.

Medium-duty bulk-erasers are almost as easy to use.

Drop a razor-blade on your unit, then turn the thing on. You'll see the blade scoot over to one area, then hover there—pulled by magnetic forces. A bulk-eraser is simply an electromagnet—in a protective housing. The spot where the blade hovered is where you'll get the maximum erasing power. Your tape should always be passed over this area. On some units, there may be areas of the erasing surface that are virtually "dead" and provide almost no erasing power.

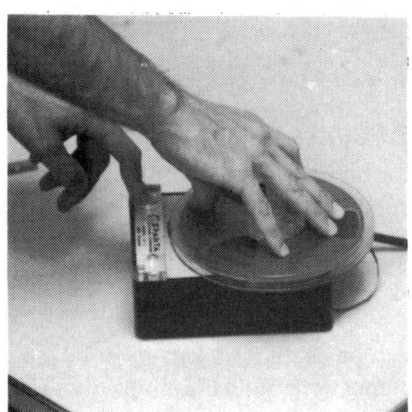   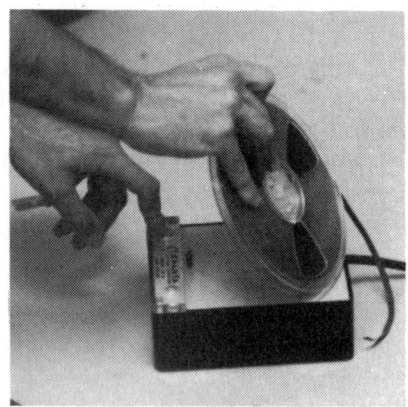

Rotating tape on the first side.   Turning tape over, with the unit *on*.

Reel tape should be put on the eraser, the power turned on, then the tape rotated through two complete turns. (The rotations should take two or three-seconds apiece.) Then—with the eraser still *on*—turn the tape over, and repeat the process. Finally, leave the eraser on, pick up the tape, and bring it three-feet away from the unit. Shut off the power, and you have a clean, noiseless tape. Remember to demagnetize the razor blade you tested, in this same way, so it doesn't put noise on tape.

A typical hand-held bulk eraser. The side button is depressed and held while the eraser is slowly wiped over the tape. *—Courtesy Nortronics*

Hand-held bulk erasers are rotated while the tape remains stationary. Generally, they are less powerful than other erasers and have a shorter "duty cycle."

On most bulk-erasers you'll find the duty cycle imprinted somewhere (perhaps on the side or bottom). This tells you how long the unit can be operated, continuously. Some small units can't take more than a minute of constant use, before they need time to cool down.

The same erasing techniques are used for the other types of tape.

Cassettes take virtually no effort. Put them on the unit for a few seconds, turn them over, then bring them three-feet away before shutting off the eraser.

Carts are handled the same way. They require two or three passes (or wipes) on top and bottom, then a couple of passes on the open end, where the tape is exposed. Be careful not to grind the plastic into the machine—you just need to make gentle contact with the bulk-eraser.

Erasing is especially critical for carts, because—unlike reel and cassette machines—cart machines do *not* have an erase head. Any noise left on cart after erasing will be on your produced cut as a "bloop-bloop" sound.

Splicing Overview

Producing good news tape involves the art of "splicing." It's nothing more than cutting out noise, stumbles, pregnant pauses, and other flaws. All splicing is done on reel-to-reel tape since, as noted, it's the most accessible.

Doing a haphazard splicing job is easy. But truly professional results often take several tries, and a cool temper. You'll find splicing is easier, if your hands are relatively clean. Skin oils, mayonnaise, and grime . . . along with thousands of other things . . . can harm the tape, and cause a splice to come un-stuck. You'll also find it easier to handle tape, if your fingernails are fairly short.

The most common splicing devices are grooved metal blocks, used with a single-edge razor blade. The original "EdiTall" brand dates from 1950. Others are now on the market and all are essentially the same.

Just a word about miscellaneous equipment. Beside the splicing block you will also need some 7/32-inch splicing tape, a grease-pencil (sometimes called a "China Marker"), and a sharp single-edge razor blade.

Scotch and a number of other manufacturers produce the splicing tape. Blaisdell and Dixon are the most common brands of grease-pencils . . . yellow and white show up best on tape. You should be able to find them at stationery or office-supply stores.

Never use regular cellophane tape, or any other kind of adhesive tape to make a splice. All of them have a very sticky glue, which can coat other layers of tape, as well as the recorder heads and mechanism. Use only splicing tape for splicing . . . it's specially designed for the purpose.

We'll assume you're using a reel machine designed for broadcast, which allows sound reproduction even though the machine is not in *play*. The most convenient models include an *Edit* button which frees up the tape reels, allowing them to be moved by hand.

Perhaps you are learning in a well-equipped studio with state-of-the-art equipment and detailed instructions on how everything works. Please be aware that very few newsrooms are elaborately equipped. This book concentrates on how to make-do.

Using a Reel-to-Reel Recorder and Control Board

Take the 7" reel of tape you erased, thread it on the recorder, and put the speed control switch (if any) at 7½ ips. If the recorder has a function selector knob or series of buttons (commonly located near the VU meter) put this in *Input* or *Record*.

Also near the VU meter—there may be a selector marked *Safe/Ready* or something like that. Put it in *Ready*. (The *Safe* position *prevents* recording—good to remember when you want to guard against accidental erasures.)

Assuming you have a microphone nearby connected to the tape recorder, get a "recording level" on yourself. You may be going directly into the recorder, and will need to adjust only the *Input* pot near the recorder's VU meter.

Splicing Step-By-Step

If you are using a board between the mike and recorder—you will need to make sure the pot is completely *off* for the recorder. And the pot for your mike will have to be *on*.

Speak into the mike and watch the VU meter(s). Adjust the pots so the loudest points on both meters are between 80% and 100% modulation. Going much beyond this will cause distortion.

Most tape machines are set up to record, when *both Record* and *Play* buttons are depressed. Once your machine is running, record yourself saying the following:

"(deep breath) This is a splicing test tape and I'm (your name)."

Wait a few seconds, then press *Stop* on the recorder. Put the function selector near the recorder's VU meter in *Output* or *Reproduce*. Then press the *Rewind* button, letting the tape go back to where you began your sentence. Press *Stop*.

If you are using a control board, turn off the microphone pot and raise the pot for the tape machine. Play back the tape by depressing the *Play* button. Adjust the volume level on the room speaker (or headphones, if you prefer) until it is comfortable.

Rewind again to the start of your sentence.

The 12 Steps of Splicing

We'll begin by removing the obnoxious breath before your first word. (In actual news work there will be breath noises, telephone line noises, coughing, paper-shuffling and dozens of other things before material you want.)

1. Find the start of the breath noise as it passes over the playback head. Use the machine controls (*Play, Rewind,* etc.) to get near that area of the tape. Then press *Stop* and, if you have it, *Edit*.
2. Put one hand on each reel and, moving them together, rock the tape over the start of the breath noise. You may need to do this

Backing up tape by hand.

several times. Immediately before the start of the noise, make a *light* grease-pencil mark on the outside of the tape, just right of the "contact point" on the playback head.

Marking just right of the "Contact Point".

3. Then put your hands back on both reels and move them counterclockwise. Once a few inches of tape pass over the playback head, you'll hear the first word. Again, rock back and forth to find the beginning, then mark immediately right of the playback head "contact point".

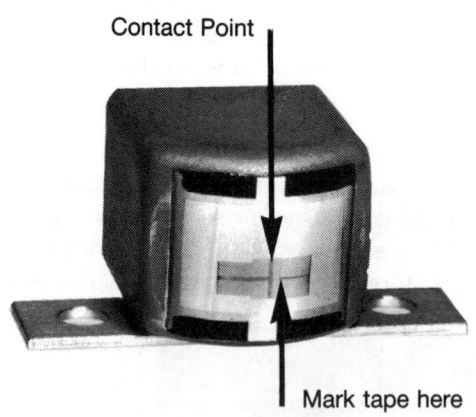

Contact Point

Mark tape here

4. Put the tape on top of the splicing block's indented channel, outside surface (with the markings) up. Once in the channel, tape can be moved with gentle fingertip pressure.
5. Align one of the grease-pencil marks on the slanted (45°) groove, not the vertical one. Glide the razor blade through the groove from back to front.

Splicing Step-By-Step

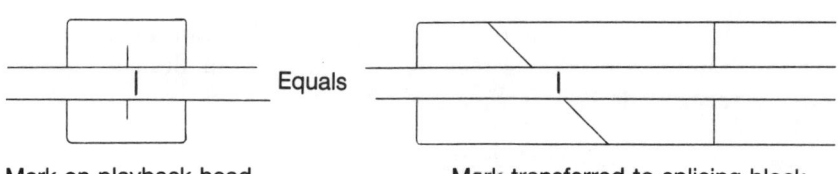

Mark on playback head.   Mark transferred to splicing block.

6. Find the other pencil mark, align and cut it the same way. Take out the tape segment that's been removed *and save it.*
7. Move the two severed tape parts to the solid part of the splicer, away from the grooves.

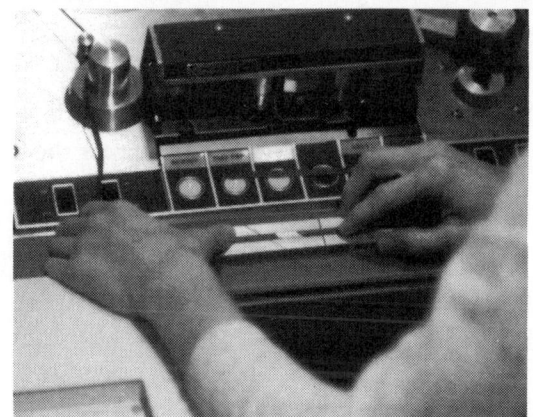

Moving the two parts together. (Note the saved tape segment just above.)

8. Join them together, so there's no gap in between.

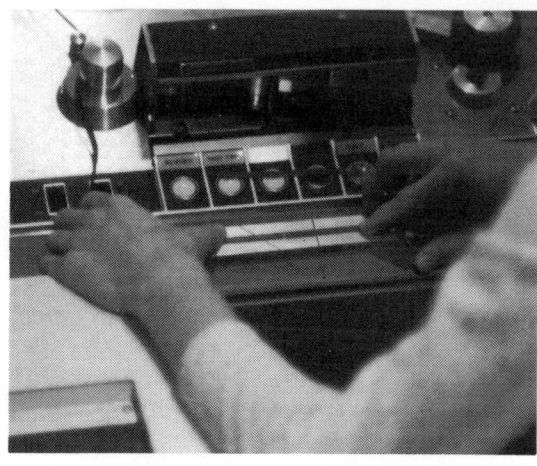

Joining the segments together.

9. Put about one-inch of splicing tape over the cut area. (You can transfer the splicing tape on your fingertip or the edge of the razor blade.)

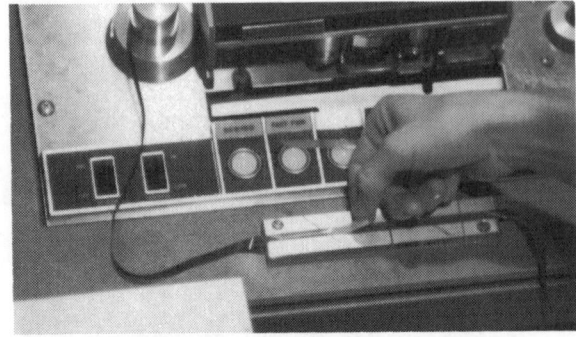

Applying splicing tape.

10. Smooth down the splicing tape with your fingernail, removing nearly all the "bubbles" under the surface.

Smoothing down the splicing tape.

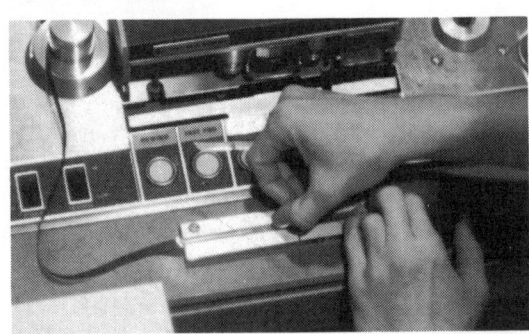

11. Remove the completed splice *gently*, by sliding the tape off to one side, rather than by pulling up.

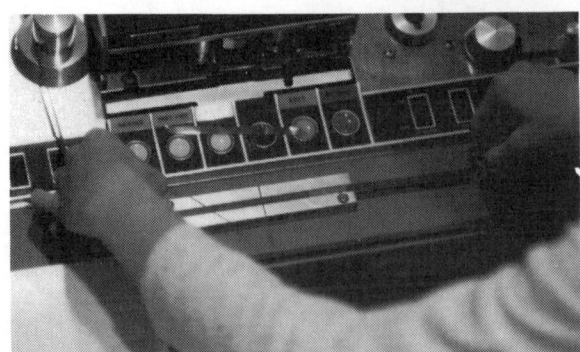

Removing the splice.

Splicing Step-By-Step

12. Put the tape on your machine and play it back. If it's not quite right, redo it.

The final test of a splice . . . playing it back.

To undo an improper splice, hold the tape *oxide* surface up and form an upside-down "U" shape. With your fingernails, grip one of the "points" created by the splice and *gently* peel back the recording tape. Then do the same to the other side. In some cases you may need to rock the tape back and forth in this inverted "U" position to loosen the points.

Never re-use splicing tape . . . get a fresh piece.

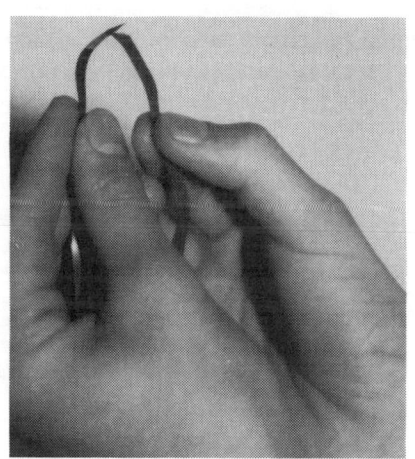

Undoing an improper splice. The oxide surface is held up, and points of the tape are peeled back.

Now, using the same sentence:

"This is a splicing test tape and I'm ---- ----"

remove the word "splicing". Use the same step-by-step procedure. Rock the tape and find the hissing sound that is the "s" at the start of "splicing". Mark right *before* it begins. Find the end of the word, which will be only a couple inches to the left.

Make your splice and listen. Again, if it's not quite right, redo it. Next—take what remains of the sentence:

"This is a test tape and I'm ---- ----"

and remove the word "test". The trick will be listening to the double "t" and cutting between "test/tape". If you slur the two words together (and many people do) you will have to cut in the middle of the sound. Remember to save all the tape you splice out—in a case like this you may need to restore some of it.

Next—if "test" is gone and you can't hear the edit, take what remains of the sentence:

"/This is a tape/and/I'm ---- ----/."

and change it into:

"I'm ---- ---- and this is a tape."

You'll need to make four editing marks, which are indicated by slashes (/) above.

This one-sentence example includes perhaps 90% of the editing techniques commonly used in news. With these basics in mind — record your own material and *practice!* Strive to get beyond the 12 steps, so editing becomes an automatic thing.

Splicing Tips and Shortcuts

Sometimes you can get by without splicing. Here's a quicker way to clean up the *beginning* of a tape cut:

1. Using the grease-pencil, mark right before the first word you want included in your cut.
2. Rewind one revolution of the supply reel.
3. Remove the tape from between the capstan and pinch roller, giving you manual control of it.
4. Turn off all audio inputs to the recorder—so it will not record anything.
5. Put the machine in *Record* (or *Record/Play*) and move the tape manually until the grease-pencil mark is on the center of the "Erase" head (which is always the far-left head on any machine). Do not go beyond!

Splicing Step-By-Step

6. Reverse your motion and wind the tape back onto the supply reel.
7. Press *Stop*. Put recorder *Input* back to normal setting and put tape back between the capstan and pinch roller.

Played back—you will have silence up to your first word, without a splice. It saves time and eliminates splice-damage to the tape.

There's a variation on this technique. On some machines you can use the *Edit* button in *Record*. The process is the same—but you don't need to remove tape from between the capstan and pinch roller.

(Still another technique, preferred by other editors, is to use a pencil-magnet. This also works well.)

You don't *always* need to make a splice before a tape cut. But unless something was recorded in a quiet studio, chances are there will be some noise before the first word, that needs to be cut off.

In the *interior* of the cut, every repairable stumble, and pregnant pause should be edited out—unless you have a valid news reason for leaving it in. The technique is the same—align, mark, slice, and splice. Make sure, when editing inside a tape cut, to allow for breathing and sentence pauses. There is a rhythm pattern to most speech, and your splicing must not disrupt it. Knowing how to handle such things takes practice, more than anything.

When editing around the consonant sounds "C," "F," "S," "X," and "Z" be especially careful. Many people elongate them in their speech.

Spend time listening to tapes at slow speed. Get to recognize the beginning and ending of words, as you manually wind tape past the heads in both forward and reverse directions. Practice cutting between words that are run together. Learn to hear the beginning of tricky letters like "F" and "S". This skill is something no instructor, and no book, can give you. It's simply a question of coordinating your ears, brain, and hands.

The splicing process is complicated at first. And it can get aggravating. But the more editing you do, the easier it gets. Honest!

If you're uncertain how much of a pause to remove, remember that you can always take out a little, then take out some more if you want. If you splice out too much, it *can* be put back in, but it's more difficult. (This is the reason for saving what you've removed from the tape.)

The *end* of a tape cut should be just as clean as the beginning, with background noise ending on the last word. But here, it may be easier to clean up, by fading the pot as you transfer your tape cut onto a cart. The volume should be faded, rapidly, *during* the last word you want included. The idea is to have the volume control all the way down, by the time the last word is completed. Once you acquire the habit, this will save time, and eliminate the need for an additional splice at the end.

But, if your speaker runs words together, you may have trouble fading in time. In this case, you use much the same erasing technique as before:

1. Mark right after the *last* word.
2. Fast-forward tape one revolution (putting marked tape on take-up reel).
3. Remove tape from between capstan/pinch roller (or use *Edit* button as explained).
4. Turn off audio inputs to recorder.
5. Put in *Record* or *Record/Play* and move tape manually until mark is centered on "Record" head. Don't go beyond!
6. Reverse motion and wind tape back on take-up reel.
7. Press *Stop*. Put recorder *Input* back to normal setting, and put tape back between capstan and pinch roller.

You should have a clean ending followed by a couple seconds of silence, allowing you plenty of time to fade after dubbing your cut.

Note that the two procedures are mirror-images of each other, with one critical change. Cleaning *before* the cut is done on the "Erase" head. Cleaning *after* the cut is done on the "Record" head. (Both are operating in either procedure—it's a question of which head makes first contact with your mark.)

All tape cuts should end on a "down" inflection, the kind that completes a spoken sentence. If for some reason you have a cut that ends with a "neutral" or even an "up" inflection, it can be changed with skillful fading of the volume control. Once you become proficient at it, a "neutral" inflection can sound "down" . . . and an "up" inflection can sound passable. (When you produce a cart that has an "up" inflection, make sure it's noted on the label or information that accompanies it.) A good newscaster can jump in and make the cut sound good . . . if he or she punches the opening word of the scripted close (or "tag") to the story.

There are three ways to shorten any tape cut:

- End it sooner.
- Chop something out of the middle
- Start it later.

The content and/or inflection may prevent you from using the first two methods on some cuts. But when that happens, you can almost always *get into* the cut later. The material you eliminate from the tape is used, instead, in the newscaster's script.

Never use non-magnetic "leader tape" in the interior of a reel of tape, for editing purposes. This tape, usually white or yellow in color, does not record. If you splice it in, you may forget to take it out—causing problems for the next person using the tape.

Splicing Step-By-Step

If there is applause or laughter, at the end of a tape cut, it should be left in. There's no sense in using the last part of a thundering address to a political convention, then splicing out the wild cheering and applause that follows. All forms of audience reaction should be gradually faded, after a few seconds. (If the speaker was given a ten-minute standing ovation, the newscaster can mention that in the script.)

When you do a lot of editing, you'll need to replace your reel-tape frequently. You can institute a regular system of discarding reels, every week or so. Sometimes you can salvage *most* of a reel, by throwing away the *first part* of the tape. It is generally used more than tape deeper into the reel. There's an easy way to eliminate used tape from the outside of a reel. Simply unravel enough until you can stick in a razor blade, and cut toward the center.

If you are getting strange "clicks" at the point where you splice tape, you may need to demagnetize your razor blades. Sometimes they build up a charge that is passed to the tape when splicing. But generally, there's no need to regularly demagnetize razor blades. They usually go dull, and need to be discarded, first.

Finally, a couple of miscellaneous pointers. You should start each day with a clean, erased, supply of tape. You'll find that the bulk-eraser is one of the most indispensable devices in any newsroom. Get a supply of clean carts and reel-tapes ready to go instantly, for breaking stories.

If you're not sure of your splicing prowess, or if you've got an irreplaceable piece of tape, dub the whole thing off to another reel. Save one copy, edit on the other.

If you notice a "drop-out" on first playing of a splice, run it through the machine another time or two in case the tape has temporarily buckled. If it doesn't improve, it will have to be re-done.

Marking Tape

There are some advantages to *not* marking tape on the head, itself. Many editors prefer, instead, to make a mark at the end of the head cover or some other standard point, then align that mark with a pre-determined point on their splicer. And there are some good reasons why:

1. No marking material gets on head.
2. Marking pressure doesn't hurt head alignment.
3. No marking material interferes with splice.

There are also some disadvantages:

1. Marks remain, causing confusion in future splices.
2. Marking material can get on other tape layers, capstan, etc.

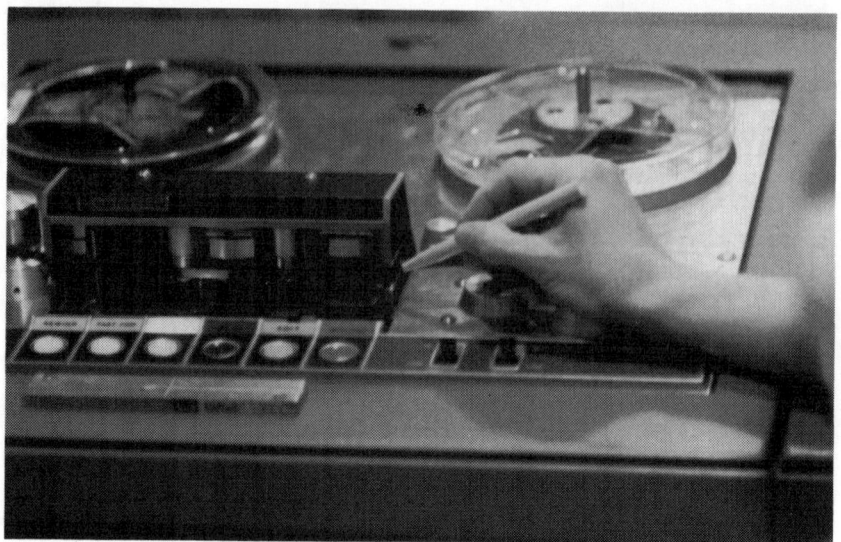
Marking at the end of the head cover has its advantages . . . and disadvantages.

3. Special measuring and marking required on some machines and splicers.

This book recommends that the mark be made to the *immediate right* of the tape's contact-point with the head gap. The gap itself is where playback takes place, and where the marking materials can cause the biggest problems.

With this method, the mark is covered by splicing tape and is unlikely to cause contamination. The solution, no matter where you mark, is to make a slight line on the tape. This way, most of the potential problems are eliminated.

Two of the best markers are a sharpened grease pencil, and a special soft pencil put out by EdiTall. Both do a good job, and go on with only light pressure. You can also use a felt-tip pen, or a liquid-marker like the "Marks-a-Lot." These, however, must be re-covered once they're used, or they soon become worthless.

Ballpoint pens and regular pencils are no good. They require too much pressure to leave a visible mark on tape. That pressure would mean a crease in the tape, and possibly damage to the head.

Get a marker that will contrast with the color of tape you use. Yellow, orange, red, and white show up best in most cases. Above all else, make a *light* mark, and make sure you don't leave a heavy accumulation of "crud" on the tape. This excess material can contaminate the head, along with adjacent tape layers, capstan, pinch roller, and guides. Frequent

Splicing Step-By-Step

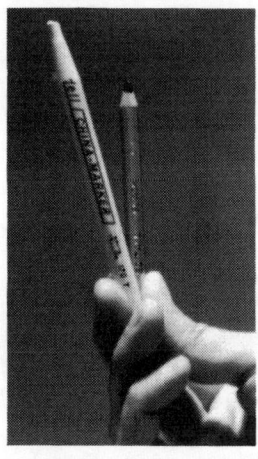

Two acceptable markers, a grease pencil, and the special EdiTall pencil.

cleaning is a daily necessity when you mark tape. Everything the marking material could possibly touch must be thoroughly wiped off.

A few (expensive) recorders solve the marking problems—by including built-in editing markers. Very few of these machines are in newsrooms.

Internal Editing

It's not always best to take out *entire* words when you splice. One of the most frequent flaws is "the stumble." Consider this sentence: "I haven't had time to go to the confirmation, er ahhh, conference yet." Chances are the word "conference" is heavily accented. And if you edit out the incorrect words "confirmation, er ahhh" the sentence will have a tell-tale accentuation.

The best method here, and in many similar cases, is to edit *within* words. Compare the incorrect word, with the correct one:

confirmation
conference

The first syllables are the same. The only difference is the first syllable of "conference" would naturally be heavily accented, after the stumble. To avoid this, you splice after the first part of:

con/firmation

into the second part of:

con/*ference.*

The result is a perfect sentence with no telltale accentuation: "I haven't had time to go to the con/ference yet."

The same little editing trick can be used in many cases just like this one. With careful marking and splicing, you can achieve perfect results.

Splicing Speeds and Angles

Good splicing eventually boils down to cutting the tape at the right place. That's hard enough at times. So make sure the odds are on your side . . . by using the fastest tape speed you have available.

Usually 7½-ips is fine for most editing. The seven-and-a-half inches that go past the heads in one second make hearing *where* to cut pretty easy, once you get used to it. At 3¾-ips, of course, your problems are doubled as you're dealing with half as much tape during a given period. And splicing at 1⅞-ips is close to impossible.

If you have trouble getting a good splice at one speed, and you've exhausted all the other methods suggested, dub the cut to a higher speed. Many broadcast recorders are capable of 15-ips. And even though 7½ is fine for most splicing, even veteran tape editors occasionally dub to the highest available speed for a difficult cut.

Normally, tape is spliced on a diagonal groove to cut down on noise. When a splice goes past the playback head, oftentimes there's poor contact. And stray oxide particles can get trapped between the two tape segments. If all the splice hits the head gap at once, it may be heard. The commonly-used 45° diagonal splice minimizes that, allowing the cut to slide by more gradually (1/30th of a second at 7½ ips). That doesn't sound like much—but it works.

Some newer editing blocks now have two diagonal grooves. Normally, either will work fine for monaural (mono) recording, which is all this book deals with. (If you ever have occasion to splice a *stereo* recording, to cut both tracks at the same time you would use the 83° groove, which is almost straight up-and-down.

Tape Thickness and Materials

Three standard thicknesses of reel-to-reel tape are available. Tape is measured in mils, or thousandths-of-an-inch. The tape most suitable for broadcast use is 1½-mil (0.0015-inch). There's also a 1-mil (0.0010-inch) and a ½-mil (0.0005 inch). These measurements reflect the thickness of the tape's "backing." The magnetic coating will add slightly more. 1-mil and ½-mil tape should not be used for editing purposes. The tape is fragile, and can break or stretch easily.

Three types of materials are used in tape "backings." Most common today is polyester. This is also known by the trade names of "Mylar" and

Splicing Step-By-Step

"Tenzar." There's also a chemical called "polyvinyl chloride" (or "PVC"), and the original tape material called "cellulose acetate" (or "acetate").

Polyester is actually the strongest, and most resistant to heat and humidity damage. But all polyester backings have a critical problem. They'll stretch greatly, before breaking. And the stretched part is worthless. This quirk of polyester means you must handle a recorder gently, not subjecting the tape to any tension that could force it to stretch.

Polyvinyl chloride is not used much any more. It is not as strong as acetate, in some respects. But it eliminates some of acetate's drawbacks.

Acetate is the granddaddy of plastic tape. It breaks easily, and is greatly affected by the weather. In hot, damp climates, it will stretch, slightly. In cold climates, it will become brittle, and break easily. And the older it gets, the worse these problems become. Some once-fine acetate tapes are almost unusable a decade later . . . because of deterioration in the box.

The only advantage acetate has over polyester is its general resistance to stretching. You can always splice a break back together. But a stretched piece of polyester will be distorted, or in many cases, totally unusable.

Splicing Devices

All splicing blocks are pretty much alike. Longer ones, which may cost $30 or up, allow more working surface. Radio Shack's catalog number 44-224 is shorter—but costs under $4. It also includes a narrower groove for splicing cassette tape.

The one splicer to avoid is the "Gibson Girl" which has been around for decades. It gets its name from the special way it cuts tape, forming a

The only splicer that hurts tape, the "Gibson Girl."

narrow "waist" at the splice. Supposedly, this cutting into the magnetic tape will prevent splicing-tape adhesive from contaminating the heads.

However, just the reverse is true. The splicing tape is *more* likely to affect the heads with this special Gibson Girl cut. (Remember that splicing tape is 1/32-inch narrower than the magnetic tape, to help prevent just such an occurrence.) The Gibson Girl makes them both the same width. Cutting into the magnetic tape also makes it weaker, and can lower sound quality, since a significant part of the oxide is being chopped off. The Gibson Girl is the only splicer that, by its very design, harms tape. Besides this, it's awkward to use, and requires regular replacement of cutting pads, and special miniature razor blades.

Splicing Materials

American technology has even given us a choice of splicing materials now. There are two types—splicing tape, which comes in different widths, and something known as the "splicing tab."

Regular old splicing tape is still the best. Keep it near the tape recorder in a convenient desk dispenser. Stick to an established brand, don't buy some unknown variety that's unmarked and unwrapped.

Scotch, for example, makes three types. "Number 41" is acetate and suitable for general newsroom work. "Number 67" and "Number 620" have a polyester base and are much more expensive. Since the life of a newsroom tape is measured in weeks—it doesn't matter that the acetate splice may become brittle in ten years.

Different widths are available. The splicing block method uses 7/32-inch.

If the splicing tape breaks, it's frequently hard to find the end. Simply draw a line around the roll with a felt-tip pen, and you'll spot it.

Any splicing tape will age when it's stored a long time. Some types may become sticky, others become very hard to cut. For this reason, don't stock up for several years, all at once. And keep the extra tape in a cool, dry place—preferably in an air-tight container—until you're ready to use it.

The "splicing tab" is put out by several firms. The splicing tape is affixed to a long strip of plastic, which is placed over the entire tape groove in the splicing block. When contact is made, the splicing tape is transferred to the recording tape, and the rest of the tab is thrown away.

The splicing tabs are *much* more expensive. Most of the tab ends up as waste. And the results are no better than what you can get by applying a piece of splicing tape, with your fingers.

The Ethics of Splicing

Once you acquire the skill of splicing, you acquire the ability to make anyone say anything. It takes only a sharp razor blade and a couple of pieces of splicing tape to distort and twist statements. This is where ethics comes in.

Our job is to polish tape cuts, to separate the newsworthy from the ordinary. Our job is *not* to distort, consciously or otherwise, anything anyone says. One method is to ask yourself, when all the splicing is done: "Has my editing distorted or slanted this person's feelings, in terms of the total speech or interview?"

In most cases, fairness and professionalism show the way. But what if you interview a candidate for office who can't speak a cohesive sentence? Do you edit out all his stuttering, stammering and pregnant pauses, to leave him sounding intelligent? What if you catch someone apparently trying to lie his way out of a question—do you leave the "well, er, ah, you see"—in the cut? If one party in a dispute calls the other a "goddamn low-down gutless skunk . . ." should all that go on the air?

There aren't any ready-made answers to these questions. One alternative is not to use the tape at all, just a copy story. Another alternative is to rely on situation ethics, basing your judgment on the story itself. Unfortunately, there's no professional code covering splicing.

4 | Dubbing Step-By-Step

The message is to do people news . . . to not use tape for tape's sake . . . to ask yourself that all-important question, "Am I, myself, really interested in what this dude is saying?" If the answer is no, you have my blessing if you take the offending cart and hurl it with vigor and force right across the newsroom.
—Dick Smyth, CHUM/Toronto
Memo to staff, July 1973

The business of transferring your produced tape cut to cart for on-air use is known as "dubbing."

Select a cart that is a little longer than the tape cut you are going to dub. An 18-second cut should go on a 20-second cart. But don't try to cram a 40-second cut onto a 40-second cart. Use the next size longer.

The Seven Steps of Dubbing

Dubbing the tape to cart is relatively simple, compared to the splicing process:

1. Erase the cart, and put it in the right side of the slot in the cart machine. On most models, a light will glow. Push the *Start* or *Play* button, and let the cart run for a second before pressing *Stop*. (This insures the cart is okay, and prevents stopping it at the same point every time it's used.) Then, momentarily push the *Set* or *Record* button until it glows.

Putting the cart machine in "record".

2. Play a few seconds of the reel tape you're going to dub, and adjust the pot, so the VU meter on the cart machine is recording at the correct level. The peaks should be between 80% and 100%. Occasionally, the meter may go slightly into the "red," above 100%

Adjusting the pot to get peaks near 100% modulation.

3. Rewind the tape to just before the start of the cut you want to dub.

Dubbing Step-By-Step 43

4. Push the *Start* or *Play* button on the cart machine, then, half-a-second later, push the *Start* or *Play* button on the reel-to-reel machine. (Activating the cart first gives it time to attain full speed, and prevents burps when it re-cues.)

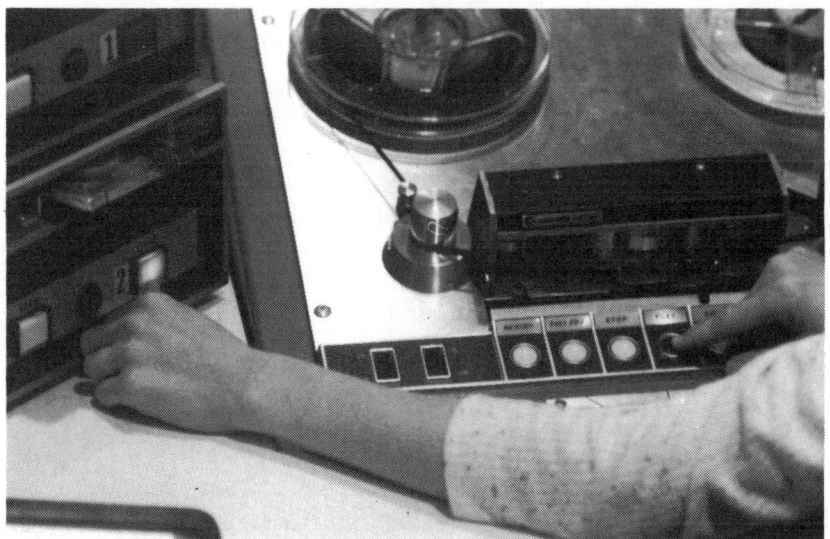

Starting the cart machine, then starting the reel machine a half-second later.

5. Dub the cart, fading the pot at the end.

Dubbing, then fading the pot at the end.

6. A few seconds after the end of the cut, stop the cart (deactivating the record mode) then start it again (without recording) to let it re-cue.

7. Listen to your produced cut. If it's not good enough, do it again. Getting the start "just right" may require some experimentation. Reel-to-reel machines respond differently. Some attain speed quickly, some don't.

On some reel machines, you may also want to spin the large metal roller on the left-hand side of the heads (known as the "idler reel" or "lollypop") counter-clockwise, just before dubbing your cut. This will help ensure that the tape is running at full speed when the cut starts.

In some custom installations, a single button starts the cart and reel machines, while resetting a count-up timer.

Quality Control

"Listening to the radio" increasingly means being enveloped in high-quality stereo sound (from either AM or FM) on Walkman-type radios and headphones. Some listeners hear *nothing but* the radio. They run the volume so high all ambient sound is excluded.

Even to listeners who aren't sound-fanatics, a single piece of poor production will really stand out. Continual lack of tape quality control could force them to switch stations in disgust. Every piece of tape should be produced cleanly. If you insist on high standards for yourself and for the tape you produce, you'll end up re-doing a lot of material that comes from your network or audio service.

The effect of a tape cut suddenly "jumping in" is extremely powerful. The instant "on-location" sound adds a great deal of impact to news. But if the cut is preceded by line noise, breathing, or other distractions . . . the effect is wrecked.

If you are dubbing through a board you can leave the cart machine pot in the "cue" position throughout. Think of "cue" as an electronic dead-end. The signal plays through a speaker, but is not part of the board output. Listening in cue, you can detect whether the cart is faulty *as* you produce it. This provides insurance in last-minute situations.

Turn the cue volume down or off near the end of the cart, so you fade the reel machine pot the *first time* you hear the outcue. (There's a lag because you are actually listening to the cart's playback head reproducing what the cart record head has just put on tape.)

Dubbing Step-By-Step

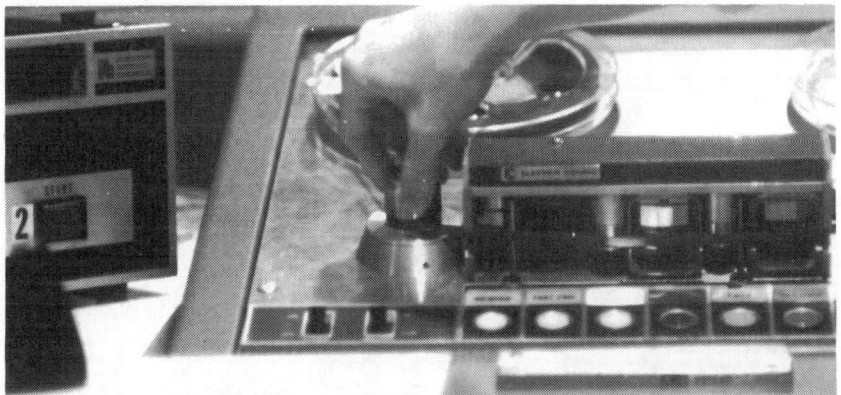

Spinning the idler wheel counter-clockwise helps the tape start at full speed — on some machines.

Everything put on cart should be consistently tight no matter which person on the staff did the editing. There shouldn't be any guesswork on the length of time between when the cart is activated, and when the audio begins (known as the "lag time"). One way to achieve this is to have a reference cart available in the newsroom, with several stop cues and brief audio cuts on it, to show how tight *all* carts should be.

Another way to simplify the "tightness" problem is to set up a uniform marking system on your reel-machines. First, find the exact start of the tape cut. Second, back it up an inch or two. Third, start the cart machine and the reel machine together. You'll have to make a mark on the reel machine, so all tapes are backed up the exact length. It may require some experimenting to find the right distance in order to get a proper start on cart.

Starting the cart and reel machine at the same time gives you a consistently "tight" sound on carts.

Unwinding tape from the take-up reel. Note the mark right below the tape "arm".

On reel units that have a tape "arm" on the right side, it's best to use this method. Unwind tape from the take-up reel until the arm drops to a certain point, then wind the excess tape back onto the supply reel, until it is tight. Then, start both reel machine and cart machine together.

Ideally, there should be a half-second lag time between pushing the start button and the time the tape cut begins. This way, the newscaster can hit the button *during* the last part of the last word in the copy. Any "click" or "thunk" caused by noisy cart machines is partially hidden by the word. And the cart won't "burp" when it re-cues, either.

Avoid starting a tape cut with a steady tone, such as a bell ringing. Some cart machines, especially the cheaper models, don't attain full speed immediately. The resulting musical sound is painful to hear.

Winding the excess onto the supply reel.

Generations of Dubs

Tape cuts lose a little quality every time they're dubbed. Here is how the various "generations" of dubs are labelled:

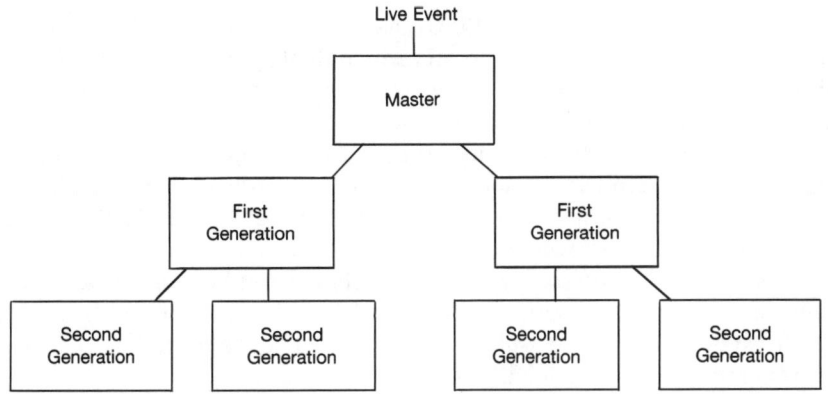

In other words, there can be *any number* of master tapes, all individually recording the event as it occurs. Any number of tapes dubbed from a master are "first generation." Any number of tapes dubbed from a "first generation" tape are "second generation" and so on.

The dubs can be reel-tapes, carts, or cassettes. As the number of generations increases, so does the muddiness, and background noise. Generally, the quality is poorer when you dub from cart or cassette. This is true on all types of equipment, especially on cheap units that are not designed for broadcast, or are bargain-basement stuff. The loss of sound quality can be compensated for somewhat, by an equalizer, as explained later in this book.

If something is recorded on cassette, it should first be dubbed to reel-to-reel, then to cart. This may seem like an unnecessary step, but it's not. It is nearly impossible to get a clean beginning to a tape cut, by going directly from cassette to cart. Many cassette machines equipped with a "pause" or "cue" button don't start cleanly.

Electronic Splicing

Some cart machines equipped with a secondary cue system can be used to splice tape electronically. This feature is helpful when a newscast deadline is breathing down your neck, and there's just no time to splice tape physically. But it's very difficult to achieve *exact* results on an electronic splice.

The procedure itself varies from machine to machine. In effect, you'll have to dub the parts of the tape cut you want to cart, in separate operations. It's the same as transferring any other cut from reel-tape to cart. But, this way, the cart has to be stopped exactly where you want the next phrase of the cut to begin.

On some machines, the various cuts are joined together electronically *as you produce them*. On some other machines, you've got to hold your finger on the *sec* button *as you play back* the produced cart, to electronically join the fragments.

Just like the physical splice, the electronic version takes practice. It's helpful in removing a long pause, or a sentence that doesn't add anything to a tape cut, when there's no time to splice physically. But in other situations, it's inadequate.

Tape with lots of background noise should not be spliced electronically under *any* circumstances. Many machines cause recording drop-outs at the splice. The noise will cause an inevitable "whoosh" as the tape starts, and goes up to speed.

Secondary (and tertiary) cues on cart machines can be set up to do many things, including triggering cue lights and activating a mike channel. And there are many ways to set up the electronic edit function. Consult a station engineer or the cart machine manufacturer for details.

Carts

There are three basic requirements for newsroom carts. They've got to be dependable, rugged, and quiet in operation. Fortunately, models introduced since the early '70s offer a big jump in quality over primitive early carts.

The only one of these still in widespread use is the original grey "Fidelipac" which dates from the 1950s. It's worth pointing out potential Fidelipac problems and ways of preventing them.

The old model Fidelipac (shown with top removed). Note that the "wire guide", which stretches over the left part of the tape, merely rests on plastic supports and is not attached to the cart itself. —*Courtesy Fidelipac*

The plastic cover may separate from the base, at the critical head openings. The cover and base are secured by only one screw, in the center of the cart. A large enough space between the two sections, combined with other inherent problems, could result in ruined tape and a technical disaster on the air. There's also a metal bar, called a "wire guide" (or "top wire") which stretches over part of the "tape coil" in the center of the cart. This guide is not firmly attached, and can make a rattling noise when the cart is played on the air. And when the top separates from the base, the bar also comes loose, frequently stopping or ruining the tape.

The plastic "corner post" regularly comes out of place, which can cause "muddy" tape, or even a halt in the tape motion. The four tiny bars of graphite (or pencil lead) that line the bottom of the tape "hub" can come loose, and rattle around. The pressure pads can come out, or bend backward, because of a lack of support.

To complicate all these problems . . . the screw holding the cart together sometimes pulls through the thin plastic in that part of the cover. Then, the cart has to be taped together, to be used.

To counter some of these Fidelipac problems, here are a few recommendations:

1. Glue corner posts into place. Pry down posts with key or paper clip if they start to rise up.
2. Check and tighten screw in center of cart with screwdriver or paper clip. This should be done every time cart is erased.
3. Check pressure pads. Gluing them into place, too, is a good idea.
4. Either throw away the "wire guide" . . . or bend it into a gentle upward arc so it will press against the rib on the plastic cover.
5. Replace any carts that separate at the head opening. These may cause major problems on-air.

The problem with most *other* carts is keeping them from ending up in the production studio. Liberal use of an indelible marker to put "NEWS" on top and bottom may help.

Another method is to have them wound to awkward lengths. A 25-second cart simply would not get used for a 30-second commercial.

Many firms rewind carts and do routine maintenance on pressure pads, etc. This is also fairly simple to do at the station level by using a "cart winder" which comes with operating instructions.

Of course, *any* cart is only as good as the tape inside it. There's no substitute for regularly checking the appearance of the tape, and its "sound" on the air. All carts should contain the same brand and type of tape, to avoid unnecessary level problems. Some tape is designed for much higher recording and output levels.

If you have a damaged cart, splicing generally isn't practical. If the cart has been wound correctly, there won't be enough "slack" tape available for you to take out a mangled piece. And if you remove one loop, you've made the cart into an odd length. Generally, your best bet is to remove *all* the tape and have some fresh tape put in.

Cart Splice-Finding

All carts contain a length of tape that is spliced together. And no matter how good the splicing job, chances are you will be able to hear some distortion at that point when a cut is recorded. There's an easy way to remedy the problem.

Several brands of "splice-finders" are on the market, many with bulk-erasing units built in. These machines commonly wind through a cart at 15 or 30 ips then stop immediately after the splice. This gives you the entire length of tape for recording, without any dropouts or distortion. You can get the same results, by *watching* the cart as it runs in a conventional machine, and stopping it after the splice. But this is both frustrating, and time-consuming. Unfortunately, splice-finders are fairly expensive (typically around $300) and are rarely used, even in major-market news operations.

Eventually, most any cart gets coated with old labels, dirt, and other marks. Most of this stuff can be removed by a cloth, soaked in paint-thinner. The cloth will take off smaller label particles by itself. It will also loosen large labels, so they can be scraped off with a razor blade. The paint-thinner will not "frost" the plastic, and your cart will end up looking like new.

A typical splice-finder runs at 15 ips, twice the normal speed. It stops carts just after the splice.

5 | Broadcast Tape Forms and Content

"It wasn't by accident that the Gettysburg Address was so short. The laws of prose writing are as immutable as those of flight, of mathematics, of physics." Ernest Hemingway, 1945
Selected Letters, p. 594

Now that *how* to record is out of the way, let's deal with *what* to record.

This chapter introduces all the tape forms, then offers content suggestions and time limits. Just as important, it looks at when tape could *harm* a newscast and should not be used.

A mere book cannot reproduce the intensity, inflection and sound of good tape cuts. So printed examples have been kept to a minimum in favor of broad guidelines. Real examples, by the hundreds, are available every day on all-news stations and network audio feeds.

The Six Basic Tape Forms

Actuality: The actual voice of a newsmaker (Fire Chief talking about 4-alarm blaze, poverty worker talking about malnutrition, President addressing Congress). In short, an actuality is first-person tape, frequently emotional and colorful, always personally involved.

Q&A: An answer from a reporter. This may come in response to a question from the newsroom, or one posed by the reporter.

Voicer: A news story told by a reporter, either on the scene, or from a studio. This is done in a formal, prepared style, frequently quoting or paraphrasing a newsmaker. This technique treats a story objectively and traditionally has formed the basis of radio news reporting.

Wraparound: This is a *combination* of the voicer and actuality. In it, the reporter begins the story, then sandwiches in a piece of actuality before coming back to close-off with his or her name and location.

Voice-Ality: A *compromise* between the voicer and actuality. This is a piece (frequently adlibbed) by a reporter telling a story in a subjective, eyewitness style. This technique is especially useful in covering stories where mood, description, and color play a large part (as in fires, riots, parades, etc.)

Sound: This is a catch-all category—also known as "Natural Sound," "Wild Sound," "Raw Sound," or just plain "Noise." It includes the roar of airplanes used to back up a scripted story, funeral music for a fallen leader, the sound of a picket-line scuffle, or demonstrators shouting. In short, "sound" is non-spoken actuality.

Remain absolutely silent, and look at the second-hand of a clock for 10, 20, and 30 seconds. Time drags . . . when it's filled with nothing. A story *with* tape almost always takes more air time than a story *without* tape. So if either the story or the tape is dull—you're better off with copy alone.

Radio is a sequential medium. One thing must follow another. News stories cannot all be presented at once, as in a newspaper or magazine. And not all listeners are going to be interested in *any* given story, no matter how good.

That's the underlying reason for the philosophy of short tape cuts, expressed in this book. Here are some general guidelines on each type of tape, and some advice about pitfalls.

Actualities

Actualities should contain *one clear, uncomplicated idea or statement*. This means, of necessity, the cuts are going to be short. 10 to 15 seconds is just about ideal, 20 to 25 seconds is a reasonable maximum.

If your actuality cuts are both clear and short, they'll be in the top 25 percent of all broadcast tape produced, nationwide. If you're dealing with a complex story, or a poor speaker, you can always paraphrase his or her ideas, or simplify them in your own words, in a voicer or Q&A.

When it's appropriate, try to get the drama and emotion of an event on tape. (Ask the winded fireman what it was like *inside* the inferno . . . get the local union boss thundering before the strike meeting . . . get tape of the cop on the beat, rather than the police PR guy in his office.) In short, go after "real" people, rather than "spokespeople."

Whenever possible, try to get background sound in your actualities. The noise of traffic, the roar of a fire, an audience laughing, cows mooing, all these add impact to tape. Get your person in a faster-paced area (without

Overhead view of reporters getting actuality from New York Governor Mario Cuomo at Democratic National Convention, 1984.

© Shmuel Thaler, photographer

noise that will obliterate him or her on tape) and chances are the answers will be more concise.

Avoid having more than one voice on an actuality cut. Reporters' questions should be edited out, unless they're *absolutely essential* to meaning, and the tape can't be cut any other way.

Do everything you can to get newsmakers to "explain it simply." Even the most long-winded news conferences can sometimes be salvaged (assuming it's a newsworthy story to begin with). Just ask one of the spokespeople to sum up, in 15 seconds, the purpose for calling in the media. It works almost every time.

When someone phones in with a prepared press release or statement, get them to sound like they're "talking" instead of "reading." Many military, government, political, and even radical organizations persist in calling up to offer a page full of gobbledygook—read in a monotone. Asking them to sum up in 15 seconds works—sometimes. But if some PR man insists on "reading" instead of doing it to *your* standards, inform him it won't get on the air. (If the story is such that you *have* to run that kind of handout, introduce it as a prepared statement, and say the organization refused to answer questions.)

One of the things we should strive for in tape is variety. Some actuality cuts, when warranted, should run 20 to 25 seconds. Others, like Richard Nixon's famous "I'm not a crook!", express a complete statement in two or three seconds. Having several cuts, of varied lengths, on a particular story gives the newscaster more options on treating it.

One more thing about actualities. They're free. You're using a volunteer to give you information or a description. They're also the only tape form a studio-bound newsperson can gather without help from an outside reporter.

Q&A

If you question a newsmaker, you get an actuality. If you question your reporter, you get a Q&A cut. Sometimes, the easiest way to handle this is to have the reporter pose the questions (as suggested leads) and then proceed to answer them. Regardless, they should sound ad-libbed and run no longer than an actuality, 20-25 seconds, maximum.

If the story is a big one, deserving of more air time, it can be very effective to have the newscaster appear on tape, asking the questions.

Voicers

Normally, a voicer runs longer than an actuality or Q&A. In theory, this makes sense because voicers are written out, and actualities or Q&A cuts are (or appear to be) ad-libbed. In a traditional five-minute newscast, voicers may have limits anywhere between 30-45 seconds.

The voicer is the most basic form of tape. Some network casts are still built around them. But many voicers come out sounding dull and irrelevant. Even well-edited actualities with only mediocre content frequently have much more impact. The reason is an actuality is first-hand, straight from the source. It contains a personal point of view and emotion. A voicer comes out second-hand through a skeptical, objective reporter. But that *doesn't* mean it has to sound cold and distant.

Ideally, a voicer should convey a story with some of the human feeling and intensity of a good actuality. That doesn't mean any objectivity has to be sacrificed.

There are many textbooks and style guides available on broadcast writing in general. Here are a few additional guidelines specifically for voicers:

- **Make your on-scene presence obvious.** Your location belongs near the beginning of any on-scene report. Include first-hand knowledge or information with the verb form "tells me."
- **Try for present tense.** Especially in your lead, look for a current angle.

- **Relate to your audience.** Think how you would want the story told if you were listening.
- **Avoid unnecessary facts.** On complex stories, concentrate on just one angle.
- **Omit unnecessary words.**
- **Don't over-attribute.** On routine stories where the source is not in question, "Capitalist Corporation says" is enough.
- **Simplify titles when appropriate.** Frequently, "spokesman" or "Vice-President" are adequate.
- **Avoid numbers.** They're potentially deadly. Round off and simplify whatever numbers you must use, and never force listeners to do any mental calculations.
- **Avoid middle names and initials.** Make exceptions only for people who actually use them, like Southerners ("Billy Bob") and women ("Jane Maiden-Married").
- **Avoid bureaucratic or artificial words.** Not "change of venue" but "moving the trial." Not "persons" but "people."

Leave the complexities and extensive backgrounding to AP, UPI and the papers. Radio news has to be simplified, sometimes oversimplified, to make it fit, and make it understandable. Voicers—in fact, all stories—should be written so someone who's been in a coma for the past decade can get something out of them. At the same time, you can't talk down to an intelligent listener who has been keeping up on the story.

Ideally, all voicers should be recorded at the scene, making full use of available background sound. That's not always possible, even in the largest operations. But there are other methods to liven up a newscast, with different sounding tape cuts:

- Do the cut on the sidewalk outside your building, next to the freeway, in a park nearby . . . in any outdoor setting that would match the mood of the story.
- Record your cut on a portable tape machine in the newsroom taking advantage of the background noise.
- Record your cut on the portable recorder while standing next to the wire machines.
- Record the cut through the telephone, using the phone mouthpiece.

Some stations consider these techniques 'faking' and forbid them. Others have had policies forbidding the opposite—in-studio voicers done from a microphone onto cart.

There is a big difference between seeking out background sound . . . and misleading your audience. You must never claim to be somewhere you're not. This is not only a cornerstone of journalistic honesty, it's also a matter of FCC regulation.

Obviously, some of these techniques are inappropriate in certain formats. You wouldn't want wire machine noise on a classical music station's newscast, but a well-done on-scene voicer would fit anywhere.

You don't see many TV reporters doing their pieces from the studio anymore, at least not when they can tape their story in an appropriate setting. (Why do you think Washington TV newspeople do their stories from the White House lawn, or from the grounds around Capitol Hill, rather than from their studios?)

Doing a story on meat prices from an "appropriate setting." An occasional "moo" from the background adds realism to the report.

And when television *can't* find a setting—reporters are put in front of control room monitors or in the newsroom to provide a visually-interesting background.

Radio has done just the opposite. It has gone from a lusty history of newsgathering, with regular on-scene reports, to drab in-studio voicers.

Voicer Variety

Voicers usually report what other people have said aloud. As a result, the verb form "says" is frequently over-worked. Here are some others that can be used, instead:

adds	declares	proposes
agrees	demands	remarks
announces	discloses	repeats
answers	emphasizes	replies
argues	holds	reports
asks	insists	shouts
believes	laughs	snaps
charges	maintains	tells
comments	observes	thinks
contends	pleads	urges
continues	points out	wants

Rather than get too flowery in a simple voicer, use a verb on this list (or another that fits the occasion) for special effects. Don't fill ordinary stories with "charges," "insists," and "snaps." The verb forms "says" and "tells me" should not be abandoned.

The tense of your story has a large part in determining its impact. If it sounds stale, when it's actually a fresh news item, you're using the wrong verb-form. Consider this example, written in a style that's straight out of a print-journalism textbook:

President Smith TODAY SAID he WOULD SIGN a mutual defense treaty with Easter Island. Last Thursday, in a speech at Peoria, Smith SAID he HAD POSTPONED his decision for a month. But today, the President TOLD reporters, he DECIDED to act immediately.

Here's the same story written in good broadcast style, minus the needless dating:

President Smith NOW SAYS he WILL SIGN a mutual defense treaty with Easter Island. Last Thursday, in a speech at Peoria, Smith WAS SAYING HE'D POSTPONE his decision for a month. But now, the President TELLS reporters, HE'LL ACT immediately.

The contractions used in the last two sentences lend a conversational tone to the story. In some other instances, it's best to use the full form, such as "he WILL act." Contractions help obscure the tense of stories, and should be used whenever possible when you're dealing with old news.

Here are the options you have in the past, present, and future tenses for the verb "say":

Past Tense:

He SAID (historical statement)
He WAS SAYING (implies continuing action)
He HAS SAID (continuing action)
He JUST SAID (recently completed action)
He HAS BEEN SAYING
He HAD SAID (historical statement)
He HAS JUST SAID (recently completed action)

All seven forms express past action. But the one most commonly used in broadcasting (He SAID) is best saved for a historical statement that has no forward action to it. For example:

"As he was strapped into the electric chair, he SAID he was innocent."

The forms WAS SAYING and HAS SAID treat the past action in continuing terms. They don't have the stodginess of SAID, and as a result, sound much better on radio. JUST SAID and HAS JUST SAID have an immediate sound, almost like present tense.

Present Tense:

He SAYS
He NOW SAYS
He JUST NOW SAYS (immediate, continuing action)
He IS SAYING (implies continuing action)
He IS NOW SAYING (continuing action)
He IS JUST NOW SAYING (immediate, continuing action)

Two other present-tense forms obscure the verb, but add brevity and a headline-effect to your writing. You won't find these in any grammar book, but they sound good on the air: "President Smith, SAYING he thinks . . ." "President Smith, NOW SAYING he thinks . . ."

Overuse of these forms, however, can be hazardous to your audience. They have a word-economizing impact that doesn't work well under all formats. Even at a breathless rock-'n-roll station, they should not be used routinely.

Just as bad is the other extreme: the needless dating of stories, newspaper style. Verb forms like SAID TODAY and TODAY SAID are good enough for the newspapers and wire services. But, for broadcast, if your speaker SAID it TODAY, the present-tense, SAYS, is appropriate. If he or she is expressing a belief, it's assumed to be continuing, so IS SAYING is appropriate.

Sometimes all the story needs is a different angle: PAST: "The victim of yesterday's small plane crash died today." PRESENT: "The victim of yesterday's small plane crash is dead."

A good choice of tense can liven up *any* story!

Future Tense:

> He WILL SAY
> He WILL BE SAYING
> He WILL HAVE BEEN SAYING (used rarely)

Avoid unnecessarily dating your tape. If you do a story on Thursday that will be used immediately, and also Friday morning, do not use the verb form "said Thursday." Instead, express time in terms of *"the afternoon"* or *"the evening."* Such a story doesn't sound awkward on the day it took place, and it also makes sense the following morning: WRONG: "The Governor said Thursday the state will have to increase its sales tax." RIGHT: "The Governor says the sales tax will have to go up. During an afternoon news conference..."

If you're dealing with a rapidly-changing story, lines like "during the past hour" are fine. But watch for dating problems on a cut that could be used later that day, or the next. All cuts that are dated should be labelled that way, and automatically killed at midnight.

Avoid using extremely short voicers. A two-sentence report followed by a sign-off sounds ridiculous. As a general rule, voicers should run at least 20-seconds. If you want to use a short cut from a reporter, eliminate the identification, and treat it as a Q&A.

Feeding Voicers

If you're outside the station covering a story, try to make your first piece of tape that is fed back a voicer or voice-ality, rather than an actuality. This will help set the scene for people who may catch several successive newscasts. It will also give the newscaster a "feel" for the story and some background information to use in writing later stories.

When you're feeding from outside, it's also best to write your *own* lead and tag material. Doing this will help the flow of a story. When you call back to the station, give a suggested one-or-two sentence lead, then count down "3-2-1" and feed your voicer. Afterward, supply a sentence or two of tag material. It means more work for *you*, but also makes it easier to meet time limits. You may have a 60-second story, but if you leave the first and last 10-seconds for the newscaster to read, you're down to 40 seconds.

Here's a possible lead:

City Airport could be getting overseas flights, beginning next summer. Reporter Tom Tape says there's only one possible hitch— the end cue: "without any gripes." Coming down in 3-2-1.
The main runways here will have to be extended another quarter-mile . . . to handle the huge jets. Airport officials tell me that shouldn't be too much of a problem. It will cost the city at least one hundred thousand dollars for the pavement. But the overseas air traffic will bring in a lot of new business and industry. And the president of the Airport Board says he thinks City Council will approve the runway project, at this week's meeting, without any gripes.
(Pause)

And a suggested tag: Reporter Tom Tape also says the international flights may force City Airport to expand its terminal in a few years.

Doing this also cuts down on lackluster leads like: "Some big changes at City Airport, Tom Tape has the story."
(The same feeding procedure should be followed for actualities, and sound, unless the cuts are completely self-explanatory. Everything should be fed with a sentence or two of lead material and tag material. The newscaster may decide to re-write it, but then again, he or she may not.)
If you make a mistake while feeding a story, don't panic. Simply pause for a few seconds, and tell the person on the other end you're starting over. Precede your second try with the words "Take Two." If you blow it again, the next try is preceded by a "Take Three", and so on.
It's never a good idea to cuss or swear on tape. A simple mistake in the newsroom could result in your botched report being aired, complete with a "Jeezus" or something worse, on the end.
Some stories just don't lend themselves to voicers. A speech is best handled with actualities, unless the speaker is notoriously bad. And, unless

the reporter covering it feels the remarks should be put into perspective with audience reaction, heckling, or something of that nature.

Then, there's the question of a sign-off. Should we bother to say, "This is Tom Tape at City Airport."? It all depends. If your station runs several taped voicers back-to-back, an identity should be included in the cuts themselves. But, in any other format, the name and location shouldn't be necessary at *any* point in the cut. If the voicer is written in the involved, first-hand style, there's no need to repeat the location. And if the studio newscaster either introduces or tags the cut with the reporter's name, that *too* is unnecessary. It's all a matter of style.

Another factor to consider is the legal one. If you say, "This is Tom Tape at City Hall" . . . you legally have to be *at* City Hall. Eliminating the sign-off will eliminate problems. In a pinch, a reporter can check on a story by phone, then record the story saying, "The mayor's office tells me . . ." and no dishonesty is involved.

Wraparounds

There are three types. The first is the *standard wraparound*. Basically, a reporter tells the story objectively, as in a voicer. But in a wraparound, he or she writes into an actuality, then comes back to sign-off.

All that can make for some confusion on the air, in a short period of time. The studio newscaster hands off to a reporter, who tosses it to a newsmaker, then back to the reporter, then to the newscaster. What you get on the air is a *double*-wraparound with the newscaster forming the outer layer.

In expanded news formats, where you may have a minute or more per story, wraparounds are well worth doing. But in shorter wraps, the Law of Diminishing Returns takes over, and you may end up with a couple of handoffs, a dwarf actuality and a sign-off.

That's not to say that wraparounds never work. But at the very least, wraps of 45 seconds or less have a great potential to be ineffective and shouldn't be used routinely.

From a manpower standpoint, when a reporter is out in the field with only a cassette recorder, a wraparound is especially difficult and time-consuming. If it is phone-fed it generally will contain two technical problem areas (before and after the insert) filled with clicks and compression noise. To maintain any kind of professional sound, these two spots must be edited, requiring yet more time in the studio.

The Standard 3-part wraparound has been joined by some newer types, that are sometimes worthwhile:

Standard Wraparound:
    V/A/V

Amputated Wraparounds:
    A/V; S/V (occasionally V/A or V/S)

Compound Wraparounds:
    V/A/V/A/V etc.
    A/V/A/A/V etc.
    S/V/A/S/V etc.

V — voice of newsperson
A — actuality
S — sound (which can also be faded under voice or actuality)

Amputated Wraparounds

Amputated Wraparounds eliminate some drawbacks of the Standard version. They work best when the actuality or sound is brief, direct, and grabbing. In effect, the reporter tells the story *through* the actuality, putting it into context:

> *Actuality:* If elected, I promise a cancer cure within ten years, and a job for everyone who wants one!

> *Voicer:* (with actuality continuing underneath) That's Joe Gazork, a long-shot candidate for Mayor, making his last-minute appeal at a North-side shopping center. Gazork is telling voters here that his opponent is a tool of big business. The crowds on Gazork's tour aren't very big today. Most people are only willing to listen for a few minutes . . . before they head off to other stores.

The Amputated Wraparound is most effective when the initial actuality (or sound) is faded and continues *under* the reporter to the end. Another way of doing them is to include the reporter's name (or name and location) immediately following the actuality or sound cut.

The occasionally-used V/A and V/S types work best with the actuality or sound material under the beginning segment, continuing until 100%

modulation at the end. They require a scripted tag by the newscaster to close out the story.

Amputated Wraparounds require special production—either in the field or back at the station.

Compound Wraparounds

Compound wraparounds have only limited uses in short newscasts. And they're time-consuming to produce. But if they're done right they have a lot of "on-scene" realism. With short cuts, and good tight writing, they move rapidly. There are some drawbacks, however. It's hard to utilize these forms over the phone, because of technical problems. And, cramming your voice and a couple of actuality or sound cuts into 30 or 40 seconds often leaves out a lot of meaning. Since our business is presenting information, the first priority is sacrificed to action-packed sound. These types of modified wraparounds are high on excitement and confusion, but generally woefully low on content, and meaning.

Wraparounds are useful for in-depth stories of several minutes in length, where plenty of production time is available. But in abbreviated time limits, many wraparounds are more confusing than informative. The technical headaches only make matters worse.

"Documentaries" are beyond the scope of this book (and the staffing limitations of most commercial U.S. radio stations). But, tape-wise many are Compound Wraparounds, whether they run 3 or 30 minutes.

Voice-alities

Think of the voice-ality as a Polaroid snapshot . . . an instant look at an unfolding scene. It must convey feeling and emotion—*your* feeling and emotion—of what it's like to be there. Your recorder will pick up what you are hearing (although you may need to explain it). When appropriate, call on senses other than sight. Smell, taste, touch all have their place.

Information content in voice-alities can be incidental. Let the newscaster convey the hard information in the lead. Save your efforts at "telling the story" for conventional voicers.

In some news operations this form is called a "Scener" or a "ROSR" (pronounced ROSE-err) which means Radio On-Scene Report. Whatever you call it, this form should sound ad-libbed. That's not to say that you can't script it beforehand.

The voice-ality is very useful in covering unfolding events where the reporter doesn't have a clear overview of the whole picture, and where mood, color, and emotion play a large part. Fires, riots, parades, and many ceremonies can all be handled this way.

In effect, you're treating the reporter as an eyewitness, sacrificing objectivity to paint a picture:

> In front of me now, the Air Force Band, led by a column of recruiters. Military music, uh, is filling the air, here at the annual Fourth of July Parade. Hundreds of children are waving small American flags at the servicemen, as they go by, dressed in their colorful uniforms, their medals gleaming from the hot sun.

Voice-alities should paint a word picture. Ross Simpson of Mutual filed this while hurricane-chasing in Florida:

"Here at St. Mark's Lighthouse on Apalachee Bay, the wind is really beginning to whip up. We're getting 85 mile per hour winds as Hurricane Elena moves toward Panama City and Pensacola. We're about 50 miles East of Panama City and it's getting very difficult to stand up. I'm leaning into the wind as Hurricane Elena rips across St. Mark's Lighthouse."

Voice-alities are most effective when they're short. In most cases, 15-20 seconds will be plenty, since you are primarily illustrating the story and the newscaster will still have to get in the facts.

Sound

The most *under*-used technique is that of just plain sound. Used occasionally, and imaginatively, it's a blockbuster. The sound can be utilized in the background of a voicer or voice-ality (as mentioned). It can also magnify the impact of an actuality.

Moreover, a tape cut of the sound by itself, can add tremendous impact to a studio newscaster's script. Noise from a strike, the crackle of a fire, the moo of a cow, can help to "bring home" a story in the listener's mind. So, whenever there's a good sound available, a separate cut of it alone should be carted and left for the newscaster.

Montages

People relate to the news when they hear other people relating to the news. This is the philosophical basis for the montage. It's nothing more than a combination of short actualities, put together to give a consensus of opinion.

The individual cuts must be short, and concise. Leave out longer actualities, they can be used separately.

A montage should contain *at least* three voices—preferably male-female-male, or female-male-female—when the story allows.

You may also want to put the cuts together so opposing viewpoints are back-to-back. In a montage on government corruption, for example, you may wind up with something like this:

>(male) I think they're all corrupt, and we'd better start prosecuting.
>(female) There are probably just a few rotten apples.
>(male) You newspeople always make our leaders look like bums.
>(female) All I know is my taxes are way up and my Congressman is always on vacation.

Perhaps the hardest part is getting a good *final* cut to use. Try to find someone who sums up the whole issue. Ideally, this will be done with a touch of sarcasm or humor (like the final cut in the example). In cuts that deal with a tragic event, such as the death of a well-liked public figure, the final cut should be an emotional and gripping one.

You can gather the cuts through personal interviews, of course. And you can also get them through the telephone, as explained in the following chapter.

No Tape

While good tape can improve a newscast, bad tape can ruin it. Here are broad guidelines on when tape should *not* be used:

- Technical quality is bad.
- Story is unimportant or dull.
- Person on tape is confusing or boring.
- You can tell the story better with script alone.

These are subjective categories, open to interpretation. In borderline cases, dump the tape! Listeners do not care how much time and effort you invested.

Let's face it, *no* amount of splicing can make some cuts fit for air use:

(**Question:** What does the outcome of the U.S. election indicate about the mood of the American people?)

Answer: Well ah (pause 1 sec) the outcome (pause 2 sec) indicates (pause 3 sec) ah (pause 8 sec) well first of all uh (pause 2 sec) ah (pause 2 sec) it indicates uh (pause 3 sec) ah (pause 2 sec) uh and ah uh no I Mr. Nixon is not particularly popular with the American people.

—Sociologist Vance Packard
in Toronto interview with the author, November 1972

Finally, don't forget that tape isn't all there is to radio news. It should tell part of the story, but not all of it. Make sure the newscaster has been given enough information to write in and out of your tape story. If he or she is creative, the tape will be woven with script to form a tapestry of sound.

6 | Telephone Newsgathering

A reporter from New York was once trying to get information on a Texas school explosion, so he phoned the sheriff. "Now, you reporters got to wait," he heard the sheriff say. "There's a man on the telephone here calling all the way from New York."
—quoted by John Brady
in *The Craft of Interviewing*

Radio is now, and has always been, the fastest news medium. TV has caught up to us in speed only on remote broadcasts. But radio alone can make full use of growing telephone technology—our best and most cost-effective weapon in the battle with TV.

Your market has been wired to your newsroom. Nearly everyone you would ever want to interview has a phone number and can be reached.

This chapter and the next will recommend some uncommon equipment and modifications to enhance telephone quality and make newsroom phones more useful. All have been tested.

Life After Ma Bell

There are far-ranging effects for radio news, from the 1984 breakup of AT&T. Prices of special phone lines and equipment immediately climbed. Charges for one-time-only "loops" for special coverage forced some stations to invest in *non*-telephone remote gear. The flood of cheap telephones degraded the technical quality of phone interviews and telephone-talk shows. Many stations trying AT&T's long-distance competitors found low prices and wretched quality.

Another side-effect has been technical confusion and buck-passing. (If you encounter unreasonable equipment or installation problems—lodge a formal written complaint with state regulators, and you may be surprised how quickly things are resolved!)

The AT&T breakup also gave us handy modular telephone instruments which can be plugged in and the promise that we may someday 'wear' a phone as we now do a wristwatch.

Even now you can talk to somebody while they float in their backyard pool, because they have a cordless extension phone. The mayor may return your call from the middle of a freeway traffic jam, because his car has a cellular phone. The local member of Congress may call you from a pay phone on board Amtrak, or a commercial jet.

There's a lot of news available by phone at minimal cost. And for many stations with skeleton news staffs and little or no outside equipment, it is the *only* way to be competitive.

Phone vs. On-Scene

Some newspeople make a big distinction between tape gathered "on the scene" and tape gathered by telephone. Most listeners don't know the difference. There's no audience "stigma" to phone tape, if it's good quality.

A telephone is not always the best way to cover stories. It can't replace personal contact and personal attendance. But remember, a telephone is already at, or near, every newsmaker or news event. All you've got to do is ring it. Here's a quick comparison:

Advantages of phone:
Quicker.
No appointment necessary.
Utilizes news staff efficiently, gets more done in less time.
Immediate interviews possible, if you sound urgent on phone.
Less expensive.

Advantages of on-scene:
Required for regular contacts with newsmakers.
Establishes yourself/station with regular newsmakers.
Only way to get personal-detail, mannerisms, etc.
Cassette quality is always good.

Disadvantages of phone:
Inadequate for regular checks with important news sources.
Lack of personal-detail, mannerisms.
Quality in some cases is not the best.

Disadvantages of on-scene:
Time-consuming process.
Appointments must be set up, can be delayed.
Can be expensive.
Ties up reporter who can't get away for fast-breaking news, if need develops.

If you're not sure whether to cover a particular story in person, or on the phone, ask yourself these two questions:

- Do we need to maintain or establish a face-to-face relationship with this person to get this story or future stories?
- Is this story so important we have to tie-up a reporter, a car, and a large amount of time to get it in person?

If you can answer "no" to both questions, you should try to get the story over the phone. If, for some reason, you don't get what you want, you can always send someone over for a personal interview.

With the short cuts required for radio, extended interviews and pages full of reporter's notes are needless. A telephone is a business instrument, it helps keep a business call from degenerating into a wasted effort. A telephone is also a medium of instant information, instant decisions, and instant interviews. And radio is the *only medium* that can totally exploit it! The phone is a great way to cut through obstacles, a quick method of getting information. People will interrupt almost *anything* to answer a ringing telephone.

Many interviews actually come out *better* over the phone than through an on-scene cassette interview. There's one principal reason—people are used to talking into telephones. They're not used to having a reporter shove a microphone into their face. Lacking an audience, many people become very reflective on the phone. The reporter on the scene (no matter

Custom telephone panel (below board) at WROK/Rockford, IL. Phone lines are controlled at left. Tone dialing pad for phone is in center. —*Courtesy WROK*

how skilled) can be a distraction, inhibiting rather than helping the flow of words.

Good quality telephone tape, properly equalized, sounds *excellent* over AM radio—and *good* over FM. It has intimate, close-talking characteristics (breathiness and all), that are an extremely effective change from studio-quality and cassette-quality. This sound alone can "grab" a napping listener, snapping him or her back into consciousness.

If you gather and process telephone material correctly, most listeners will not suspect it came from an ordinary phone call. The sound will be totally different from the sharp, metallic sound they get from the components in a phone receiver.

Legalities

Most phone calls in radio news are made with tape, or live broadcast, in mind. You want information *and* authorization to use a person's voice on-the-air. This falls under Section 73.1206 of the FCC Rules:

> "Before recording a telephone conversation for broadcast, or broadcasting such a conversation simultaneously with its occurrence, a licensee shall inform any party to the call of the licensee's intention to broadcast the conversation . . ."

The FCC Secretary's Office clarified it further:

> "The obvious object of the Rule is to give the party called a real opportunity to refuse to have his conversation broadcast while not yet on the air."
>
> —Secretary Ben Waple
> (in letter to KKEY/Portland, OR, 6 December 1972)

Here's how you go about it. As soon as the phone rings, adjust your level to the person answering. Be personable in opening the call, identify yourself and your station. If necessary, explain why you're calling and then use one of these time-tested "permission sentences":

- "I'd like to record our conversation and maybe use some of it on-the-air . . . is that okay?"
- "I'd like to put you on-the-air live, is that okay?"

The FCC does not specify any language, but these two versions cover any situation. Try to sound matter-of-fact, and avoid the words "permission" or "interview", which scare many people.

If the person says "no" to taped or live broadcast, gently try to find out why and overcome the objection. Failing that, you can agree not to put them on-the-air and still get quotes:

- "Okay, I won't use your voice—but let me get some information..."

Then start your recorder! Under Federal and nearly all State laws, you don't need their permission to merely record off the phone. You cannot broadcast the tape, but the words on it are fair game for quotation and attribution unless they specify otherwise (and you agree).

Laws in a handful of states require consent from *all* parties involved in a phone conversation. Stations there can't record until getting a "yes" answer to the permission sentence, which takes care of both State law (permission to record) and FCC Rules (permission to broadcast).

But—where legal—taping gives you a record of the quotes.

In Canada, stations are only required to get permission before broadcasting (not taping). So the interview can be done first—with permission at the end.

In 1985, the FCC looked at a similar policy, but no changes were made. Even if U.S. rules are relaxed eventually, there's something to be said for being "up front" with what you want to do. Even if you don't tell them—many people are going to suspect they're being taped.

Old-fashioned "beep tones" are no longer required. They are distracting and do not serve any purpose under current U.S. or Canadian broadcast regulations.

No permission is needed in two cases:

- Call-in programs (or news call-in lines) where listeners are making an effort to get on-the-air.
- Calls to (or from) station employees, news stringers, etc.

There is one additional caution on *live* broadcasts. This may seem petty—but make sure the opening "Hello", etc., from the person you call is not aired. Use your side of the conversation *alone* while you do the standard permission sentence. Only after you get the okay can you put someone on-the-air. The FCC has imposed $2000 fines for violations.

To Tape—or Not To Tape?

Under a 1968 U.S. law, telephone recording is legal as long as you are one of the parties in the conversation. Permission of the other person(s) is not necessary. But your state may have passed a more restrictive law and telephone recording without permission may be a serious offense. Consult your station attorney, or the state attorney-general's office.

Frequently, it seems, a government figure or business person will tape *private* phone conversations which later get made public, embarrassing everyone involved. Even though taping may have been legal, a confidence has been breached.

To some, taping without notification smacks of Big Brother or Richard Nixon's White House. Some news operations have policies forbidding taping without permission.

To others (myself included) a tape recorder is simply a modern-day notepad. If you have properly identified yourself as a reporter—the conversation is automatically *not private*. It is absolutely fair game for quotation unless you agree in advance to keep it "off the record" or "not for attribution". You should never *offer* to do this.

Rolling a tape allows you to concentrate on interviewing, not stenography. You also have protection against later charges of "I was misquoted" or "You took that out of context".

Equipment for Gathering

Two types of devices connect a phone line with broadcast equipment. The simplest is a "QKT" coupler. All it does is isolate phone lines from station equipment, and provide a jack where the station can plug in. It has only four components, and costs around $40.

The other device is a metal box filled with four-pounds of circuitry called a "RCZ" Recorder-Connector. This amplifies the incoming sound, provides automatic or manual gain control, and an optional beep tone (which you don't need). This is the professional set-up for phone recording and costs around $200.

Telephones for broadcast use have a "push-to-talk" switch. Actually it's a spring-loaded button which you depress to turn on the phone handset microphone. The rest of the time the phone mike is off—so your recording picks up only the person you're interviewing, not your breathing and newsroom noise.

But with a typical push-to-talk switch, many interviews go like this:

You: (with newsroom noise in background) "What's your feeling about that?" (Click—then dead silence).
Interviewee: "Hello, you still there?"

The way to prevent this involves adding one part, costing less than $1. It's best left to an engineer. This modification allows normal operation of the push-to-talk switch and provides a quick fade instead of a click and

Telephone Newsgathering

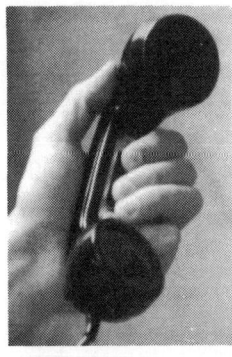

The "push-to-talk" switch cuts off the phone mouthpiece, eliminating noise on your end from the recording.

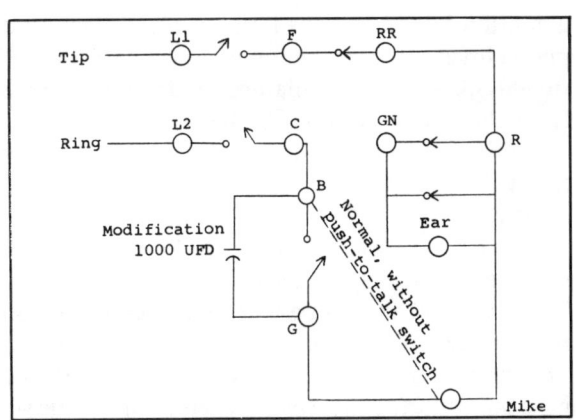

Telephone 425E Network. Normally, push-to-talk switch is in *series* with microphone connections. Capacitor, 1000 MFD rated at 16V, is placed in *parallel* across the switch.

dropout. Release the switch two or three words *before* the end of your question.

This modification eliminates one more obstacle to getting information and putting people at ease as they talk.

There are many ways to get good quality from *both* sides of the phone conversation. If your station is set up for this you may encounter speakerphones, hybrids and other equipment used in telephone-talk programming.

If you don't have this hardware around and you want to do long-form interviews, or just retain your questions in the final product, roll a separate tape. You will need to talk both into the phone handset, and a mike — but this second tape will record *only* the mike output. You can then go back and splice the two tapes together or "cross-fade" them on the board, bringing up the on-mike questions then rapidly fading and bringing up the telephone answers.

(Your newsroom and/or news studio also should be set up to *feed* down the phone, by throwing a switch. This is a simple wiring job for an engineer. Ideally, you should be able to feed through the news studio board and any other equipment. As explained later, this is very important when you swap tape with stations in other markets, or feed a network.)

Equalising Tape

Equalization is simply re-arranging the relationship of sound frequencies. It is most useful on telephone tape where — even under the best conditions—much of the human voice is lost. Under optimum conditions, phone lines will pass frequencies between 200-3,400 Hz. Many are limited to 300-3,000 Hz. As explained in Chapter 8, the human "speaking range" is much wider—75 to 8,000 Hz.

Every piece of phone tape can be improved by equalization and sometimes the difference is astounding. Phone-fed *cassette* tape also benefits greatly.

Five or seven-band "Graphic Equalizers" allow plenty of control at a reasonable cost ($30-$100).

An equalizer can be wired between the incoming phone line and the reel recorder. A more-useful way is to use it as the final step before carting. This way *all* your audio (not just the phone) can go through it. And you have the opportunity to play back reel tape while you adjust for correct EQ.

Units with separate *stereo* channels allow twice the adjustment range for stations doing news in *mono*. Output of one channel is wired into input of the other channel. Occasionally you'll need all that range to compensate for someone talking on a cheapo phone or down inferior rural phone lines.

EQ helps in other cases, making the frequency blend more-normal. Here are general guidelines:

Tinny-sounding Tape:	Lower treble
	Raise bass
Muddy-sounding Tape:	Lower bass
	Raise treble
Tape with "hum":	Lower fader for (or nearest to) 60 Hz.
Off-Mike Tape:	Raise fader for (or nearest to) 1000 Hz.
	Adjust others to compensate.

Once you've gotten the equalization to where it sounds good, add just a little more "crispness" by increasing the treble, slightly. Then, dub the tape onto cart. (Tape loses a little high-frequency quality when it's dubbed, especially to cart, so the added "crispness" compensates.)

The highest-pitched sounds produced in normal speaking are the letters "C," "S," "X," and "Z". In all, there's a certain amount of hissing as the "S" sound is made: "sscee" "ssss" "ekxss" "szzee"

Your equalization must capture this added high-frequency dimension. Otherwise, the tape cut becomes dull and hard to understand, simply because we're not used to hearing speech without the overtones. Avoid going to extremes, however. The "S" sounds should not whistle. Strive to make the speech quality natural, and intelligible.

If the material is perfect as it came in, EQ controls are set in the middle or "0" and the equalizer will not alter the sound balance.

The monitor speaker must be wired so you can hear effects of the equalizer. Headphones are *not* recommended, nor is a huge speaker. A

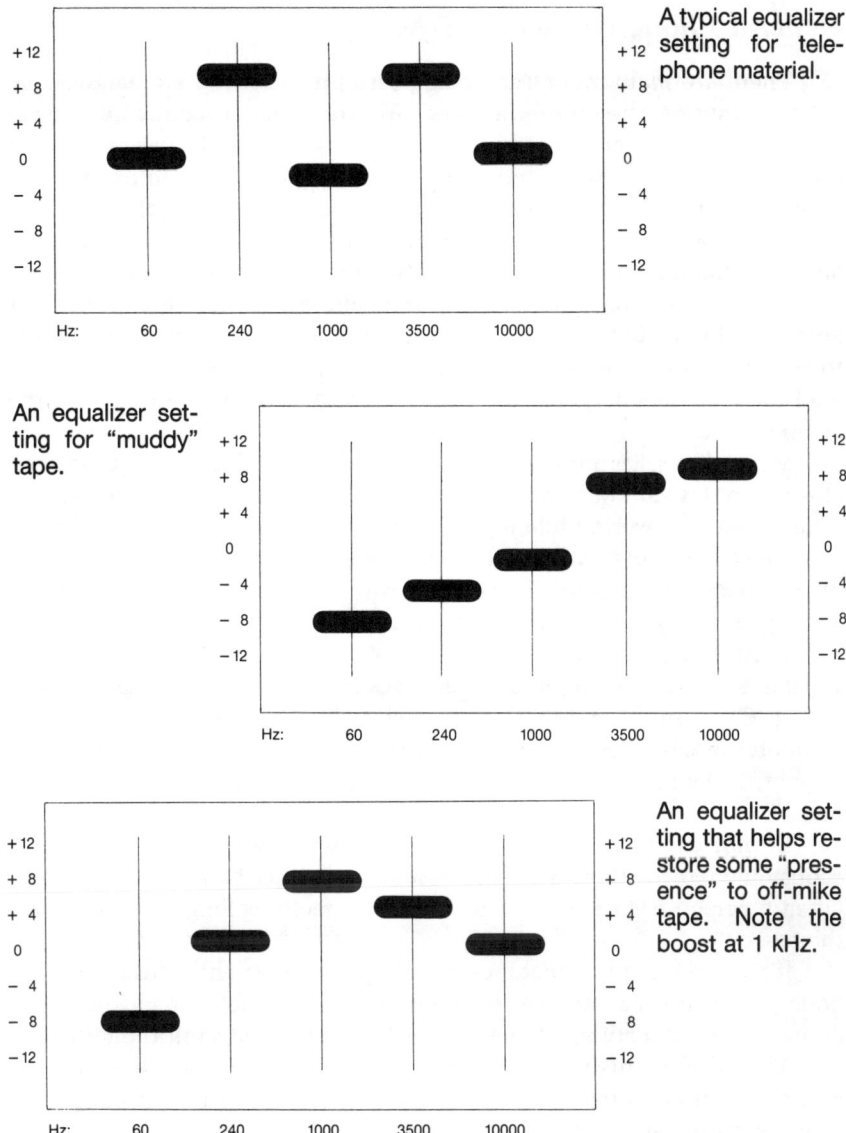

A typical equalizer setting for telephone material.

An equalizer setting for "muddy" tape.

An equalizer setting that helps restore some "presence" to off-mike tape. Note the boost at 1 kHz.

good compromise is a speaker equivalent to that in an average home stereo system.

Audio processing on the station's signal may undo EQ work by increasing noise, especially on phone tape. Manuals for some processing units offer suggestions on this problem—consult your station engineer. Or, since the processing is adding its own EQ, you can simply back off on newsroom EQ settings.

General Phone-Gathering Tips

There are many news-gathering possibilities on the phone. Most involve actualities, the only basic tape form that doesn't require an outside reporter. But you can also improve your news product by swapping with other news shops in your state, province or region. They can provide you with material in exchange for your offer to do the same for them.

Keep a list of key stations in nearby markets. Have their news hotline and switchboard numbers handy—also, the time of the hour they do newscasts. Don't call right before their deadline. If a story breaks in their area, ask them what tape they can feed. Have them do any voice reports to your style and standards. If you end up dealing with a person who can't read (and it happens!) ask him or her a few questions, then just use the answers.

Many times, it's helpful to set up regular "beat" calls of stations in close-by cities, to swap tape. Sometimes, setting up "exclusive" trading arrangements is worthwhile to both stations concerned.

Many tape cuts gathered by telephone will sound very poor, fed by phone to another station. The quality will be reduced by the phone line so they're hardly worth using at the second station.

To get tape of newsmakers, and people thrust into the news suddenly, you'll need a set of local phone directories (white and yellow pages), along with a City Guide and/or Cross-Street Index. You should also keep a computer or card file of key newsmakers, along with their office and home phones. Make sure the file is regularly checked to remove outdated numbers.

Do not use the word "interview" unless the person you're calling is accustomed to dealing with the media, and thus being "interviewed". Often a person frightened by the term is perfectly willing to "talk about" the story.

If you encounter reluctance to talk, or an outright refusal, say you hope you "won't have to use the *other side* alone." Tell the person you're doing a *favor* by calling, giving him or her a chance to tell their story.

After you've finished asking questions, ask the person if he or she wants to add anything. Sometimes the person will. If not, it brings the call to a quick, and natural, conclusion.

On unlisted and unpublished numbers, an operator can place the call, and ask the party to call you back. Check with the operator to make sure the message got through. If a phone number rings "busy" constantly, someone may be trying to avoid you. Get the operator to check the number, it may be off the hook. If it is, you're free to use that fact on the air. Some phone companies now impose separate charges for these services.

If you can't get hold of the person you want, you may want to leave a message for him or her to call back. When you do, always find out the time that person is expected back in. If the time has passed, and you haven't been called, place another call.

If your person is involved in an unfavorable story, your call-back, messages may be ignored. In this case—keep trying—and keep track of how many calls you make (and how many different excuses you get). You may want to use those facts on the air: "So far, there's no reaction from Capitalist Corporation to that massive anti-pollution lawsuit. We've called the company's headquarters more than a dozen times. Secretaries say all the top people are in a meeting, and can't talk."

It's easy for someone to ignore a little piece of paper that contains your call-back message. It's not so easy for them to ignore a persistent, live, newsperson on the line. Be obnoxious, if that's the only way to get the story.

Avoid making calls through a switchboard, whenever possible. They're frequently the source of annoying hum, clicks, and buzzes that can drown out voice material. Many phones are now set up so you can call an extension number directly, avoiding the switchboard operator.

Spot-News Via Phone

Most of your dealings with ordinary citizens will be on spot-news stories or random-reaction cuts. That includes everything from a plane crash down the block, to their feelings on the high cost of meat. These "folks" have no reason to suspect that a reporter would suddenly want to talk to them. Many times they're surprised . . . in many spot-news situations they're nervous and bewildered.

Never use the word "interview" on these types of calls. Talk to these people in their type of language. If you have a deep radio voice, don't use it. Make the recording legalities quick and casual. You may have to ask very simple questions: "What did you see?" . . . "What did it sound like?" . . . "How do you feel?"

Start with the basics and give people lots of freedom to express themselves on tape. Avoid questions that can be answered "yes" or "no". Once you have enough good tape, go back and pin down any specific details that aren't clear.

If the "folks" won't talk, it's generally out of nervousness, or a feeling of inferiority. You must flatter the reluctant person. Tell him or her how much listeners depend on them for information. Say: "You can help tell us what's going on." . . . "You'll be able to hear yourself on the radio." . . . "We don't have to use your name, if you don't want."

To reach people on a spot-news story, check the City Guide or Cross Street Index to find a location near the scene. Use names that are listed, and find them in the phone book. This generally works best on businesses.

They're most likely to have listed phones, and least likely to move to another location. You might also keep a list of *pay* phone locations (and numbers) at key locations. Some local phone companies may have a list available.

Depending on the story, and your own newsroom policies, you might want to call the actual location of the spot-news story. Be sure, however, that you are not interfering with police or fire operations, and are not jeopardizing lives. You might be doing exactly that by phoning the gunman who's holding hostages.

If you are chasing spot-news in an unfamiliar small town or rural area and law enforcement (or fire) people are not available for information, here are some options:

- Virtually every county will have at least a weekly newspaper, perhaps even a radio station. You might be better off avoiding Directory Assistance charges and seeing what is in your station's "Broadcasting Yearbook" or "SRDS". Both are invaluable newsroom reference tools.
- Ask the Directory Assistance operator to look up the name of the town (or county). For "Greenville" there might be the Greenville Cafe, Greenville Motel, etc.
- Ask for the Post Office (this will frequently double as a store and community center in small towns).
- Ask for a 7/11 Store (open late, perhaps 24-hours), a Denny's (24 hours), or a McDonald's. They'll be listed by company name, with addresses below.
- In a farm area try for a Co-op, or perhaps a grain elevator.
- Try the American Legion; Knights of Columbus; or Veterans of Foreign Wars. One of these may double as the local social club.
- Tell the local Directory Assistance operator you will talk with *anybody* in the area. This may put you one or two calls away from somebody at or near the scene.

News Conferences via Phone

Frequently, run-of-the-mill news conferences can be worked on the phone. Many people are willing to talk the day (or night) before. They see it as extra publicity. For you—it's a chance to use tape of the scheduled 10 AM news conference material in the 7 AM and 8 AM newscasts.

Another method is to work the phone an hour (or even a few minutes) before—with the idea of airing something *as* the news conference is held. If you already have a news release or other background information, all you need are two or three good answers.

Or—as a last resort—arrange a phone interview *after* the news conference.

The same technique can be used with *some* speeches . . . if you can get through to the speaker before or after. The phone interview can deal with issues raised in the speech.

If you simply have no outside staff, there's no reason *not* to use these techniques. But stations with a news image certainly wouldn't want to jeopardize a working relationship with important local figures by ignoring their news conferences or speeches in favor of a quickie phone interview.

Overseas Calling

Foreign calls can be dialed directly to most of the non-Communist world. Prices are surprisingly low—sometimes less than calling across the state.

You can get foreign numbers by calling "O", your local operator, and asking for "Directory Assistance" in the city and country you want. The charge for this, in 1987, ranged up to 50¢.

Calls to *non*-direct dial countries take longer. Call "O" and ask for the International Operator. Identify yourself by station and say it's a "Press Emergency" call which will speed completion. You'll be called back in minutes—or hours—when a circuit is free and when the other party has answered.

AT&T offers more information at 1-800-874-4000, and will send literature free on request.

Calls from the U.S. to Canada (and Canada to the U.S.) are ordinary Long Distance and are dialed "1 + area code".

Callbacks

```
                    C A L L B A C K   F O R M
    At time: _____   ☐ Exactly    ☐ Approximately
    ☐ Please Call  ☐ Expect Call From
    Name: _____  Title: _____
    Organization/Company: _____
    Location: _____  Phone: _____
    Questions:
    1)
    2)
    3)
    4)
    5)
    After interview please  ☐ Air tape  ☐ Hold for me  ☐ _____
    Your name: _____
```

Naturally the person you want to interview is not in. And you have an assignment and will be out of the shop for hours. This form (or something similar) can allow someone else in the newsroom to do the job.

As a general rule, the person who does the interview—whether over the phone or on-scene—should cut the tape. Sharing the work is inefficient and a source of potential mistakes.

News Hotlines and Tipsters

A news "hotline" or "tipline" can enable you to beat the competition— and hype your station's news prowess, as well. You simply ask listeners to phone in when they eyewitness a spot-news story. This saves you time and effort in checking directories to call the location.

The hotline number, itself, should ring directly in your newsroom (without going through the main switchboard). It should not be used for *outgoing* news calls. For effectiveness . . . you may want to arrange a number that ends with the digits "6-3-9-7" or "N-E-W-S." You might also try to get a hotline that ends with your station call letters.

Inventive promotion of a hotline number should give you a great deal of input from eyewitnesses. And their tips will sometimes enable you not only to beat the competition, but also the police or fire department, to a story.

You'll probably find it helpful to have a hotline form prepared, so all the necessary information is written down, and nothing important is omitted. It's also helpful to have a tape-recorder within reach, hooked up to the phone line.

```
WLW RADIO NEWS
DATE _____   TIME RECEIVED _____
TIP  _____
     _____
     _____
TIPSTER'S NAME _____   PHONE _____
        ADDRESS _____   CITY _____
EDITOR _____   TIP NO. _____
```

—Courtesy WLW/Cincinnati

A good form can simplify the handling of hotline tips.

Some stations use an incentive—either a prize, or cash—for the best tip of the week. Some offer up to $1,000 for the best yearly tip. The hotline can be promoted every time you use a spot-news story, whether or not it came from a tip: "When you see a story like that, call the news hotline . . . 7-8-9-N-E-W-S. You could win a prize for the best news tip of the week." Or, the hotline announcement can be used as a reminder, at the end of a newscast.

The big danger is the phony news tip. You can weed out some of them—by getting the tipster's name, address, and phone number. But you must have a hard rule—not to air any story received down the hotline, until it's been confirmed. There's an old saying: "Get it first, but first get it right" that applies very well.

The hotline, correctly promoted, will generate a lot of spot-news tips. You may also be pestered with giggling kids, calls about fender-bender accidents, and distraught people begging you to use their lost-dog announcements. But if your station is "into" car wrecks, fires, and the like, a hotline is invaluable. It can also put you ahead on major disaster stories (plane crashes, explosions, and the like) that any station would use.

Opinion Lines

A major story breaks in your market. You expect a big public reaction, so out goes a (reluctant) member of the news staff—recorder and microphone in hand—for the infamous "Man-on-the-Street Interview". The reporter has to find someone willing to talk, then explain the new development and hope the person has an intelligent comment.

```
KAAM Direct Line...386-6130...Question Log:

Month of:  August 1980

Date:      Question:

7-Thurs    Have you changed your family planning--because of the
           high cost of having children?

10-Mon     Would you consider living along the coast? (f/up to Hurricane)

13-Mon     Will you parents be glad to get kids back to school (1 wk till
           DISD starts classes).

19-Tues    Do you think Cowboy's Tony Dorsett deserves more money?
(evening)

22-Fri     Do we need more military power (as Reagan claims)--are you
           willing to pay for it?

25-Mon     Do you think school starts too early?

28-Thurs   Should the City of Dallas spend more money--trying to keep
           Love Field closed to commercial flights?

29-Fri     Should we make another attempt to get our hostages out
           of Iran, with a raid? (Ties in w/300th day of captivity)
```

As this log from a Dallas station shows, listener opinion does not have to be reserved for cataclysmic events. Three questions were on hard news stories, three on lifestyle/family, one on sports and one on weather.

The reporter is taken away from something else. Depending on logistics, there may or may not be tape on the next newscast.

The other option involves phone equipment—a line and answering machine. The better consumer models provide good quality and proven dual cassette reliability for $100 or less.

No outside work is needed, the same person doing the newscast can handle on-air promotion, auditioning and dubbing of incoming calls.

The machine is connected to a direct outside line (not through a switchboard) and runs unattended. A story breaking at night could, for example, generate calls from all-night listeners. You could be airing fresh reaction tape in morning-drive newscasts the next day—even though the newsroom was shut down overnight.

As in talk-radio, people react to both the question—and the reactions of other people. One good cut aired in a newscast, plus an invitation to call your station, could mean dozens of reactions over the next hour.

If you use it just once or twice a week, the answering machine system is much cheaper. The speed, and ease of use, may mean listener reaction becomes a frequent part of your newscasts.

Call-ins, however, cannot be used for *polling* with any degree of accuracy. It would be far too easy for one side of an issue to 'pack' the line with callers.

There is no "permission to broadcast" needed. Listeners are calling for the purpose of getting on the air, as on a telephone-talk show.

7 | Telephone Feeding

> ... *that's all we ever dreamed about, to be as fast as radio.*
> —Pat Polillo, VP, Westinghouse TV station group,
> *Broadcasting* Jan 5, 1976

No matter what kind of outside equipment a station has for newsgathering, there are times when a standard dial-up phone call is the quickest and most practical way to relay tape or live reports back to the newsroom. For some stations it is the *only* way.

For purposes of this chapter, we'll assume telephone feeding is—or will be—a regular newsgathering tool, worth the investment of a few extra dollars.

We'll also assume you already have a cassette recorder, which will be necessary to demonstrate phone-feeding techniques. Almost all cassette machines have standard input and output connectors known as "mini-jacks" which are also used with "patch cords" that terminate in "mini-plugs". (If you're not sure about your machine—consult the pictures under "Audio Connectors" in Chapter Eight.)

Equalizing Revisited

The same techniques that work for phone tape in the newsroom also apply on the feeding end. Unfortunately, at publication, only a few cassette recorders had built-in variable EQ.

Consumer electronics graphic EQ units, the size of a cigarette pack, are now available for as little as $15-$20. (A comparable Sony unit, the SEQ-50, is around $40.) Testing for this book shows they are extremely cost-effective and worth carrying as standard equipment if you feed by phone.

Typically they operate off one or two batteries and have five bands, generally with ±10 dB. In non-technical language—that's a pretty good adjustment range. As a general rule, you'll want to increase the controls for (or nearest) 300 Hz and 3000 Hz. Each phone line is different, and you'll need to get the opinion of the newsroom person taking in your material.

These portable EQs are stereo, but for our purposes only one channel is used. Check a local record/tape or electronics store for availability. 47th Street Photo in New York sells the Sony SEQ-50. At publication, Radio Shack did not have a comparable model.

How Phone Feeding is Done

There are now four methods of feeding material through a telephone. Two were developed for this book, along with a simple kit that will cover the best three methods. Equipment for the fourth (used on pay phones) is commercially available.

According to one estimate, 75% of the phones now in use are "modular", and the percentage of *non*-modular phones grows smaller each year. All modular phones can be unplugged at the "line cord" which connects to the "modular jack" typically on the baseboard or wall.

Modular phones with a separate handset may have a "handset cord" with modular plugs at both ends. Note that although plugs *look* the same on both line and handset cords—they are not. Line cord plugs are slightly wider and will not fit handset jacks.

But the two modular connectors . . . line plugs and jacks . . . and handset plugs and jacks . . . are standard industry-wide and will work on equipment from *any* phone company.

Some older phones are not modular. But because they're still fairly common, our kit includes a way to feed tape through most of them—called "alligator clips". All the feeding methods will be explained in their turn.

Radio station engineers may have many of these parts available. But if you have to purchase them, the complete list will cost $25. at Radio Shack (perhaps $15-$20. at other electronics or phone stores). This will give you the components for *two* "Octopus" feeding devices.

If you know how to strip wire you can build the first Octopus kit yourself in minutes. There is no soldering, no schematic, and it's as easy as hooking up your stereo.

Building the "Octopus" kit.

Tools required: Standard screwdriver
Wire Cutters
Electrical, cloth, or duct tape.

Parts: 1 - 2-position terminal strip (Radio Shack 274-663) 2/99¢
1 - 12" Modular to spade line cord (RS 279-391) $1.29
1 - Modular handset cord (RS 279-301) $5.95
1 - Lightweight headphone with miniplug, preferably mono (RS 33-1000) $5.
2 - Mini-plug to alligator clip patch cords (RS 42-2421) $2.29 ea.
1 - ⅛ Dual Jack Adapter (RS 274-310) $1.59
1 - Modular Duplex Jack (RS 279-357) $5.

Radio Shack parts numbers and prices are for reference only. (FCC Part 68 registration not required under Public Notice 20851 and Form 730 Rules, May 1985.)

This will give you all necessary equipment and parts for phone feeding. It's enough to build the Octopus kit *and* a smaller, companion kit explained in Chapter Eight. All unused parts, cord pieces etc., must be saved.

1) On modular to spade line cord, leave spades for red and green wires intact. Cut off spades for yellow and black wires (which will not be used).
2) Stretch coiled modular handset cord at one end and cut it approximately 2-feet from the plug. Strip away one-inch of outer insulation. Although cord appears to be round, 4 wires are actually flat in a row. You will strip the two *outer* wires back 1/2-inch to expose the delicate metal foil and synthetic fiber inside. (The two *inside* wires are not used and should be cut off.)
3) Next, cut one mini plug to alligator clips patch cord in half. Strip off insulation on each section, next to the cut, to expose 1/2-inch of metal on all wires.
4) You now have four patch cords. Arrange, so two are on each side of terminal strip.
5) One wire from each cord goes on each terminal. (No - it doesn't matter which one.)
6) Tighten screws, making sure the delicate modular handset wires are secure. Test the Octopus, using procedures outlined in this chapter.
7) Once test is complete, wrap terminal block with electrical or other tape. One cord should dangle from each corner of terminal strip, and all must be tightly secured in place with tape.

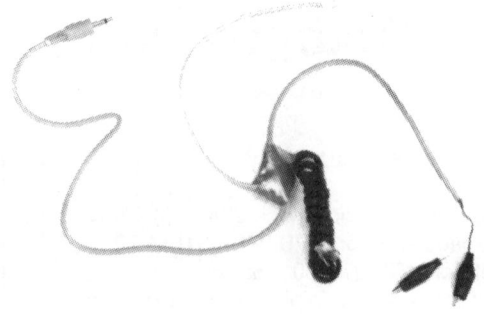

The Octopus is perhaps the world's ugliest patch cord.

Here are feeding procedures for all three methods covered in the Octopus kit. Let's say you've recorded an interview and want to phone-feed it to your station. (We'll discuss *live* feeding later in this chapter.)

- Rewind your cassette to beginning of interview and put volume control about halfway.
- Take the "Dual Jack Adapter" you bought and plug it into the graphic EQ output jack (which may be marked "monitor", "headphones", etc.) The EQ input is then connected to the output jack on your cassette recorder. (If you don't have an EQ unit yet, the "Dual Jack Adapter" goes directly into your cassette recorder's output jack, marked "monitor", "headphones", etc.)
- Your earphones are plugged in either side of the "Dual Jack Adapter". The mini-plug from the Octopus goes in the other side. (After you connect to the phone, you'll be able to hear your material and, at low level, hear the newsroom.)

This general set-up procedure applies to *any* Octopus feeding method.

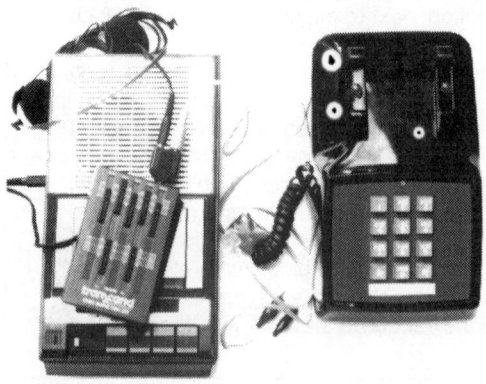

Modular Handset Feeds. Overhead view shows cassette recorder feeding EQ (on top). EQ output is split by Dual Jack Adapter, goes into headphones (top left) and Octopus (next to phone). Modular Handset Plug on Octopus goes into base of phone.

Modular Handset Feeds

(Use when phones have modular handset cords.)

1. Call newsroom using phone as on any other call.
2. Once newsroom is ready for level and EQ test, grasp handset cord where it enters base of phone. Slip your fingernail under little plastic tab right below the plug. Lift up and hold while pulling out plug. Put handset and cord nearby (*not* back on phone cradle).
3. Insert Octopus modular handset plug (which is on a coiled cord), into base of phone.
4. Feed tape by depressing *Play* button on cassette machine. Stop tape every 5-seconds, listen on headphones for instructions on adjusting level and tone quality. When newsroom is satisfied, re-cue tape and feed.
5. Confirm afterward by unplugging Octopus modular handset cord and reattaching phone handset.

This is the quickest and easiest feeding method—and should be used whenever you have the option.

Modular Line Cord Feeds

(Use for phones detachable at wall-jack only, including one-piece modular phones and modular phones with "hard wired" handsets.)

1. Disconnect phone at wall jack and plug in "Modular Duplex Jack" you purchased. Reconnect phone to either side of adapter.
2. Call newsroom using phone as on any other call.
3. Once newsroom is ready for level and EQ test, plug in Octopus modular *line* cord to other side of "Modular Duplex Jack".
4. Unplug the phone from the adapter. (That's right—unplug the phone!) Feed test material. Stop tape every 5-seconds and listen to headphones for level and EQ instructions. When the newsroom is satisfied, re-cue your tape and feed.
5. After feed, reconnect phone by plugging into adapter.
6. Once phone is in, disconnect Octopus modular line plug.
7. Talk on phone to confirm.

Caution—steps 5-7 must be done in just this order to avoid breaking the connection. In addition, with this method only, the Octopus must

Modular Line Cord Feeds. Overhead view shows setup before removing phone. Cassette recorder feeds EQ, output goes into headphones and Octopus. Octopus Line Cord plugs into Modular Duplex Jack, entering telephone Wall Jack (top right).

not remain connected after you or the newsroom hang up the phone. Electricity on the line is only 6 volts DC during a call with *any* of these feeding methods. But with Modular Line Cord Feeding only, it will jump to over 50 volts DC the second the call ends, and 90 volts if it should ring. Either could damage your equipment. (An engineer can put a 2.0-5.0 ufd capacitor in series to block DC voltage through the Octopus, if desired.)

Testing shows feeding volume is somewhat lower using this method, but it did not present a problem. Quality was comparable.

One Microcassette recorder tested would not "hold the line" when the phone was unplugged. If you encounter this problem—the phone *can* be left in. The handset mike will then operate at *very* low volume and you can easily cover it with your hand while feeding.

Alligator Clip Feeds

(Use on standard non-modular phones that have removable handset mouthpieces.)

1. Call newsroom using phone as on any other call.
2. Once newsroom is ready for level and EQ test, unscrew round plastic mouthpiece, turning it counter-clockwise. It may need a few taps on a hard surface to loosen.

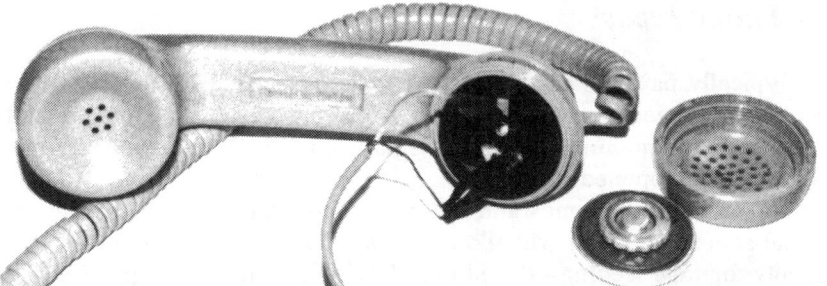

Alligator Clip Feeds. Traditional phone mouthpiece is unscrewed, clips are put on both metal contacts. Old-type carbon microphone is next to mouthpiece cover.

3. Take off plastic mouthpiece cover. There may be an unattached metal "carbon microphone" disc inside. Remove it and you'll see two metal prongs, bars, or some other pair of contacts. On some newer phones, you must turn the handset upside down and let the entire microphone element fall out of place, revealing two screw terminals on the backside.
4. Put one Octopus alligator clip on each metal prong, bar, or screw terminal. The clip jaws should be open and gripping the edges, not a flat surface. (If metal parts of the clips are touching, sound will be cut off.)
5. Feed test. Stop tape every five-seconds, and listen on headphones for level and EQ instructions. When the newsroom is satisfied, re-cue your tape and feed.
6. Once feed is over, disconnect alligator clips, replace mike and reattach plastic mouthpiece cover by turning clockwise.
7. Talk on phone to confirm.

This is the older method of tape feeding, more cumbersome than plugging in. The percentage of phones allowing easy access by alligator clips is steadily diminishing.

Some GTE equipment, like this pay phone, uses overlapping metal bars. One alligator clip is attached to each.

Pay Phone Feeds

Typically, pay phones on the AT&T system (made by Western Electric) have mouthpieces glued with epoxy to prevent vandalism. And special vandal-resistant microphone covers degrade quality. (Many non-AT&T pay phones *can* be opened.)

For sealed pay phones and older non-modular decorator phones, a special acoustic coupler will allow access. There is one model made specifically for tape feeding—the Shure 50AC ($40). It fits snugly over the phone mouthpiece and sends sound through the carbon mike. Therein lies the drawback. Quality may, at times, be good—but won't be up to that of a wired connection.

Shure's 50AC, a telephone feeding device of last resort. A strap (not shown) holds the acoustic coupler in place. —*Courtesy Shure*

Since this is a method of last resort, you may have trouble justifying so much money for a device you *don't* want to use. A far cheaper version, developed for this book, produces fair-to-good quality on a phone line for $3 (assuming you elect to carry a portable graphic equalizer as recommended). Even without the EQ, quality is useable.

The prototype is based on a "Budget Pillow Speaker" (Radio Shack 33-206 $3.) which is pried apart with a screwdriver. The grill is used only as a protective case in your kit. The speaker is a perfect match in size with a conventional phone mouthpiece. It is placed directly on the plastic mouthpiece cover and secured with a thick rubber band.

Assuming you have good quality cassette material to begin with—the following EQ settings are a guide:

    100 Hz (0); 300 Hz (+10 dB); 1 kHz (-8 dB); 3 kHz (+4 dB); 10 kHz (-10 dB)

Telephone Feeding

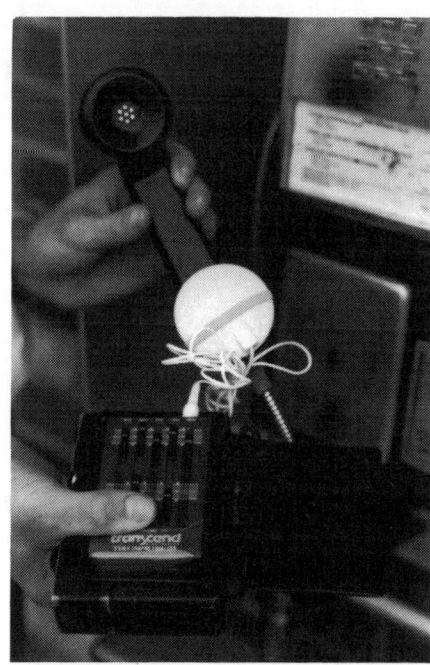

A cheap, but effective, way to feed down a sealed pay phone. Heavily-equalized cassette tape goes through the $3 "Pillow Speaker" attached to the phone mouthpiece.

With these extreme settings, you can see how much of a difference the EQ makes. Naturally, this will vary depending on phone line conditions and what you have recorded. "Tweaking" (making little adjustments) on the equipment will make a big difference with this method.

This is far better than an older technique, which involved using giant pliers to unscrew the mouthpiece.

Last (and least) you can try feeding over the cassette machine speaker. This works *only* if you have a good recording and a good phone line to the newsroom. Put your cassette machine's tone control on full bass. Hold it just a couple inches from the phone mouthpiece, and have the newsroom check sound quality as you feed tape. You may want to cup your hands over the cassette speaker. This method requires some experimenting, but it does work.

Obviously, the ideal solution would be for pay phones to contain modular jacks on the front, allowing direct connection of equipment—including cassette recorders and portable computers. (This was suggested to several phone companies beginning in 1984. There were no results at publication.)

By the way, pay phone calls from outside your local area should always be made collect, or on a credit card. There have been at least two national network bulletin stories done live from a pay phone, complete with the operator interrupting to demand more change!

Some pay phones are now restricted to *outgoing* calls only and won't ring (although the other end will hear the "ring back" sound in the handset). So the newsroom may not be able to reach a reporter who is standing by at a pay phone either waiting to feed, or to go live.

Problem Phones

Non-modular phones with sealed mouthpieces

The pay phone method works, but is a last resort. If you can get permission to open up the phone with a standard screwdriver, do the following:

- Loosen screws holding plastic case (2 screws in most standard size phones, near front and rear of bottom plate, or hidden under removable plastic cover over phone number.)
- Remove plastic case, establish call, then use Octopus alligator clips to patch onto network terminals "B" and "E2". Cover phone mouthpiece with your hand during feeding:

If this fails, you can use a variation on the Modular Line Cord technique and patch directly to the line. On *single*-line phones this will be "L1" and "L2" on the network terminals. On a typical 6-button business phone, whatever line you're using is switched to "L2" and "9"—which is where you patch. Again, you will have to put your hand over the phone mouthpiece. And the Octopus will have to be disconnected *before* you or the newsroom hang up. (See caution note for Modular Line Cord Feeding.)

Party-Line Phones

They look harmless enough, but some play dead when we patch on. Even the FCC can't establish uniform national standards because of what it calls a "great difference in the design of party lines within and among telephone companies". If a direct connection fails for no apparent reason— you may have to use the inferior pay phone method.

Other Useful Phone Equipment

For reporters doing a lot of street work, and relying on phone feeding, it's now feasible to *carry* a phone. This allows you access to any modular jack where a phone is not in place.

Telephone Feeding

Voice quality on the phone really doesn't matter—it's only used to establish the call, then the Modular Line Cord method takes over and the phone is disconnected. If you consider doing this—pick a rotary dial phone, or a push-button model allowing "pulse dialing". Both can be used on *any* line. Push-button phones that generate tone will work only on lines equipped for this.

Carrying your own one-piece phone gives you another option—installing a jack in the phone allowing you to feed tape and simultaneously mute the mike. This is delicate work and should be left to an engineer.

There are several drawbacks to using this as your *only* feeding method:

- Some phones are still hard-wired with no modular connectors.
- Many one and two-piece phones are "quarter modular" and have only one of four potential modular connectors—at the wall end of the line cord. Thus, you may have to move furniture to unplug this phone so you can plug in your own.
- The phone is far larger than the Octopus.

A final handy piece of gear is a small plastic adapter to hook your Octopus modular line cord to a 4-prong jack, which is widely used in older buildings. (RS 279-351 $3.19.)

Talk-Through

So far, this chapter has dealt with getting *into* phones. Now comes a companion technique for getting more *out of* phones.

Cassette and Microcassette recorders don't just record and playback tape. They can also amplify the microphone when *no* recording is taking place. This is known as "talk-through" (or "feed-through") and it's an easy way to improve the quality of live voicers, Q&A and voice-alities fed down the phone. We bypass the cheap telephone mike and use our own.

In talk-through the recorder's VU meter or LEDs will respond normally to your voice on mike, but the tape will *not* run.

First, insert an erased cassette into the machine. Then, try using normal pressure to depress the *Record* button alone. On some machines this will be all you need to do.

If *Record* won't go down by itself, depress the *Pause* button or switch, so the tape will not move. Then depress both *Record* and *Play*.

(If your machine has no *Pause* function, you can still use talk-through by installing a customized cassette or Microcassette. You make it by cutting or removing the tape inside, then using *Record* and *Play*. Be sure this cassette or Microcassette is well-labelled, so you don't attempt to record on it.)

If your machine has a choice between automatic and manual recording levels, use manual.

Talk-through works with any of the phone feeding methods just described. Equipment is set up the same way for both recorded and live material.

Talk-through is also very handy if you are feeding a number of tape cuts and want to "billboard" them in between. You would use the cassette containing your recorded material, and cue up the first cut before entering talk-through right at that point. The newsroom will need to get a level on the tape (which won't necessarily match the talk-through level). To feed tape, here's how you get out of talk-through:

- Press *Stop*. If *Pause* was used, release it. Then press *Play*.

As mentioned earlier, wraparounds are awkward to do on the phone, and are not recommended for routine use. Instead of a blank cassette, you would use the one containing the actuality "meat" for your wraparound "sandwich".

First you would write your wraparound, noting the actuality "incue" (first few words) and "outcue" (last few words). Then you cue the cassette to the incue.

- Patch into the phone, go into talk-through, and call the newsroom.
- Feed a test of your voice level.
- Feed a test of the actuality level. (It won't necessarily be the same.) After the newsroom is satisfied, go back to the actuality incue.
- Use talk-through and feed your live beginning.
- When it's time for the actuality, press *Stop*, if *Pause* was used, release it, and press *Play*.
- Immediately after the actuality, press *Stop*.
- Go back into talk-through and feed your live close.

It's a long process, but the report still is not ready for air use! You created dead air and noise going in and out of talk-through, so the newsroom will have to splice out those flaws before airing.

One final caution: some reports fed by talk-through will not sound as good as ones *recorded* on cassette and fed down the phone. This is especially true on cheaper consumer-grade recorders. A few minutes of testing will determine how your machine performs.

Mixing Without A Mixer

The "⅛-inch Dual Jack Adapter" you invested in earlier does double-duty in your kit. As explained, it allows simultaneous feeding and monitoring through your EQ or cassette output.

Telephone Feeding

It will also work *sideways* to combine the output of two recorders. This is frequently helpful in putting your voice over music or some other background sound. The only tricky part is getting the right balance between the two.

Sound is cued up on cassette recorder 'A' and must be at roughly the same level throughout. You will use recorder 'B' in talk-through to do a report over the sound. You'll also need a mini-plug to mini-plug patch cord, which is supplied with many recorders. (RS 42-2420 $2.29.)

Here's the procedure:

1. Plug one end of the mini-to-mini patch cord in output jack for recorder 'A' (sound) and the other end in one side of the ⅛-inch Dual Jack Adapter.
2. Plug the adapter in the output jack of recorder 'B' (talk-through).
3. From here, a standard hook-up is made to your graphic EQ and the Octopus kit.

Because you will need to hear newsroom instructions on level and EQ settings, it is easiest to feed via the Modular Line Cord or Alligator Clips (leaving the handset in place while you test).

You will at least be able to raise or lower playback level on machine 'A'. If recorder 'B' has manual level, you should have control over volume in talk-through and can adjust that as well.

This procedure is also useful for phone-fed wraparounds. The actuality is cued up on machine 'A', which is put in *Pause* and *Play*. Machine 'B' does the talk-through. Inserting the actuality is as simple as releasing *Pause* and letting the tape play. You then engage *Pause* to stop it, while simultaneously beginning your live close.

Done smoothly enough, no splicing will be necessary in the newsroom.

This basic mixing technique isn't necessarily limited to the phone. But on much of the other equipment we use for feeding news, mixing provisions are built-in.

Action Central in Your Basement

You or an engineer can change a phone into a handy tape-gathering and feeding center for $2.-$3. A conventional modular desk phone is the easiest kind to work on. A push-to-talk switch with the no-noise modification described in the last chapter is recommended. Switches that are commercially installed are "Momentary push-button, normally open". (Several Radio Shack models are available depending on space available in your handset.)

Feeding and recording are both done with the Octopus kit. Feeding methods have already been described. Recording uses the Modular Line

Cord method. You observe all steps, except you plug the Octopus mini-plug patch cord into your cassette recorder's *mike* input jack, and you leave the phone in place instead of removing it.

If your recorder has manual level control—use it. Adjust to get 100% modulation on the interviewee. Depending on the phone you use, *your* level on tape will be extremely hot and may distort even if you lower the volume control while you are talking. So don't plan on using tape of your voice.

The Octopus must be disconnected before either of you hangs up. Refer to the caution earlier under the Modular Line Cord Feeding method.

Still another recording method involves a phone answering machine in combination with the push-to-talk. Consult the owner's manual for instructions.

Voice-Act

This widely used piece of radio news gear made its appearance in 1972. It's a good quality microphone and transistor amplifier contained in an ungainly hunk of black plastic, which is screwed onto an old-model phone handset. It draws power from the phone line—no batteries are necessary.

The Voice-Act contains a mini-jack and three-position switch labelled "Mix, External and Mike". In "Mix" the mini-jack feeds sound from a

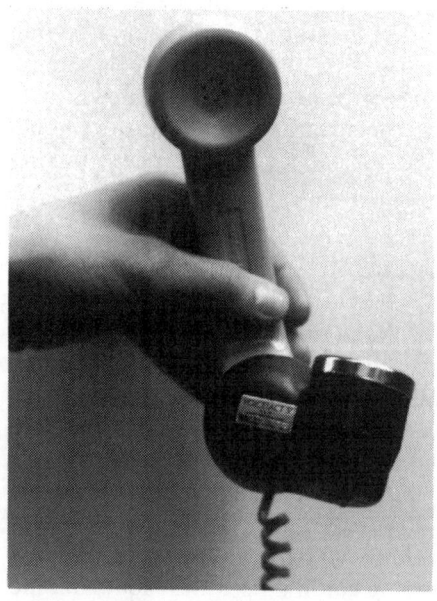

The Voice-Act provides a high-quality phone mouthpiece and input jack, but works only on standard handsets.

cassette recorder and the mike operates in a close-talking mode with a distinct "telephone" quality. Wraparound feeding is easy this way, the actuality can be inserted by using the cassette machine's *Pause* control to start and stop the tape. But, typically, the actuality will sound better than your voice.

In "External" only the mini-jack is on, and tests for this book show the Voice-Act improves quality of cassette material and provides more volume. In "Mike" the Voice-Act delivers good quality with the mike held three or more inches from the mouth. In this position it does not sound so much like a telephone.

Prices range from $80.-$90. depending on the model. One fits only standard AT&T "500-series" phones (with screw-off mouthpieces). The oither fits only standard GTE phones (with two metal bars).

Obviously, this is the big drawback. The Voice-Act works well—but if you can't find the right type of phone, it is useless.

If you do reports live through the Voice-Act you have no control over output volume. You also have no control over frequency response. Your cassette recorder (which you need to carry anyhow) already has adjustable volume in playback, and some models allow it in live "talk through". And carrying an inexpensive graphic equalizer allows you to customize the feed for each phone line.

In testing for this book, a standard EV 635A mike, a Sony cassette recorder and a $15. graphic EQ produced slightly better frequency response then a Voice-Act. Testing involved local and long distance AT&T and Contel lines.

Other Improvement Devices

The cheap carbon microphone is a major limiting factor in most conventional phones. Replacement electret condenser mikes, designed for phone handset use, are available for as little as $7. Manufacturers such as Walker Equipment have several models offering broader frequency response and/or noise-cancellation features. This may be helpful in improving quality of reports from, say, a local stock broker. These mikes are now standard equipment on many of the better electronic phones with "K" type handsets.

If local phone conditions are *really* rotten—it may be worth considering amplified handsets which combine electret condenser mikes with adjustable gain. The Walker W7-500, for example, offers up to 16 dB gain at a cost of $40.

A handy device called the "Microtel" by Gentner Engineering offers many features of the Octopus kit, plus several others, for $200. It replaces the modular phone handset and operates as a mike-to-line level amplifier.

The Microtel contains its own amplification and does basic mixing.
—*Courtesy Gentner Engineering*

It allows variable output and headphone levels and will also work in reverse—to record off a phone line. Microtel is slightly larger than a cigarette pack and uses 9-volt batteries or an optional AC adapter.

Frequency Extenders

These units are used at both ends of the phone call, to shift the sound range of material, allowing more of it to pass over the 300-3,000 Hz range of a standard phone line. Comrex is the best-known company, and equipment using its system is said to be "Comrex-compatible."

The commonly-used Comrex one line systems extend low frequency response, so 50-3,000 Hz is possible on a standard phone line. (If you think of a piano—this is an extra 2½ octaves of sound, which adds depth and naturalness.)

Comrex one-line systems are widely used by networks, which must contend with reports filed by phone worldwide. The basic LX-T and LX-R

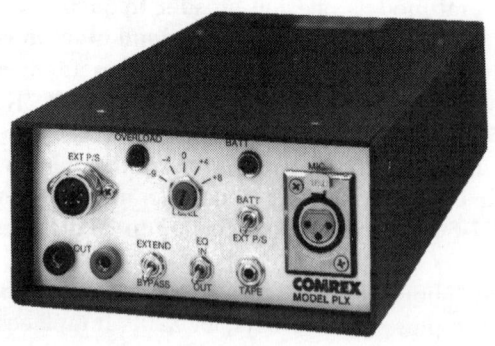

The Comrex PLX broadens frequency response on a standard phone line by up to 2½ octaves, restoring much of the voice's lower range.
—*Courtesy Comrex*

system involves a unit the size of a cigar box at both ends of the phone call. They require AC power and cannot run off batteries. The combined price begins at $1000. A truly portable system, using the battery-operated PLX unit in the field would cost $2000.

Frequency extenders also come in two-line types, like the Comrex PTLX, which improves both low *and* high-frequency sound. This would give you a 50-5,000 Hz response out of *two* standard dial-up phone lines used together. The transmit-receive package runs $9000.

Both types are helpful on long distance phone work, sports, and other long-form programming that must go by phone. But they're certainly not necessary to feed voicers and actualities from across town or from the next county.

Feeding the Networks

To a great extent all the national and state networks rely on their affiliates for local tape. A little extra work could mean frequent supplemental paychecks and the satisfaction of having your material heard statewide or nationwide.

People who supply tape to the nets are known as "stringers". Most work for affiliate stations, but generally nets will consider material from anyone.

Stringer Mike Rogers has sold material from hundreds of locations, to most of the U.S. networks. He's a music conductor and arranger who travels constantly and calls radio news "the most enjoyable activity in my life."

Here's his advice:

When you want to pitch a story, ask yourself: "Is this going to be informative and interesting to the listener in San Diego, Panama City, Florida or Waco, Texas?" If you can answer yes, pitch the story. Try to be as succinct as possible. Look for ways to contribute to the network. Finally, don't let an editor's rejection of a story offend you.

Before you try to "sell" tape—you should be aware of what's wanted based on the tape forms explained in Chapter 5, and your net's time limits. In other words: "listen". Several nets have written guidelines which you can request from the News Department or (if there is one) the Affiliate Relations Department.

Generally, it costs you nothing to pitch a story. Some nets have toll-free 800 numbers, others accept collect calls. Major national and some state nets are staffed 24-hours every day.

If you're in the field, you feed material as you would in calling your own station. On a breaking story nobody expects a perfectly-billboarded package.

If you are pitching a major spot-news story—*don't wait*. Call immediately with tape if you sense the net might be interested. If you can beat the wires, so much the better. (Actually, you may have better luck in selling tape if the story has just moved on the wires.)

Be ready to sell your story in a sentence: "This is Tom Tape of affiliate W---, and I've got . . ."

At this point, generally one of three things will happen:

- The material will be rejected.
- It will be accepted "on spec" (speculation). This means it will be taken in and evaluated. If the net uses it, you'll be paid. If not—there's no payment.
- The net will buy your material at the standard fee.

Assuming the material is bought or taken "on spec" you will next be transferred to a tape room person who will need your:

- Legal Name
- Station call letters (if any)
- Social Security Number
- Mailing Address
- Phone Number

All this is paperwork for payment. You'll then need to billboard what you're feeding, spelling out any names of people interviewed.

The major national nets also are set up for taking in Comrex (or Comrex-compatible) material. Some like to do it at half-speed. Check beforehand.

Then you feed your material . . . and wait for your payment. Prices vary, you may be paid for each piece, or for a complete feed. Promptness of payment also varies. If the net sends out a printed billboard, save it in case of disputes.

If the net calls beforehand and *requests* coverage on a story, it has in a sense already "bought" it. You'll be paid, assuming you fulfill the assignment.

Be aware of some quirks common to networks:

- Material you gather by phone may not be accepted, depending on network policy, because phone tape frequently sounds bad when it's re-fed.

- You may have a perfectly good story—but if there's bigger news breaking in Beirut or Bombay, the net may decline. Everything is relative. With the national commercial nets there is generally a lot of material to be crammed into a very limited amount of time.
- Just as in local radio—there are slow days and busy days. You stand a greater chance of getting material accepted at nights and on weekends, all other things being equal.
- Even though a major newsmaker, like a Federal official, is in your market—the *national* nets probably won't be interested unless he/she says something new. Nets become saturated with these people when they're back in Washington or New York. A *state* net might, however, be very interested in the story.
- Both national and state nets can almost always use good "illustration" tape. This is true on all sorts of consumer and economic stories, that have a national or state tie-in (such as monthly unemployment figures).

And nets don't just feed *news*. You may be able to provide sports, features, and material for specialized shows covering medicine, religion, and entertainment. Check the network feeding schedule to see what's going out.

Ubiquitous stringer Mike Rogers says if there's *sound* available, frequently it can be made into a story:

> I have interviewed beekeepers right by their hives to get some good sound, crawled under police cars to get sound in gangland wars and drug raids, lived in a cardboard box near a railroad track to do a piece about today's hoboes, and many more incidents that let reporters live life to the fullest.

8 | Portable Recorders and Equipment

Give us the tools, and we will finish the job.
—Sir Winston Churchill,
Radio Broadcast, February 9, 1941.

It's gotten so that reporting on the radio is no more cumbersome than listening to the radio. With just a few ounces of equipment in a shirt pocket or purse, you're ready for most any assignment.

A complete outside kit with everything you would ever need for taping and live broadcast can fit in an attache case.

While outside reporting techniques are basically the some for both taped and live news, we'll examine the equipment separately in two chapters.

Human Equipment

Normal human sound contains both low and high-pitched material. It varies, of course, from male to female, and voice to voice. The overall speech range is roughly 75 to 8,000 vibrations per second. This is referred to as "Hertz" or "cycles". By comparison, a piano produces from 27½ to 4,186 Hertz.

The "fundamental frequency" of a typically deep male voice will be around 130 hz, with a total speaking range varying from 80 to 400 Hz. For a female, the fundamental frequency is usually twice as high—around 260 Hz—and the speaking range is roughly 190 to 1,050 Hz.

Both men and women produce sounds past 6,000 Hz, when pronouncing "C", "S", "X", and "Z". But, in addition, there are multiples of the basic frequencies present, known as "harmonics" or "overtones". These go as far above the normal speaking range, adding a fullness and "presence" to the voice. Normal human hearing, at a maximum, stretches from 15 Hz to 20,000 Hz.

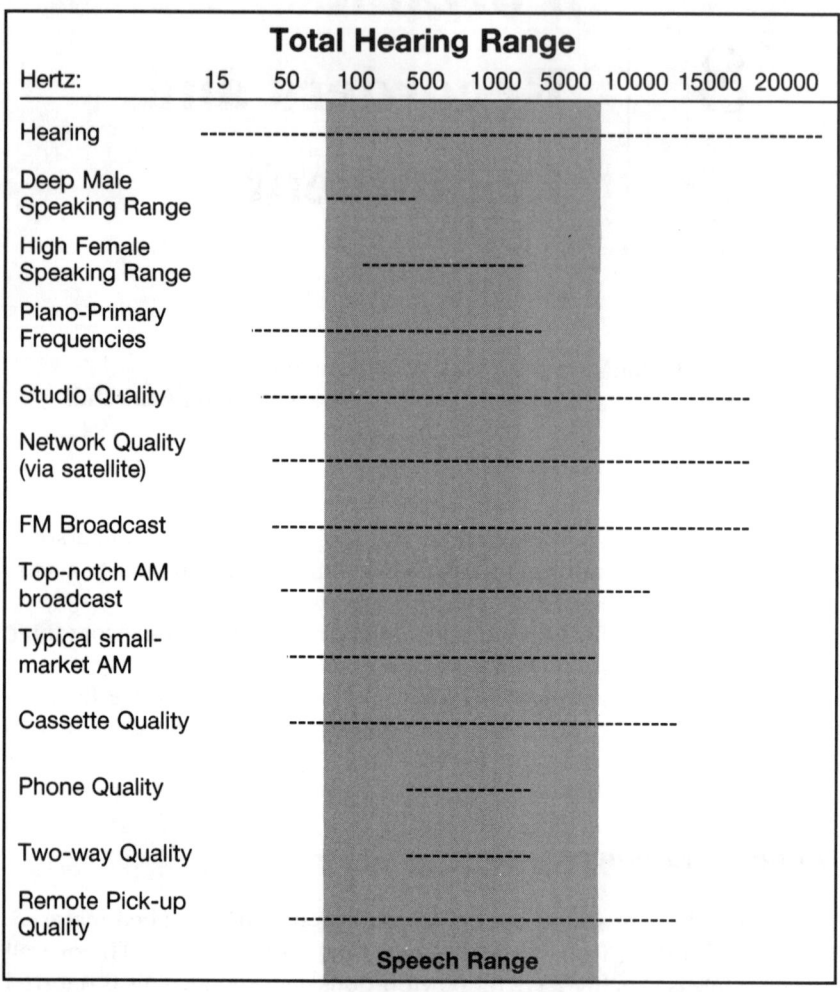

Audio Connectors

There are three main types of connectors used to link tape equipment. All consist of a male part, known as a "plug", and a female part, known as a "jack" or "receptacle". As you may have guessed, the male part fits inside the female part.

The first main group is the most common. These connectors are used in most battery-operated tape recorders, and many sound systems. The

Portable Recorders and Equipment   105

Common audio connectors
  shown *actual size*.
From left to right:
Miniature Plug (Mini-Plug)
Sub-miniature Plug (Sub-mini Plug)
¼-inch Phone Plug
RCA Plug (Phono Plug)
Paper clip, for size comparison purposes.
                              —*Courtesy Switchcraft*

"miniature plug" or "mini-plug" is standard on cassette recorders. Nearly all input and output jacks (except the remote mike one) take this connector. Radio Shack prefers to call this the ⅛-inch plug.

The "sub-miniature plug" or "sub-mini plug" is the same thing only smaller. The only common use for it, is the remote microphone input jack on a cassette recorder. It is not actually used to carry audio material, and only connects the on-off switch on the microphone, to the recorder.

The third type is used on many studio recorders and sound systems. It's known as a "¼-inch phone plug" or "phone plug". The plug, itself, is ¼-inch in diameter. (This is *not* the same as a similar-looking plug used on patch panels.)

The last type in this group is known as an "RCA plug" or a "phono plug". It's not widely used for tape equipment, but is found on sound systems and some older tape machines, along with record players and turntables.

The second main group is widely used for professional microphones and sound systems. These are most commonly known as "XLR" or "Cannon" connectors. Male and female versions come with between 3 and 7 pins or sockets. They'll only match-up with a connector that has the same number.

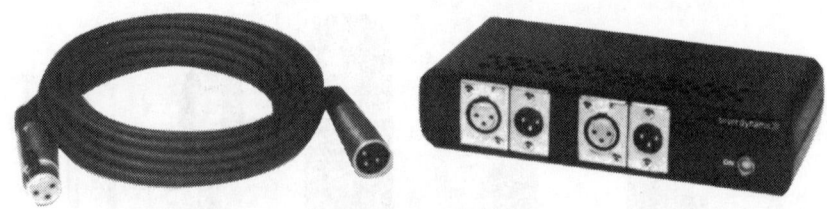

XLR (or Cannon) connectors shown on a cable and on equipment.
—*Courtesy Electro Voice/Beyer Dynamic*

To further complicate things, there's also a *miniature* version with between 3-5 pins or sockets.

With all these combinations—you will seldom encounter more than 4 pins or sockets used in sound systems. And if you don't have adapters in your kit—you can patch off the pins on a male connector, using your alligator clip patch cord (which is your backup for telephone feeding).

The third group of male and female connectors is found only on foreign machines, mostly from Europe. These are the "DIN" series, containing several different-looking types of plugs and jacks. But all have a standard 1-8 pins or sockets. DIN connectors are most commonly found on German, and Norelco (or Philips) recorders.

Just for the record, here are the other types of connectors in common use around radio stations. The "banana plug" is commonly found on test equipment. And the "tip, ring, and sleeve" is frequently used on patch panels—often in pairs of two, which are connected together. They are similar in basic appearance to a "¼-inch phone plug".

An assortment of DIN plugs and jacks.   —*Courtesy Switchcraft*

The "tip, ring and sleeve".

The "banana plug".
—*Courtesy Switchcraft*

The only oddball connectors are the "alligators clips" and something known as the "bare wire" lead. It usually has a plug at one end, and two strands of exposed wire at the other. The wire is screwed into place on a terminal block or some other sound source. In most cases, the alligator clips can do the same job—and a "bare wire" patch cord isn't really necessary.

Equipment Kits

Because news stories have a habit of breaking at awkward times—news equipment has to be ready around the clock. And if you are ready to cover a commercial jetliner crash you'll also be ready for more-mundane things (perhaps even a feature story you stumble across).

The complete Level I Kit, with everything you need to gather actualities and write voicers in the field, plus relay them to your station. This version fits in a man's shirt pocket.

It is now possible to *wear* all the basic reporting equipment. We'll call this a "Level I Kit". It's just enough to cover a breaking story and feed back voicers and actualities.

In smallest form this would include a Microcassette recorder with built-in mike (explained later in this chapter). A miniature version of the Octopus goes in a plastic sandwich bag, which doubles as rain protection for the recorder. Some 3x5 cards complete the kit—and everything fits in a vinyl glasses case small enough to be carried in a man's shirt pocket.

You'd also need a pen, and digital watch with elapsed-time function which gives you a stopwatch.

(If you have more room, such as in a purse, a small conventional cassette recorder is a better choice than the Microcassette unit.)

When you make a decision on what to carry, you can have the second Octopus built. If you opt for a compact kit, the Octopus will have to be really small. If you have more room it can be identical to the Octopus you built before.

When you have time to pre-plan coverage of a routine story, you should also take what we'll call a "Level II Kit". Assuming you keep all the Level I equipment and telephone gear from Chapter 7 with you, this would include:

- Loaded cassette recorder with good batteries
- Erased and rewound spare cassette(s) in box
- Professional-quality microphone with windscreen and cord
- Mike stand or clamp plus mike holder
- Mini-plug to mini-plug patch cord
- Extra batteries for both recorders
- A radio (for cues if you do live reports)
- Line-to-mike-level adapter plug (Radio Shack 274-300 $2.00) if your machines don't have line-input jacks
- Paper or note pad
- Pocket pager

The extra equipment can fit in the pouch that comes with some cassette machines. Larger, padded pouches are available from camera stores and will fit on some cassette machine carrying straps.

You have backup protection from two recorders and duplicates of all essential phone equipment. And the Level II Kit is compact enough to be carried in one hand.

Carrying a second recorder allows the luxury of dubbing in the field. If your news format calls for nothing but short tape cuts you can feed a clean package of them, complete with a billboard. You won't be tying up

Portable Recorders and Equipment

a person (and recorder) at the station while you hunt for cuts on the original tape.

In formats calling for long-form reports, you can dub a cassette of tape cuts in order, each separated by a second or two of silence. You would provide the scripted material inbetween while handling the *Pause* or *Stop/Play* functions of the machine. It's *almost* as convenient as having a cart machine with you.

And, as mentioned in Chapter 7, a second recorder allows you basic mixing capabilities over the phone line.

(But whenever possible, avoid recording a cassette on one machine then playing it back on another. Even between the same model of recorder, tiny alignment and speed control differences may give you a bad sound.)

Many full-time street reporters typically carry more gear which is stowed in an attache case, camera case, or some other container. Beside the suggested kits here's a list of other useful tape-related material for outside reporting:

> Spare cassettes (Microcassettes) erased and rewound, in boxes . . . tape machine AC power supply . . . long shielded mike cord (coiled guitar cord works nicely) . . . extra batteries in protective container . . . gooseneck to fit your mike stand or clamp . . . remote start/stop switch for cassette recorder . . . assorted patch cord adapters (XLR to mini, etc) . . . electrical tape . . . wire cutter . . . small screwdriver set (standard and Phillips heads) . . . "fishpole" mike holder . . . gaffers tape . . . Velcro strips, or strong rubber bands for keeping patch cords together and attaching mikes in unusual set-ups.

The best place, locally, to find specialty gear such as mike stand clamps and equipment bags is likely to be a camera store. An incredible number of gadgets are made for photographers and many are adaptable for radio news.

When possible, reporters should be assigned equipment to keep with them, instead of taking from a common pool every day. This way any malfunctions are likely to be fixed, and batteries replaced. There's also much less chance of overlooking something (like a mike cord or spare cassette).

All valuable equipment should be prominently marked with your station's call letters and/or engraved. Serial numbers should be registered in case of theft.

Also—important phone numbers should be kept in the kit. These would include your station newsline and switchboard, and perhaps home numbers of key station personnel and your network's newsline.

Choosing a Cassette Recorder

Any major equipment purchase should involve your station engineers, since they are the people who may be stuck with repairs—after the warranty period expires.

Rapid changes in recorder models and technology make a *rating* of cassette recorders impractical. Instead, here are features to consider in selecting a model (listed in approximate order of importance):

1. **Mono or Stereo?** Over the next 5 years, will your station be doing news in stereo? Stereo machines are generally larger, and more expensive, but offer better quality.
2. **Frequency Response.** Determine how much quality you need—AM listeners won't know if your equipment records up to 16,000 Hz.
3. **Size and Weight.** A big bulky cassette recorder may be only one of several things a reporter has to carry.
4. **Construction.** Metal may be best—but there is also hard plastic (like Lexan). Cheaper machines may use low-grade plastic that will need to be protected with a good case.
5. **Warranty/repairs.** Can you get service locally? Will your engineers want to do routine maintenance?
6. **Pause button.** It should lock into position allowing tight cueing for live reports.
7. **Heads.** 3-head machines allow monitoring of what's actually on tape during recording. 2-head machines do not.
8. **Mixing Provision.** On some models you can use two mikes, with separate levels—or one mike and one line input—and mix them.
9. **AGC and Switchable Manual Level.** AGC ("Automatic Gain Control") will suck up any sound, and will make editing more difficult. It is helpful when there is no set-up time. In all other cases you should run level manually.
10. **Rolloff Switches.** A low-frequency rolloff can cut hum and rumble. A high-frequency rolloff can cut whines. (This can be done later—on an equalizer.)
11. **Variable Speed.** Helpful when batteries were weak during recording.
12. **Connectors.** The best, for reliable contact, are XLR type which lock into place. Next best—¼" phone jacks. Last—mini-jacks.
13. **Noise Reduction.** Dolby, Dolby B, Dolby C, and "dbx" all reduce tape noise (hiss) not actual background noise. Available typically on stereo recorders. But most stereo machines can be run in mono—with mike feeding both channels.

14. **Tape Types.** Currently there are four, all recorders will operate on Type I, referred to as "normal". Others, on more-expensive machines, allow higher output and/or more-brilliant upper-frequency sound. Type II is "High Level" or "Chrome" tape. Type III is "Ferrichrome". Type IV is "Metal Tape".
15. **Live Talk-Through.** How do you feed your voice live through the phone? The best arrangement is depressing one button only. Others may require a cassette in place, and use of *record, play* and *pause*. On machines with manual level control, you should be able to adjust output volume.

    There's a great difference in performance under this category. Ironically, some small Microcassette recorders tested had the loudest output level! Cheaper machines, with only AGC, typically operate at fixed volume in talk-through. As a general rule, audio quality on talk-through was not as good as on cassette playback, a problem noted on many field reports (especially wraparounds) over the years.

    Most machines are built with no thought of this capability in mind. (You won't find mention of talk-through in the Owner's Manual.) If you are "inheriting" equipment on the job, try feeding both ways, live and taped, down a phone line to determine how severe the quality differences are.
16. **Interference.** Some models skimp on internal shielding and will pick up RF (Radio Frequency) interference and/or fluorescent light buzzing.
17. **Audible Cueing.** Some models allow the tape to stay in "Play" yet be moved by "Rewind" or "Fast Forward". This will give you sound to help locate material.
18. **Built-in Mike.** A nice emergency back-up provision.
19. **Counter.** Check accuracy in locating material.
20. **Batteries.** How many, what kind, what is expected life with machine in constant use?
21. **Carrying Case.** Canvas should be more durable than plastic.
22. **Two-Speeds.** All cassette recorders have $1\frac{7}{8}$ ips. Some portable machines offer $^{15}/_{16}$ ips as well. This allows recording at standard speed, and playback over phone lines at half-speed. Result is better frequency response and lower phone line noise—when station tape is played back at twice recording speed. A much better solution (not available on portable machines at publication) would be $1\frac{7}{8}$ ips and $3\frac{3}{4}$ ips.
23. **Remote Control Jack.** Allows use of remote on/off switch.
24. **Tape End Indicator.** A blinking light is good, but models that "beep" can intrude onto recording.

25. **Auto Shutoff.** Recording or play stops when cassette ends.
26. **Tone Control.** Of little or no use, typically rolls off treble only, and operates during playback—not recording. Cassettes should be dubbed (or phone fed) at full-treble.
27. **Easy Telephone Feeding.** Marantz has made a start with its PMD-201 and PMD-221 models, introduced in 1985, which have a built-in modular jack for direct connection to the phone. But (at publication) no professional cassette recorder had built-in graphic equalization.

Cassettes

There are certainly hundreds, perhaps thousands, of companies making cassettes. All are nearly identical, using a design patented by the Philips Company of the Netherlands. But there's an enormous difference in quality and internal construction.

Most will do a tolerably good job of recording voice material. This simplifies our problems, as we don't have to worry about capturing the additional high-frequency sounds present in music. But some "bargain-basement" cassettes perform only marginally.

As a general rule, don't buy a brand of cassette you have never heard of before. And don't buy cassettes that aren't labelled. These may be rejects, and the pennies you save could mean an important interview or story down the drain because your cassette "crapped out".

Here's another good rule of thumb. Check the little rectangular window between the two tape hubs. If the window is made out of flimsy plastic, and bends easily, don't buy the cassette. It's an indication there could have been other cost-cutting in the manufacture that will give you a below-par cassette.

Cassettes come in many lengths with extremes of C-02 (1 minute per side) to C-180 (90 minutes per side). For news work, C-60's are perhaps most common. Avoid using C-120 or longer cassettes—they use thinner tape.

All cassettes should be labelled. If the manufacturer's label doesn't provide space, a file folder label can be used. Also make sure to start out each day with a bulk-erased supply of cassettes. This will prevent problems in case the erase head on your machine is not functioning up to par.

Nearly all cassettes have a short piece of leader tape on both ends, which connects the magnetic tape to the hubs. It is best to wind past this and perhaps 15-seconds into the magnetic tape to get past any disturbances that may be near the splice.

All cassettes can also be preserved from accidental recording later. If you have an important interview on one side of a cassette, take it out of the machine, and hold it with the head openings facing you. On the upper left-hand edge of the cassette, you'll see a little tab. Punch it out, and you'll be unable to accidentally record on that side or "track" because of an interlock device in all cassette machines. The other track on the machine (when the cassette is flipped over) is not affected. It is controlled by the other tab, at the other end. If you later want to record on the cassette, you can simply cover up the hole you've punched out with a piece of adhesive tape.

Cassette Repairs

Despite what you may have heard, it *is* possible to repair any cassette made. Even those that are sonically-welded can be split apart and fixed. But don't attempt the job, unless you've got a lot of patience, and a lot invested in the cassette. It's frustrating work, even with the right equipment.

The most common failure in cassettes is broken or mangled tape. The Scotch Tape folks make an inexpensive "Cassette Editing and Repair Kit" that is well worth getting. It contains a plastic splicing block, along with a supply of pre-cut splicing tape segments. Most importantly, the kit has a number of polyester tabs with adhesive on the end. These can be pushed into a sealed cassette, to retrieve a broken tape end. Using these tabs eliminates the need for opening a cassette, to repair the tape. And since this 3M kit (ERK-130) only costs around $3.00 it's a good investment.

When you splice, remember that the oxide side faces *outward,* unlike reel tape. Do the best job you can, and handle the tape as little as possible. Splicing a cassette is difficult work, even with some kind of device to hold the tape. The result will be a noticeable dropout, no matter how good a job you do. Be careful to trim excess splicing tape away from the edges. Close tolerances inside the cassette can turn a sloppy splice into a major disaster.

Because of the narrow, fragile tape and the 1⅞ ips speed, cassettes cannot be *edited.* Splicing is done only to correct a major physical problem. Still, a supply of cassette-width splicing tape (like .130-inch Scotch #620) may be worthwhile in larger stations. Because of infrequent use, it should be stored in an air-tight container.

If your cassette has jammed, you may be able to loosen it up by rapping it on a hard surface. A few moderate jolts should be sufficient, accompanied by mild profanity. If that doesn't work repeat the process by rapping the cassette on the reverse side, and increasing the profanity. The blows frequently loosen something that has become stuck inside.

Here's how to repair a cassette *with good tape* that does not run properly.

- On models that simply screw together, remove the screws.
- To unseal a conventional welded cassette, you'll need a standard screwdriver with a thin tip. A screwdriver at least six-inches long is recommended, to give you leverage. Break out one of the tabs on the edge of the cassette, insert the screwdriver, and pry gently, forcing the two halves of the casing apart. Slide the screwdriver in the opening you've made, and begin working it further around the edge. Continue going around the cassette, being careful not to put the screwdriver on the tape itself. Tolerances inside a cassette are extremely tight. Some cassettes will require only a little effort to open. Others may take several minutes of delicate prying, depending on the plastic and the welding.

Don't attempt to re-use the same cassette shell. Cut your losses and put the good tape in a "Cassette Housing" which contains everything except the magnetic tape. (Radio Shack #44-626 is $1.19). Instructions are included. It's a good idea to have a couple of these around the newsroom (plus a small screwdriver) for emergencies.

Cassettes must be stored out of direct sunlight. Don't keep extras in the glove compartment of the news unit—summer heat will wreck them. Cassettes are also vulnerable to dust. They should be kept in their plastic storage boxes both before and after use.

Cassettes stored for long periods should be fully rewound, so that all tape is on the hub. Magnetic tape spanning the head openings tends to drop and stretch.

Microcassette Recorders

Take a cassette, shrink it to ¼ size, rearrange it slightly and you have the "Microcassette". For years these units were sold primarily for dictation. But now, because of quality improvements, they are suitable for broadcast work.

Portable Recorders and Equipment

When there is no set-up time, a tiny Microcassette recorder with built-in mike and one-button recording is ideal. It should be easy enough for one-hand operation in the dark.

The main advantage of the Microcassette is size. Many are smaller than a 100mm cigarette pack and even in a protective vinyl case can be carried in a man's shirt pocket.

There's a second advantage, it can be much less intimidating for interviewees to speak into what looks like a dictation machine.

The main drawback of the Microcassette recorder is incompatibility with your other recorder. If one machine dies, you can't play back already-recorded material on the other. And the Microcassettes themselves are somewhat more expensive than cassettes.

This chart compares a professional cassette machine (Sony TCM-5000) with one of the better Microcassette models (Olympus Pearlcorder S910):

	TCM-5000 Cassette	S910 Microcassette
Frequency Response	90-9,000 Hz	300-6,000 Hz
Tape Speed	1⅞ ips	twice as slow, plus switchable speed 4-times as slow
Inputs	2 mike (mini-jacks) 1 line (mini-jack)	1 mike (mini-jack)
Mikes	1 built in	1 built in
Output	1 mini-jack	1 mini-jack
Recording Methods	Full manual or Full AGC	Manual or variable voice-activation
Pause Button	yes	yes
Counter	3-digit	3-digit

You can get better bass response by using a good quality *cardioid*-pattern mike. The "proximity effect" will add bass when the mike is worked close-up.

Cheaper consumer-model Microcassettes typically leave off the counter, pause button, sometimes even the mike jack—meaning you have to use the built-in mike. Typically, they have only AGC recording, with no provision for any kind of manual control.

A microcassette recorder may be no bigger than a pack of cigarettes. This 4½-inch tall model is shown with a tiny Octopus which includes a modular handset plug and alligator clips.

Don't judge quality by listening to the built-in speaker, which may be only the size of a quarter. Dub a test recording onto reel-tape or cart.

Microcassettes are gradually becoming available for *music* recording and playback. Metal tape models with improved frequency response are on the market. The continued consumer demand for small personal tape machines might give this miniature unit the edge over cassettes.

To further confuse the issue, in 1985 Dictaphone introduced a slightly smaller capstan-drive machine called the "Picocassette" ($400.) It uses its own smaller tape and offers no real advantage for radio news.

There is also a similar-looking recorder called a "*Mini*-Cassette". It operates by rim-drive (instead of capstan and pinch-roller). These recorders, and the tape they use are entirely different. Speed variations make the "Mini-Cassette" unsuitable for broadcast.

There is something to be said for using the *standard* cassette size including the generally-better quality, and ability to play back on one machine if the other goes bad.

If size is not that much of a concern on a Level I Kit (for a woman who always carries a purse, or a man who always wears a sport coat) a small standard cassette recorder will work fine. But the idea is to stay 'wired for sound' even on your routine Saturday burger run to McDonald's ... where, in 1984, a gunman massacred 21 people.

Microcassettes

Microcassettes share most of the same features of cassettes, in a much smaller package. Supply and take-up reels are reversed—so

Microcassettes operate backward compared to cassettes. And they contain two pressure pads, instead of one.

Recording tape is identical to cassette but typically there is no leader tape on the ends. Microcassette lengths range from MC-40 (20 minutes per side at fast speed) to MC-90 (45 min. per side). The most-practical length for news is the MC-60.

Extremely tight tolerances (and sonically-welded plastic) make repairs difficult. If tape becomes broken, the Scotch cassette kit (ERK-130) may help. The only other option is prying apart the housing and (at publication) no empty housings were commercially available.

Care and Feeding of Outside Recorders

Every recorder made, can be wrecked by dust and sand. The particles can destroy heads and other critical parts. Recorders should also be kept out of strong sunlight, and away from high moisture (like heaters, or vaporizers).

In cold climates, all recorders have problems. You'll just have to keep the machine as warm as possible, inside your coat, when the temperature dips below freezing. And, before recording, make sure the machine is running at full speed—by alternately depressing the *fast forward*, and *rewind* buttons, to get it limbered up. When temperatures dip below zero, this may take a minute or longer. It helps to have fresh batteries, and to keep the machine in good running order, with frequent servicing.

Cassette and Microcassette machines also need routine cleaning and demagnetizing, as explained under "Maintenance and Trouble-Shooting" in Chapter 2.

Microphone Types

If an external mike came with your recorder—chances are it's a cheap plastic one. It will probably be a serviceable *spare,* but you also should carry a good microphone or mike system.

There are many ways of transforming sound, into electrical energy. Some work better than others, for different purposes. That's why, of the six types of microphones listed here, only two are in general use for broadcasting today.

In many telephones you're using a *carbon microphone.* It's inexpensive, and rugged. Sound strikes the carbon granules, changing the electrical current that flows through them. These mikes, found commonly in phones and two-way radios, are suitable only for basic voice transmissions.

Crystal mikes aren't used much anymore. They used to be supplied with inexpensive tape recorders, as standard equipment.

The most common low-cost microphones now available are the *ceramics*. They do a mediocre job of recording normal voice material.

Dynamic microphones are in widespread use today for broadcasting. They're especially good for outside news coverage, because of their ruggedness, and resistance to shock. Sound strikes the microphone's diaphragm, which is attached to a coil, generating an electrical current. Some dynamics have a frequency response from 40 Hz to 20,000 Hz. One of the most popular models, the EV 635A, picks up sound from 80 Hz to 13,000 Hz. Prices on dynamic microphones vary widely—from under $10 to over $300.

Condenser microphones are generally the best available for studio work. Some top-of-the-line dynamics, however, have a frequency response every bit as good. Condenser microphones require their own power supply, which can involve a separate unit, or just a small battery in some models. Some of the battery-powered units are known as "electret condenser microphones". The best condensers, like the best dynamics, can pickup from 40 Hz to 20,000 Hz. Costs range widely—a unit capable of 20 Hz to 13,000 Hz is available for under $20, while the better, studio-quality units run into the hundreds of dollars.

The *ribbon microphones* used to be the best in the industry. For years, there was nothing comparable for studio work. Today, however, they're being replaced by condensers, and the best dynamics. Ribbon mikes (also known as "velocity mikes") contain a thin strip of metal that is suspended in a magnetic field. When sound waves strike the ribbon, electric current is generated. The problem is that ribbon mikes are extremely delicate. Even a loud studio sound can cause the metal ribbon to break. Of course, they can't be used at all for outside coverage.

If you use a dynamic microphone for outside news coverage, it won't need any maintenance. Condenser mikes, however, require a power supply, or in the case of most used for remote purposes, a battery. This needs to be checked every month or so, depending on how much use the mike receives.

Mike Impedance

The measure of a microphone's electrical resistance is known as "impedance" or the abbreviation "Z". There are two general categories: low and high. The "mike" input jack of cassette and Microcassette recorders is designed for use with low-impedance (low-Z) microphones.

High-impedance mikes are more susceptible to picking up hums and buzzes and, as a general rule, cannot be used with more than 20-feet of cable.

Portable Recorders and Equipment

The key point is: your mike has to match what it's plugged into. Otherwise, a "mismatch" may lead to bad sound or bad levels.

A few mikes, like the Electro-Voice 627C and 681, are switchable between low and high. And "Impedance Matching Transformers" are available from microphone manufacturers.

Line-Level Mikes

Levels refer to the electrical output strength in a mike. Most, regardless of impedance, have a low "mike output" level which must be greatly amplified by another device, such as a cassette recorder. But "line-level mikes" contain their own amplification and produce a much higher output. (Some can be switched between mike and line levels.)

There are some advantages to line-level mikes. Once a phone call is established they will drive and hold the line, just as a cassette recorder would in talk-through. Nothing else is needed to amplify the signal.

The best-known models, Shure SM-82, Electro-Voice RE30 and RE34, are foot-long condenser mikes with built-in limiters. They were designed for remote news and sports applications. These three models can provide an "on-air" signal through a built-in or optional light. Prices are close to $400.

Mike Patterns

Not all microphones pick up sound from all areas. Some are designed to reject or "null" sound coming from one or more directions. This means that even in a noisy situation only what *you* want to record will come through clearly. Basically, there are four "pick-up patterns".

The *omni-directional* microphone picks up sound equally well from all directions. This pattern is very common in all types of microphones. But it does have drawbacks in outside recording, because it can pick up background noise from a news conference or audience, as well as the speaker.

The second pattern is a *cardioid*, named that way because it is heart-shaped. This is produced artificially in the microphone, by blocking off sounds which come from behind. This pattern is especially useful in outside coverage. The null reduces background sounds, while the "lobe" of the pickup pattern is concentrated to the front and sides of the mike. There's also a pattern called the "super-cardioid" which is the same thing, with more of a null, and a more concentrated lobe.

(In special cases where you need omni-directional coverage you can get it by pointing the cardioid mike straight up. The null will then be facing the floor.)

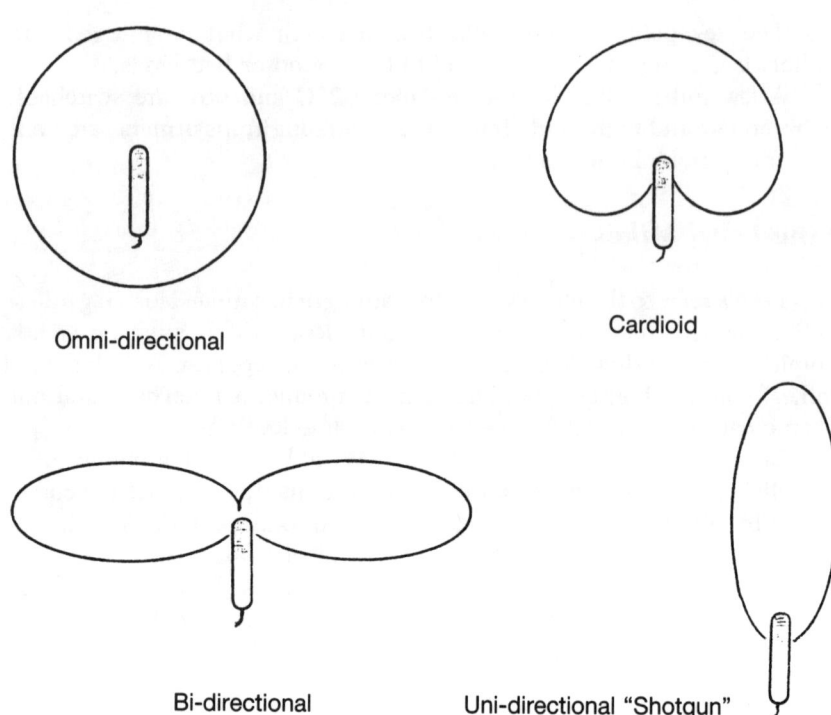

Omni-directional

Cardioid

Bi-directional

Uni-directional "Shotgun"

The third pattern is rapidly fading from the scene. It's called a *bi-directional* or "figure eight". This is the natural pattern for the old "ribbon" or "velocity" mikes. Many could be switched from this pattern to an omni-directional one. For outside coverage, it's as useless as the fragile ribbon mike.

The final microphone pattern is the *uni-directional* or "shot-gun". This is commonly found on expensive, highly-directional mikes. It is used to record sound over unusually long distances, or in extremely noisy situations. These mikes are typically long, to cancel out sounds from the sides and back. They are also expensive.

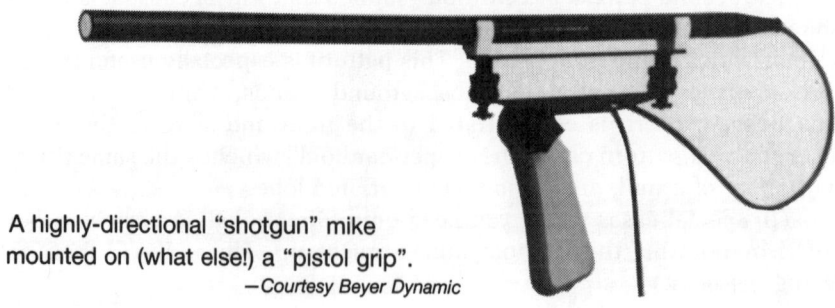

A highly-directional "shotgun" mike mounted on (what else!) a "pistol grip".
—*Courtesy Beyer Dynamic*

Mike Systems

Another option is the modular mike system. Companies including Beyer, Nakamichi, Neumann and Sennheiser offer units that can be converted from one pattern to another, all the way from a basic cardioid desk mike to a long shot-gun. Depending on your needs this may be cheaper than carrying separate mikes. Components can be purchased individually.

If you are going to invest in just *one all-purpose* mike, the best choice is a cardioid-pattern dynamic made of metal. There are several good ones priced near $100.

Wind and Other Problems

Any microphone has trouble when it's used outside. (Don't believe everything you read about the effectiveness of built-in "pop-filters".) Even the slightest breeze can ruin your tape, by causing small "explosions" as it strikes the microphone grill. This is especially true with a built-in Automatic Gain Control on your recorder. The wind enters at a very high level, and the AGC forces everything, including your sound material, down to compensate. In cases like this, AGC hurts rather than helps your recording.

Many professional-quality microphones have optional windscreens available from the manufacturer. Most are in the $5.00-$10.00 range. Radio Shack sells a multi-purpose acoustic foam windscreen, the 33-373, for $1.49.

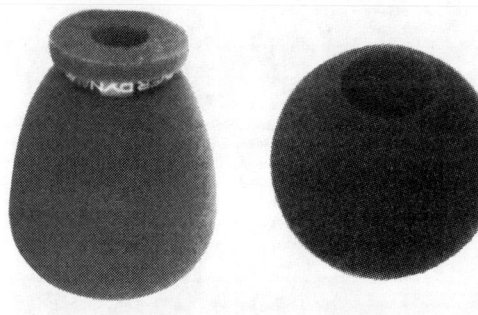

Typical acoustic foam windscreens designed to fit mikes with similar exterior dimensions.
—*Courtesy Beyer Dynamic*

Most of the quality lost from the windscreen can be regained in an equalizer. But even a noticeable loss in high-frequency reproduction is preferable to wind blasts, which can *destroy* an otherwise good tape.

If mike cords and connectors were as sturdy and reliable as most broadcast microphones, we'd be in good shape. Since that's not the case, check out your cord, first, when something goes wrong. Wiggle the cord around the plugs, while recording some test material. Often a poor connection within the plug will cause the sound to cut-out.

There's a common problem with using microphones . . . so common that we have a name for it: "Popping your P's". Put your hand a few inches in front of your mouth and speak the letter "P" aloud. Notice the blast of air. This is where the mike should *not* be placed, when you record yourself or anyone else.

Move your hand around and notice how the air blast disappears a few inches up, down, or to any side. Proper mike placement will vary greatly depending on your speaking technique, mike construction and mike pattern.

Try having the mike slightly below you, or people you interview, about level with the chin. Sound should go across the microphone grill—or windscreen—not directly into it.

Most mikes should be placed roughly six inches from the mouth. In a noisy environment (factory, locker room, etc.) get the mike within one or two inches and, if you can, control recording levels manually.

Batteries

Just like any other piece of equipment, different types of batteries work best for different applications. The drug store batteries you buy for a transistor radio may give months of dependable service. But, chances

Once you locate the right *size* of battery, the biggest problem is still ahead. The wrong battery *type* can leave your recorder "dead" at a critical time.

Portable Recorders and Equipment

are, they won't be much good in a tape-recorder. Recorders, by their very nature, drain a lot of "juice" from batteries. They not only contain electronic circuitry (as a radio does) but also a motor, and other mechanical parts. Tape must be wound, and re-wound—requiring yet more power. So the battery you buy for a radio or flashlight may not have enough energy to run your tape-recorder for more than a few hours.

Generally, the cheapest available batteries at any store are made out of carbon-zinc. These do a good job in applications where there's not much "drain", such as radios and flashlights.

The second major type has some broadcast uses. These are the "alkaline" batteries. They cost far more than the carbon-zinc, but they usually last four or five times longer. Most of these batteries cannot be recharged more than a few times. Some other alkalines, which cost still more, are good for perhaps a hundred charges before they go dead.

"Mercury" batteries are the oddball. They last a long time—but when they begin to die, they go very quickly. The high initial cost of this battery pays off in months of good service, especially in hot weather. But voltage from a mercury battery isn't always the same as the other types, which deliver close to 1½ volts per cell (no matter what size). So, some recorders can't use mercury cells.

When you do buy any of these types of batteries, stay away from those that are made overseas—a great deal of their charge may have been lost in the trip over here, plus the usual loss on the shelf. Despite the generally-higher prices, American-made batteries are usually a better buy.

The last type is the most expensive—the "nicad" or "nickel-cadmium" variety. Their initial cost is quickly regained, however. They're completely rechargeable.

But because nicads typically deliver less power than conventional batteries of the same size, they don't perform well in *some* recorders. In this case, you'd be better off with alkalines.

If you can use them, nicads are the least expensive by far. Recharging can be done overnight. If the machine isn't used at all over the period of a week, batteries should be recharged anyway—to keep them at their peak.

Whenever you change (or recharge) batteries in a cassette machine, it's also a good idea to put on a label showing the date. This is especially helpful if machines are kept in a common pool of equipment, with no regular user.

Mixers

A portable mixer can be invaluable for long-form reports or anchoring coverage of a major pre-planned event. Many models in the $25-$100 price

A high-quality battery-operated mixer designed for news gathering. It weighs just over two pounds and is smaller than many cassette machines.
—*Courtesy Shure*

range allow the flexibility of four or more sound sources ("channels") along with acceptably low distortion and noise.

Some of these consumer-market mixers are comparable in size and weight to cassette recorders. Many operate from wall current or standard batteries.

A mixer will allow complex production and (theoretically) a smooth on-air sound. It can allow several mikes to be used with one cassette recorder. When feeding live or taped reports to the station, it allows live mikes and tape sources to be combined in a cleanly-engineered package.

Mixers can also be used to feed telephones, in combination with any of the equipment detailed in Chapter 7.

There are also a few specialized mixing tools which may be useful:

- A two-channel recorder, such as the Sony TCM-5000, allows use of two mikes feeding one tape track. Note that once the sounds are combined on tape they cannot be separated or mixed differently.
- If your recorder has a ¼" microphone jack, Switchcraft makes a handy pair of "Mini-Mix" adapter plugs (310Pl and 311Pl $30.) Either will allow two mike inputs, each with a separate tiny volume control for mixing onto one tape track.
- Lastly, you can delegate the mixing to the newsroom. Feed sound (and/or taped inserts) then feed your voice material separately. The newsroom will combine and mix. (Any background sound should be fed at 100% modulation to avoid line noise.)

9 | Live Broadcasting and Equipment

> *To me, radio is the most challenging medium because there are no props—no pictures to support the words, no points of reference to go back to.*
>
> —Merrilee Cox, ABC
> (*Rip 'N Read,* January 28, 1986)

Long before there was such a thing as tape, radio had live reporting. Stories were done over the phone. Bulky tube equipment was lugged outside. There were even stupid "no recording rules" networks imposed on themselves requiring overseas reports to be done live.

Now a reporter can be wired for both live broadcast and taping by carrying just six pounds of equipment. Remote production with both can be done in the field—relaying high-quality sound to the station. That is what this chapter is all about.

As shown, it *is* possible to do some radio news 'on the cheap' by aggressive phone work. Doing live news requires a lot more— both in equipment and personnel.

This chapter explains in non-technical terms, the equipment used to feed live (and taped) material. Then, drawing on experiences of stations equipped for live news, it examines format considerations and potential technical problems in live broadcasts.

One radio-TV equipment magazine created a meaningless term for all this—"Radio Electronic News Gathering" or "RENG". This is like specifying "printed newspaper," or "TV with picture". Radio news gathering has *always* been electronic (except for pencil and notepad).

In many cases a station may have to make do with less than state-of-the-art outside equipment (or none at all). In this case many of the live reporting techniques can be used over the telephone instead, with the inexpensive equipment detailed in Chapter 7.

Mobile Equipment

Four radio systems will give you ability to feed live or taped material from a car. There's a great deal of difference among them in quality and operation.

Two-Way Radios

The most familiar system is known as the two-way. This is a basic radio set-up, with a "base station" at the studio, and one or more "mobile units" located in cars, or other vehicles.

Traditionally, two-ways suffer from a lack of sound quality. They were developed for police dispatching and other similar uses and only took hold in radio because, at the time, there was no other technology available. On conventional two-ways, even good-quality cassette tape may sound marginal by the time it reaches the studio.

Some newer units can be modified to allow increased frequency response. KFWB/Los Angeles gets flat response from 20-5,000 Hz out of its J-ngineering modified conventional Motorola two-ways. And there's only a gentle roll-off in sound out to 7,500 Hz, near the upper end of the "speech range".

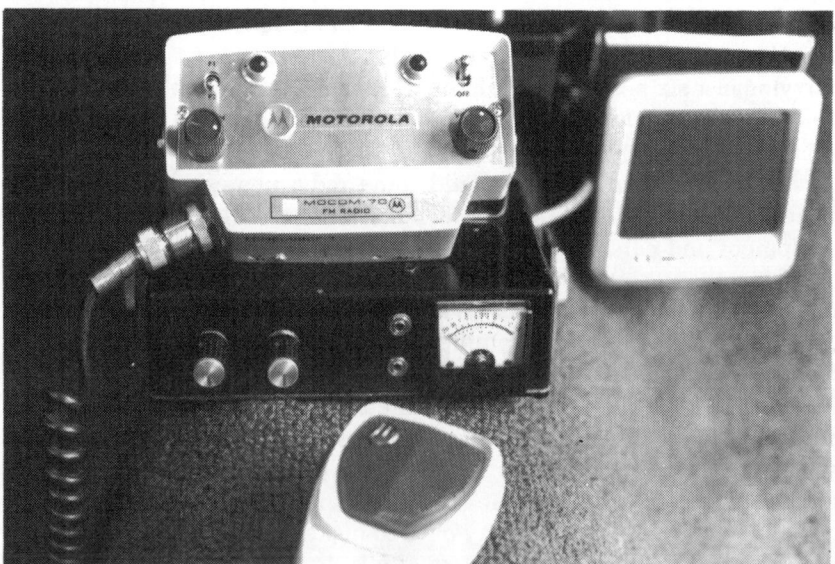

A typical two-way radio (top) with custom mixer (bottom) used to feed from mike or cassette recorder.
—*Courtesy WGAR/Cleveland*

Live Broadcasting and Equipment 127

Even *without* modifications, two-ways should achieve a frequency response of 300-3,000 Hz, equal to that of a telephone (although the sound will be different). Quality below this may mean adjustments are needed.

With some two-way equipment, it's possible to "slave" a hand-held walkie-talkie to the car. This allows the car to pick up, and re-broadcast, the walkie-talkie signal with higher power, giving you better quality back at the station. Two-way units can be modified to accept a patch-cord, for feeding tape from a recorder.

A couple additional features extend the coverage and usefulness of two-ways. Briefly they are:

- **Repeaters** — remote-receiving stations strategically located on high buildings, mountains, etc. Signals picked up there are relayed to the newsroom, extending the range reporters can travel and still stay in radio contact.

- **Phone Patches** — equipment allowing you to dial phone calls from your two-way.

- **Scramblers** — new digital technology designed to prevent competitors from monitoring your communications. Scrambling converts sound to noise which is then converted back to sound at your base station only. The process lowers sound quality, and some stations use it only to set-up reports which are then transmitted "in the clear" for broadcast.

Mobile Telephones

The second type of in-car system is a mobile telephone. This is just what the name implies—a radio unit that connects with telephone equipment, hooking your signal into the phone wires, for transmission to the station. The quality is generally about comparable to the two-way. But the mobile phone is subject to interference and limitations, from *both* the radio waves, and telephone lines.

It does have an extra advantage, however. With a mobile phone, you can call anyone, anywhere. This is especially helpful on spot-news assignments. It allows you to check with the police and fire agencies. Mobile telephones are capable, in most areas, of producing roughly 300 Hz to 3,000 Hz.

To feed tape down a mobile phone, you unscrew the mouthpiece, and use it just like any other phone, or a special adapter can be built.

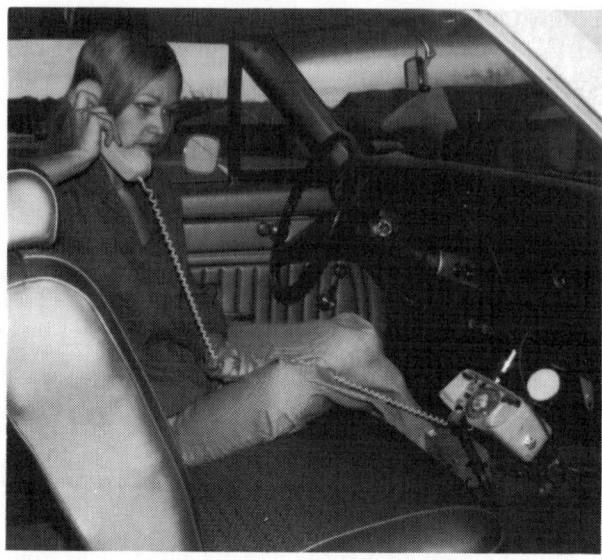

The conventional "mobile telephone" allows you to call anyone ... if you can find a vacant channel. It is generally not practical in large cities.

Mobile phones can either be purchased, or leased. Long waiting lists are common in many parts of the country. Monthly leasing charges can run upwards of $100. and there is frequently a time-limit on how many minutes you can talk, per month. Anything above this is subject to more charges. In some areas, you dial your own calls—in others, you must go through a special operator. Quality of service, availability of units, and rates, vary widely. Because of overcrowded channels it has taken over an hour to get a call through in some larger cities, making the mobile phone useless for breaking news. Fortunately, better technology has come to the rescue.

Cellular Telephones

The third in-car system almost seems like it was designed for radio news. Now being installed in larger cities, this combines the basic idea of an old-fashioned mobile telephone with a computer-controlled network of ground stations. A metropolitan area is divided into "cells" and as cars travel the calls are automatically (and silently) transferred from one ground station to another.

The result is that far more users can share limited frequencies. Overcrowding is eased, and quality improved.

Cellular phones use newer technology to replace the old carbon microphone. As a result, sound quality is generally *better* than a standard wired phone!

Live Broadcasting and Equipment

Through the cellular phone, you direct-dial calls on the built-in tone pad. On some units it is not possible to feed tape through patch cords and a modification kit will be necessary. This may pose a problem with phones that are leased.

The cellular phone offers better flexibilty than any other system. Beside feeding material, you can advance the story and check other angles by phone from your car.

Purchase prices begin around $800. Typical leases begin around $20 per month. Charges apply by the minute on local calling.

Remote Pickups

RPU's, unlike the three other types, were designed for broadcast. In the best cases frequency response will extend from 20 to 15,000 Hz — which is studio quality. But on some bands frequency response is much less and ranges down to an extreme of only 20-3,000 Hz.

On the better bands, RPUs are widely used for sponsored remote broadcasts, and sports play-by-play. They can quickly pay for themselves in non-news areas.

RPUs are also increasingly popular as stations avoid rising telephone company charges for one-time-only broadcast lines.

Most RPUs can be removed from cars, and run off AC current. This allows feeding of live or taped material from the scene, with fairly easy set-up and without the added cost of hand-held units.

A basic mixer is already included on standard in-car RPUs. All have inputs for at least one mike and one line source, such as a cassette recorder.

Remote pickups effectively transform a news car into a studio on wheels. And hand-held units can be "slaved" to the more-powerful car unit, which relays and rebroadcasts the signal to the station.

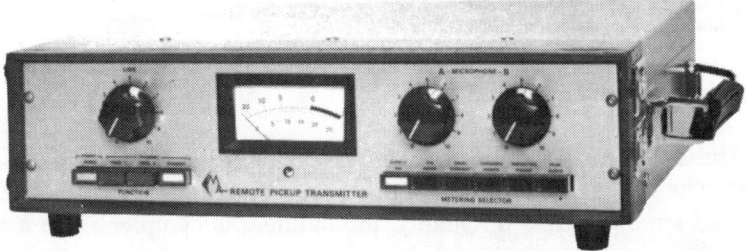

This 16-pound RPU produces 10-watts of power. It will operate off a car's electrical system — or wall current. It can function both in a mobile unit and in on-scene work, providing there is a source of electricity nearby.

—*Courtesy Moseley Associates, Inc.*

There are two problems. One—in urban areas, interference can make some frequencies unusable. And RPUs frequently make reports sound too much like they were done in the studio! So, depending on the station's format, you may have to seek out background sound to get that on-location effect.

Prices for a basic one-way package (allowing the mobile unit to talk to the studio) start at $3,000. A system allowing communication both ways will run $5,000 and up.

Portable Equipment

Each of the four in-car systems has a companion portable system that offers the same (or slightly lower) quality.

Walkie-talkie used with car two-way radio. The station called this its "Mighty Mike".
—*Courtesy WSB/Atlanta*

Walkie-Talkies

These hand-held units are simply portable two-ways with lower power. They were developed for police communications and other similar uses and are quite rugged. Quality, unmodified, is comparable to a telephone. They can operate in direct communication with the station from nearby or be "slaved" to a two-way unit in a car.

A professional model will run close to $1,000. and must be custom-modified to feed tape.

Hand-Held Mobile Telephones

These are self-contained phones that do *not* get re-broadcast by companion units in cars. Some are hand-held, others range up to briefcase size. All the advantages, and disadvantages, of in-car mobile phones are present. And since a higher-power car unit is not relaying the signal—portable mobile phones can be almost impossible to use from inside buildings, or even on the streets of congested urban areas. Purchase and leasing prices vary widely and there are charges by the minute for local calls.

Hand-Held Cellular Phones

Like the mobile telephone, these units are not slaved to a car. They transmit and receive directly via a radio link to the nearest cellular base station. At publication, units as small as 7½ x 2 inches were available, easily transported in a briefcase or other equipment kit.

Perhaps the best in cellular technology is a combination unit, such as the Motorola 8000S, that operates both in and out of the car. While driving it is plugged in with a modular cord, and powered by the car battery. Reception and transmission is through an outside whip antenna. When unplugged and used outside it runs off internal batteries (recharged in the car) and a short built-in rubberized antenna.

This cellular phone operates as a hand-held portable. For car use it plugs in and operates off an outside antenna. —*Courtesy Motorola*

Performance will depend on how many base stations are used in your market. If only a handful now cover a wide area, there may be "dead spots" where a hand-held cellular phone will not work.

Batteries are also a big limiting factor. Fully charged, the Motorola hand-held units are rated at only 30-minutes of "active talk time". The cellular phones can run up to 8-hours in "normal operation" during which they are on and waiting for incoming calls.

Tape can be fed over hand-held cellular phones through acoustic couplers (chapter 6) or a custom modification.

Purchase prices begin around $1,100. and leases are also available. Charges by the minute for local calls typically apply.

Hand-Held RPU's

The truly "hand-held" models contain internal batteries and weigh only five to ten-pounds. They produce up to 3-watts of power and most stations using them slave the signal through an in-car RPU. This provides the twin benefits of higher power and (frequently) a directional antenna beamed at the station's RPU system receiver.

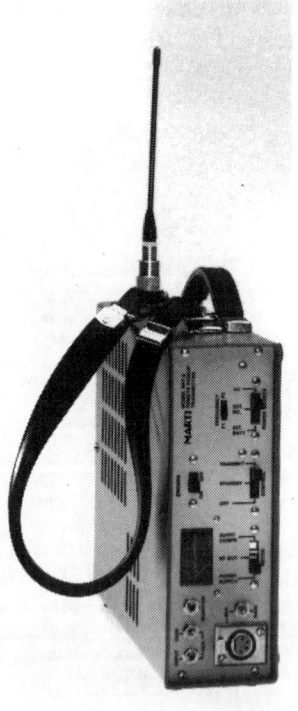

This 5¼-pound hand-held RPU produces 2½ watts of power. Depending on the operating frequency band, audio response of this unit can range up to 50-15,000 Hz... in other words "studio quality". —*Courtesy Marti*

But under the right conditions, the hand-helds can go 10-15 miles across flat terrain. These units allow basic mixing through separate mike and line inputs. Prices range from $850.-$1,300.

In some cases you may be able to get limited mobility out of the communications unit in your car. Simply buy a long, shielded, microphone cable that can be added when needed. If you can get the car reasonably close to an outside news story, you simply attach the extra cord, plug in your microphone, and carry it to the event.

Before making any decision on mobile equipment, you should check on the quality of service, and experience of others in your area. Local factors such as population, tall buildings, hilliness, telephone lines and so on, make a difference. A system that works perfectly on the Kansas prairie, may bomb out in San Francisco.

Cordless Telephones and Wireless Microphones

Both cordless telephones and wireless mikes consist of two parts—a base unit which must be plugged in, and an un-wired handset or microphone.

Both allow mobility up to 1,500 feet (about ¼ mile) under the best line-of-sight conditions. In a building, range will be considerably less.

While this doesn't begin to compare with other systems—it does allow some freedom to roam. A wireless mike might, for example, be on the podium at a city hall news conference while the base unit remains at the station's city hall bureau, feeding sound live down the line to the newsroom. Typically, quality is comparable to that of a good-quality conventional microphone.

A cordless phone base unit plugs directly into a modular jack and allows a similar range, but with a phone handset instead of a microphone. Quality can be as good as a wired telephone.

Live Reporting Problems

Although radio has had live reporting capability since the 1920's, much of the technology is relatively new.

The first hand-held RPU came out in 1976. Commercial modification of two-ways to allow broadcast quality began in 1979. Cellular phones began appearing in selected markets in the early 1980's. And the AT&T breakup of 1984 revolutionized the phone industry, greatly complicating the ordering of one-time-only lines.

In a survey for this book, stations doing live reporting were asked what problems they're having. Some typical responses:

Often our two-way reports will break up and we have to dump out of them.
—KOMO/Seattle

Two-way range is short. Q&A with anchors can be difficult.
—WMAY/Springfield IL

On election nights we have had trouble with the phone company. They just don't set things up in enough time to have them checked.
—WOBM/Toms River NJ

Break up of audio due to "positioning".
—WIBC/Indianapolis

Lack of coordination between field reporter and home base (phone-in went ignored).
—KUPD-KUKQ/Tempe AZ

Making sure jocks patch us in okay.
—KOLO/Reno NV

Lack of training in live techniques on part of reporters. Lack of willingness to broadcast live elections, emergency news cut-ins.
—KYNO/Fresno CA

Severe interference with remote Marti (RPU) broadcasts as well as some with regular two-way transmissions.
—WHDH/Boston

Getting out of two-way range (35 miles).
—KWKH/Shreveport LA

Technical difficulties are the biggest problem. A live two-way report might cut out in the middle. An alligator clip can also slip during a live phone report.
—KCMO/Kansas City

> *Because of our terrain our (hand-held) portables will conk out quicker and once we get over the hill, our mobile unit doesn't go as far as it would in flatter territory.*
> —KDAL/Duluth MN

> *On occasion (the) live story doesn't amount to as big a deal as originally thought, but that is infrequent and probably (an) acceptable hazard.*
> —WGY/Schenectady NY

Live or Tape?

You retain some measure of quality control by taping. Technical problems and flubs can be taken care of by splicing or re-doing altogether. Bad live reports, for whatever reason, are a tune-out and an embarrassment. It is best not to even attempt a live report when you are near the end of your signal range or in an area known to have troublesome interference.

This is doubly true when the story doesn't *demand* live reporting. Often nothing is lost if the report is fed five or ten-mintues prior to air time and used with an intro like "Tom Tape is at the scene" or "Here's a late report from Tom Tape". Without actually saying "live" you convey the basic idea of having fresh on-scene news.

Live reports pose special dangers in situations like riots or hostage-takings where you could be turning over your station to people breaking the law. Taping allows you some control of events—instead of the other way around.

Monitoring on Live Broadcasts

To do a live report you must know when to start talking. If the format calls for Q&A with the anchor, you've got to hear well enough to understand the questions.

The most basic monitoring method is to take a portable radio with you and listen with headphones. Normally this works well. But if your station delivers a weak signal to the story location, you may be out of luck. Or—if your station has a telephone "program line" set up, you can call this to get the air signal.

The best method is the same way K-Mart interrupts music to announce "Blue Light Specials" over the store PA system. For broadcasting we have given this a name—"IFB" for "Interruptable Foldback". Programming (music) is played down the line and cues or information (Blue Light Specials) are relayed in place of, or on *top* of, the programming.

For a live report on a jock show, for example, you would be given station programming down the line and told, say, 30-seconds prior to your report to "stand by". You would hear the introduction to your report on this channel—you'd hear yourself doing it—and hear any questions afterward.

IFB can be made to work with any of the systems in this chapter, and with the telephone as well.

Last, and least, there is the crude "Squelch Tail" method. As a cue—someone at the station turns on, or "keys" the two-way microphone for a fraction of a second. This produces a half-second burst of noise (the squelch tail) on the two-way which is your cue to begin talking.

Format Considerations

Live outside reports are a wild card in today's structured formats. Several stations doing them point out the need to plan, and guard against overly-long stories. Here's a sampling of live report formats:

> *"Announcer plays sounder, reporter takes cue and opens with name and location, etc."*
>
> —KRNT/Des Moines IA

> *"Anchor does a story tease and intros field reporter. Q&A usually follows."*
>
> —WMAZ/Macon GA

> *"Just standardized intros/outros ("Live from the State Capitol I'm ---- ----, WGY News"). Usually they are lead stories."*
>
> —WGY/Schenectady NY

> *"The report is filed one of two ways . . . Q&A (or) free-standing. Our outcue is "Live and Direct from ---- this is ---- for KDAL News".*
>
> —KDAL/Duluth MN

Sometimes the newscast and the live report are one and the same. At WJNC-WRCM in Jacksonville NC, News Director Glenn Hargett handles all the local news from the mobile unit as he makes his rounds:

> The majority of the morning newscasts are done from either the Police Department, Sheriff's Department, the State Highway

Patrol office or the downtown local government complex. It's become quite an acknowledged fact that we report from these locations. At least three times, I have interviewed someone live from the car during a breaking story.

The news from the previous day is entered on a Radio Shack lap-size computer. Tape cuts are played from the station by the on-duty announcer, who also reads state and regional news—to round out the package.

On many live stories you may want tape for later newscasts. This can be handled a number of ways, using a reel or cassette machine dedicated to your RPU or two-way frequency. Or a "skimmer" reel or cassette machine can record everything coming out of the news studio.

Satellites and the Future

Today, few locations are too remote for a well-equipped radio news operation to cover. Outside of RPU range, the cellular phone system may get your report on the air. As a last resort there's almost always a pay phone or private phone you can borrow. (Areas completely without communications are also likely to be without much news.)

Once again, television is playing catch-up to radio . . . this time using satellite technology to expand live news coverage beyond the range of microwaves (comparable to RPUs). Small truck-mounted "uplinks" shoot the live TV signal to a satellite, where it is bounced back to a dish at the station.

The availability of satellite time, and rented uplinks, now offers radio an opportunity to get full studio quality from beyond RPU range. For both local stations and networks, satellites have replaced standard 5 or 8 kHz telephone "broadcast lines" on many planned remotes, including political conventions, Super Bowls and Olympics.

If costs continue to drop, owning a satellite uplink truck may be worthwhile for some radio stations doing frequent remotes across a wide geographic area.

Smaller uplink units the size of several suitcases are now available. As early as 1984, 100-pound 'portable' uplinks were on the market, allowing phone calls to be bounced off a satellite. In the devastating 1985 Mexico City earthquake these phone-quality uplinks (and Ham radio) were the only direct news links to the world.

But something even more far-reaching is happening at our fingertips. Computers and magnetic memory soon should allow us to combine the wire machines, typewriter, telephone, reel recorder, splicing block and cart machine—all in one desk-top unit.

A potentially important step was the 1986 introduction of the Apple IIGS, the first desktop computer capable of storing, rearranging and reproducing audio that actually sounds "human". (Computers are already replacing wire machines, typewriters, even dialing and answering phones.)

We may be on the threshold of putting an entire newsroom into a relatively inexpensive desktop computer that will cost less than the equipment it replaces.

Although some technical skills will become obsolete with new technology—journalistic skills will not. And whether you pound an ancient Underwood or a sleek computer keyboard, the only thing that will matter is what listeners hear on the air.

10 | Reporting Situations

> ... radio is like a coloring book. It supplies the guidelines, the words, the sounds. If they are intriguing enough, the audience will become the artist—visualize the total picture, color it and ultimately bring it to life.
> —the late Orson Welles, 1971

This chapter introduces the major types of outside assignments and offers advice on live broadcast and taping procedures. But first—a message about the sponsors of many alleged 'news stories.'

Public Relations

The men and women who work for PR offices often have titles like "Community Relations Advisor", "News Services Manager", "Public Information Specialist" and so on. Their jobs boil down to making their employer look as good as possible, regardless of the story.

While you may be given some of the truth some of the time, other common techniques include blarney, evasion, deception, and outright lying. And it may come from a PR-person who, for better pay and security, crossed over from the news media.

PR performs a necessary information and image function for the employer. In some corporations and agencies, interviews cannot be set up without going through PR. And in some cases nobody else will talk to the media.

But it's important to remember that we can be used by PR-people (among others) and they have some insidious techniques to get favorable news coverage.

Free Tape

One of the most effective, and dangerous, PR devices is the "taped handout." You must call on the phone to get some of the handouts. (Often, a toll-free number is provided.) Some other handouts are phoned in to your newsroom, whether you want them or not. Still others are mailed. All generally contain a capsulized story and a free actuality of a PR-person or top official putting their organization in the best possible light.

You can bet the words have been carefully chosen, the piece carefully recorded for public consumption. Even if it's taken from a public speech, it promotes what the organization wants promoted. Some outfits crank out conventional voicers or wraparounds, with a PR-type playing reporter (sometimes even signing-off with your call letters!).

If a free handout is used, it's even better than a free commercial or "spot." A PR item in a newscast gives it an aura of believability and impartiality that's missing in most paid commercials. And since the handout is done in a totally controlled environment, it's a totally managed product. Newspeople don't even have a chance to question the taped pronouncement as they would have in a news conference.

Here's what a standard college textbook advises aspiring PR-types:

> By providing news for the radio newscast, the publicist can get a wide hearing for his story within the audience limits of a given station or set of stations . . . Good results in radio news can be obtained by supplying tape-recorded interviews and news events. . . . Many institutions have found it profitable to equip their publicists with cassette tape recorders so they can record interviews for (a) newscast.
> — Scott Cutlip and Allen Center, *Effective Public Relations,*
> Fourth Edition (Prentice-Hall)

The only time a piece of handout tape really is justifiable, is when you identify it on the air as a prepared statement. If the Justice Department files a lawsuit against Capitalist Corporation, chances are there will be a prepared statement ready to go within minutes, either live or taped from the company PR office. In a case like this, it's generally acceptable to use the canned reaction, providing you identify it as a prepared statement. You should also try to get through to corporate officials, and if they won't say anything more, *use that fact as well.*

Politicians regularly make heavy use of handouts. You may find your local congressman, and others trying for public office, seem to have an abundance of free tape prior to an election. Though this stuff may be an excerpt from a public speech, it's still the product of a PR judgment, rather than a news judgment, on what's important. And you can bet you

If local radio news is worth a damn, it's worth $75 to be in it.

For six years now, InfoNet has successfully delivered top-quality broadcast news stories via audio feeds to some 150 Texas radio news directors. The cost to you, the newsmaker or public relations professional, ran $265 for a 60-second feed.

But what about **regional** stories?

The hottest story of the day in Houston may not be news in Dallas. Or, in a practical vein, you may want coverage in only one specific market.

For you there's our $75 "worth a damn" special. For $75 we'll tape and edit "the big story", add professional news voice open and close, and put it right in the newsroom of 10 stations in the market you designate. It can be a trade area, franchise area or city — we'll trust your knowledge of the territory.

Naturally, we're not making any money on this. The "worth a damn" special is good only once. For first-timers, radio news skeptics, and folks with $75 and a story to tell. If you don't qualify on the latter, we'll even tell you — and let you keep your $75.

By the way, InfoNet radio releases have worked for U.S. Sens. Lloyd Bentsen and John Tower, Lt. Gov. William Hobby, Atty. Gen. John Hill, Central Power & Light, Ford Motor Co., Pearl Brewery, Texas Monthly and Tracor Inc. You might check us out with them.

If you're already convinced, curious or sold, telephone Jim Haynes or Charles Ward, 512-478-9315.

A division of Media Communications, Inc.
500 Mutual Savings Building, Austin, Texas 78701. 512-478-9315
TWX 910-874-1395.

This ad appeared in publications aimed at corporate executives and others who might benefit from free plugs on a newscast.

—Courtesy InfoNet, Austin, Texas

won't be fed the part of the speech where the politician is booed, or where he makes a fool of himself.

It goes without saying that if all radio stations suddenly imposed a total ban on handout tape, the practice of providing it would cease. But it's not quite that easy. Free tape on a worthwhile story is hard to pass up, at any station. The use is really a matter of individual judgment . . . of situation news ethics. But every time a piece of handout tape is used, PR people gain a little more control over a supposedly free press. The use of handout tape, except in very rare instances, is journalistic prostitution.

News Conferences

The difference between a news conference and a handout is a fundamental one. A news conference involves questioning . . . a handout does not. However, most news conferences are staged events, managed by people who want publicity. The atmosphere, many times even the format of questioning, has been shaped by the people holding it. (Other news conferences, such as those held by a local press club, or governmental leaders following a major vote, etc., are generally much less staged.)

When possible, arrive 10 or 15 minutes before the news conference is scheduled—to get set up and get acquainted with the story. Place your mike roughly six-inches from the person who will talk. Once you have the mike and recorder set up, give it a test. Don't *assume* it's functioning, because it worked all right back at the station. Check to see you have enough power left in the batteries. Make sure your cassette is rewound, and has a full left-hand spool of tape.

On pre-arranged stories like news conferences (along with most interviews and speeches) you can arrange to sit next to your recorder. Whenever this is the case, manual gain control is preferable. Otherwise tape can be subjected to AGC three times—by the recorder, in phone or radio equipment, and finally, processing at the transmitter. The first two are pretty crude and the combination can make it sound on-air like your person is trying to talk over a vacuum cleaner.

Try to jot down the counter number, in-cue, time, and out-cue of cuts you'd like to use on the air. Whenever you start a new cassette, the counter should be reset to "000".

Getting to the conference early may give you a chance to chat with the person holding it. If you've thought up a few good questions, you can get them answered while no other reporters are around. Then, you simply highlight the resulting "exclusive" cuts on the air—while your competiton runs news conference material. You can also use this occasion to get some undated cuts for weekend use, on a related subject. Many times, PR people will have a news release or a background sheet all ready for you. Take time to jot down a few relevant questions . . . if you haven't done so already.

You have a right to ask any question you want . . . that's what a news conference is for. Even if the subject says beforehand he or she won't take any questions on a particular touchy topic . . . you can still ask the question, and get the person begging off, on tape.

Avoid jumping in over the last words of the subject's answer . . . to ask your next question. Allowing a little pause makes editing much easier—for you, and everyone else.

If the conference is an important one, you may want to feed back a voicer, while it's still in progress. Get your important questions answered . . . then write your story . . . and phone in, using the regular phone mouthpiece. Leave all your equipment in place, so nothing is missed.

After the news conference is over, play back a few seconds of the tape to make *sure* you got something. If your recorder did "crap out" for one reason or another, you may be able to remedy the problem, and do a quick interview right then. If not, you may be able to steer the subject of the conference to a phone for a quick interview to be taped by a newsroom machine. (Of course, if you carry a second recorder, this won't be necessary.)

If you arrive late for a news conference, there's generally no need to interfere with everyone else, by shoving your mike up front. Simply take your "mini-plug to mini-plug" patch cord and plug one end into the "Aux" or "Line" jack in your cassette machine. The other end goes into the "Speaker" "Output" or "Monitor" jack of a machine that's already recording. This will give you a "master" recording, since your input is coming directly from the circuitry, not from the tape in the first machine. When your unit is placed in "record," the VU meter should bounce at normal levels. It's best to check the quality with earphones to make sure. This recording method won't disrupt the other tape, and your own will come out just as well.

One final thing, avoid the term *"press* conference." It's a throwback to the days before radio and television. The term "news conference" includes both electronic and print media, while "press conference" includes print only.

Speeches

You'll have to deal with hundreds of different speakers, and speaking situations. But the same reporting techniques are valid for the local PTA meeting, or a presidential campaign swing.

The first thing to remember is to park your car where you can get to it, and get away in it, once the event is over. This may mean leaving it some distance away, or in an obscure place when you're covering a major event.

If you will be feeding material by phone—search out what's available in the building. Try making quick friends with a worker there, to get access to a private phone, preferably modular. (Some reporters have been known to reserve pay phones by scrawling an "Out of Order" note or even using the official phone company version, a gummed label that goes over the coin slot.)

As a general rule, whenever possible, set up your *own* mike. Don't rely on a sound system, unless it's a professional one, operated by professionals. In a large auditorium, or in a place where pool news coverage has been arranged, you can generally rely on the quality.

On occasions where there will be a horde of reporters present, a "mult box" may be set up. This allows just one or two microphones to take care of feeding all recorders—through outputs on the mult box. Typically, they

A typical "mult box" with 18 outputs.
—*Courtesy Opamp Labs*

require XLR (or Cannon) connectors—so you should carry a patch cord that will go from this into your cassette recorder.

But sound systems carted in for the occasion, and the cheap public address systems commonly used in hotel meeting rooms, schools, and churches are notoriously bad. If you record off one of these, you may have problems with hum, or other electronic malfunctions. Don't take a chance—set up, test, and trust your own equipment.

If you have a long extension cord for your mike, use it. Try to get backstage or in the front row of the audience. There you can watch your cassette machine . . . and check on the tape, the VU meter, and the digital counter.

Advance copies of speeches are customarily provided for major figures, and for speakers at many conventions. Try to get one, go through and mark tape cuts that might be worthwhile. You may want to tape only those parts—if the speech is too long—or generally not very relevant. Mark your speech (or notes) with the digital counter numbers and approximate running times of the cuts you record. However, by taping only part, you run the risk of missing something important the speaker may decide to suddenly include. If you think there *is* a chance of this happening, it's best to roll your tape during the entire thing—relying on your digital counter to find relevant parts later.

Quick Tape

Depending on the worth of the story—and your own schedule—you may have to catch a speech hurriedly, then move on across town to another story. If this is the case, your best bet is to get backstage, or near a *small* sound-system speaker. If you can plug into the sound system easily, that's the best way.

Or, you may want to "tap" a speaker. Use your alligator clips, and put one on each "lead" to the speaker (where the wires are attached in the rear). You'll need to check for impedance problems—on some speakers the patch cord needs to be plugged into the high-impedance "Line" or "Aux" input of your cassette machine. In most cases, it should go into the low-impedance "Mike" input.

Another alternative is to put your mike a normal recording distance from the speaker. (The ideal situation is a speaker that is the same volume as a normal human voice.) This technique can also work with a regular auditorium loudspeaker. But you'll have to move away, and probably make several test recordings before you get a decent level.

In some cases, when all else fails, you may want to tap the volume or tone controls on a sound system. But this can entail a shock hazard in some cases. Don't attempt this unless you know electronics, and unless you have no other way of getting the tape.

If the speech hasn't already begun, you might try to get a quick interview. Tell the person you'd like cuts to use in an upcoming newscast, while the speech is being delivered.

Late Tape

If you *arrive* during a speech, try to find a way to get tape of the speaker, without setting up your gear in front and disrupting things. If another reporter has a cassette unit in use, take your mini-plug to mini-plug patch cord and use it.

If there's no other way, don't hesitate to go up quietly, and put your mike in front of whoever's speaking. You may disrupt things, but you're probably increasing the person's audience many times. Similarly, if you need to tear down your equipment before something is over . . . do so as quietly and unobtrusively as possible.

On major speeches, you can do double-duty, if you've packed two machines. Set up one to catch the main event. Use the other to go into the audience, backstage, perhaps even outside. You can do a scene-setting piece, describing the speaker's habit of moving his feet, tapping his fingers on the podium—or commenting on how the audience is taking it all. You can record side-bar actualities of outside demonstrators, or someone standing in back of the audience, reacting. In some cases, the speech may only be incidental to the *real* story.

With a second machine you can also tape material of the speech itself to feed back, as the thing is in progress. Either record off the sound system, or a speaker—or use your mini-plug to mini-plug patch cord hooked up to your first machine, which remains in "Record" and doesn't miss a thing.

Personal Interviews

Interviews are the backbone of journalism. They're far more than just questions and answers. They're actually an exercise in human relations and conversation.

When setting up in-person interviews, remember that a telephone conversation usually suffices for radio (see Chapter 6). Use in-person interviews only on stories where they're required. Routine stories should be handled by phone, to save time and effort.

The ultimate goal in radio news interviews is to steer your subject into giving you good tape cuts. A police lieutenant and a college professor think and talk on a different level, and you must deal with both on their own terms. You must take whatever role you need, to get your tape. Some people just want to have a friendly chat with you, others will expect and require tough questioning.

If you're dealing with a complicated topic, remind your person beforehand to keep it simple. Get in a place that doesn't have annoying, loud, background noises, unless this is important to your story. (An interview with the bartender after the drunken knife fight is better when it's done with the jukebox on, and with the sound of clinking glasses in the background.)

Reporting Situations

If you need to, have questions jotted out beforehand and use them as a guide to areas you want to explore. Don't be rigidly bound by them—follow up questions logically, instead of going down your list.

In most cases, avoid questions that can be answered "yes" or "no". Instead of asking, "Do you want limits on downtown parking?" put it this way: "What do you think about limits on downtown parking?" The resulting answer should give you more possibilities for creative leads, when you write your story. If you get a wishy-washy answer, *then* it's time to go after "yes" or "no".

If you can keep your person on his or her feet, the interview will probably come out better. Your person will be more concise, and to the point, and will tend to give you the short answers you need. Give them an idea what you'd like to cover beforehand, and make sure they understand the answers must be short.

If you do the interview sitting down, have your mike on a stand, facing the subject. In most cases, *your* voice is not necessary on tape. Keep the mike pointed at the subject—your question will still be picked up, but there won't be the noise of a shifting microphone, or an off-mike answer from the person you're interviewing.

In a stand-up situation, hold the mike yourself. If your person tries to grasp the mike, don't relax your grip. Interrupt, and say you'll have to keep the mike a proper distance away for a good recording—then ask him or her to start over. Don't shift your grip on the microphone—that movement will be picked up on tape. Avoid wearing jewelry on the hand you use to hold the mike. Bracelets and rings can strike it and cause devastating noise problems.

Make note of mannerisms or personality characteristics that can lend a human angle to your story. If your subject chomped on a cigar all the way through, use that fact in your voicer—and let the newscaster use it in the scripts. If the Mayor put his feet on the desk during the interview, use that fact.

Keep quiet while your subject answers. But don't forget that an interview is a one-on-one dialogue. Don't lose eye contact. Nod your head when appropriate, give your subject a quiet audience. Be relaxed, and soon most subjects will stop talking to the microphone and start talking to *you*. If your subject utters something important, wait until the thought is complete. Then get him or her to repeat it by interjecting: "In other words, you're saying . . ." The answer will be the same thing, repeated, giving you another piece of tape.

Keep in mind your final goal—polished actualities—that will ideally run 10 to 15 seconds each. If you can, jot these down as you come across them, along with the in-cue, running time and out-cue, and the number on the digital counter of your tape machine. But be cautious—note-taking frequently disturbs people, especially those not used to dealing with the media. If this is the case, put away your paper, and make your notes "mentally."

When you're through, ask your subject if there's anything else he or she would like to add. You may have forgotten to ask something. Or, in many cases, the person will just sum up the story with a few well-chosen remarks. Often, this last comment is the best thing in the whole interview.

Once you get good enough at it, you'll progress beyond doing "interviews" into having "dialogues" or "conversations" with newsmakers. This doesn't mean a business-like atmosphere will degenerate into a bull-session. But your technique will improve to the point where you treat interview subjects as individual people—and you merely talk to them, to obtain results on tape.

Either before or after your interview, get the person's name and title *on tape,* in case you forget, or in case someone else has to chop up the tape back at the station. When everything is completed, thank your subject—and give him or her your business card, if you have one.

Tough Tape

If you're interviewing someone involved in an unfavorable story, you may want to start with easy questions—just to get the answers coming. Once your subject has spewed forth some easy stuff, pop the big question. Even if the answer is "no comment," you've got it on tape.

The same trick works when setting up the interview. Arrange to talk about an easy subject. Once you're there, ask some easy questions—then go after the big story.

In some cases—when you're given what appears to be a bold-faced lie for an answer—you can turn it around. A follow-up question like "You're actually serious about that?" or "You expect people to believe that?" may produce a telling answer, even from a seasoned PR man. Or, you may choose just to remain silent, staring at your subject—which may produce the same results.

Save the entire tape of interviews that may be needed later, for reference, or for possible legal troubles. On a highly-charged issue, the full cassette of the interview may get you out of hot water—if your subject claims to have been mis-quoted, or quoted out of context.

Mark your cassettes with file-folder labels. Even routine interviews and stories should be marked, and not erased, at least for that working day. File folder labels can be peeled off, or covered with fresh labels, as required. Unlabelled cassettes are dangerous to have around!

Follow up appropriate interviews with opposing viewpoints. News generates news, generates news.

Tape On-the-Run

There are three main types of tape that are gathered hurriedly.

Random-Reaction Cut

This is a quick chat with an average person who's reacting to the news. It can be a shopper paying high prices for meat, a man on the street saddened by news of the President's death, or a college student giving his opinion on the latest cheating scandal. These people individually aren't *making* news. But through their comments your audience gets a perspective on how a particular event is *affecting* others.

The people you're talking to probably have never been on the radio before (and may never be again). When you approach them, it's generally best to have your tape-recorder running. Rather than get them flustered and nervous about their sudden luck, walk up and say (with the recorder on, mike in hand): "Hi, I'm from W----News, what do you think about these meat prices?"

Keep your mike aimed at the subject; don't swing it back and forth to ask your questions. If you need to have your questions appear on tape, stand close to the person you're interviewing. Keep the mike in position between you, but make sure you can see the grill of the mike, and speak toward it. Your questions will be picked up, without an off-mike answer and the sound of a shifting microphone.

Your main problem will be people who can't string a cohesive sentence together, who respond with two- or three-word answers, as a child would. You may have to ask them several consecutive questions, in order to get a complete answer that can be spliced together. Some of the brief comments may fit well in a montage. When you run into someone who is an articulate speaker, get enough tape for several cuts.

Eyewitness Actuality

An eyewitness actuality is a chance to grab some action-packed tape on a fast-breaking story. This can be a fireman just out of the raging four-alarmer, a passer-by who watched the bus and train collide, or the farmer who saw the plane go down in his "back 40." With your recorder running, identify yourself, "I'm from W----News" and put the mike in front of your subject.

The first and most obvious question to ask these people is: "What happened?" or "What did it look like?" Other questions will logically follow, but it's best to start out with these time-honored ones. This is especially true if you have just arrived at the scene, and haven't had time to figure out what's going on. Your subject may just babble on with the same answer, expressed different ways. This will give you several different cuts.

If your person claims he or she is too busy and starts to walk or run away, follow and do your interview on the run. The labored breathing you get on tape will add to the on-scene effect. But don't disrupt the work of officials in a life-or-death situation. In these cases you can generally find someone else to talk to. Many people, especially women, will have trouble controlling their emotions in a spot-news situation. So, if your format calls for this material, seek out people who appear upset.

In especially large spot-news events, there may have been a loud noise—from an explosion, the impact of a bus and train, and so on. Ask your person what it sounded like, what he or she thought was happening at the time. It's generally best not to have your person describe what the scene presently looks like. You're better qualified to do that yourself—in a voicer, voice-ality, or Q&A.

If you are on-scene as a story is developing, keep your tape recorder rolling. You may have only one chance to pick up gunfire, or a building wall collapsing.

Confrontation Situation

This is your chance to grab some tape of the accused mass-murderer as he goes into court, your chance to talk to union and management bargainers as they emerge tight-lipped from the bargaining session. Have your tape recorder running, and be as aggressive as you reasonably need to be.

Never, under *any* circumstances ask the question: "Do you have any comment?" The obvious answer is "no". If there are several newspeople around, and "no comment" answers are expected, you might plan to more-or-less block the exit with your bodies and microphones. This way, you may get a 10-second cut before being rudely brushed aside.

Have some quick questions thought out. Ask the accused killer: "How are they treating you in jail?" "How is the jury reacting to your story?" Ask the bargainers: "Do you have anything to celebrate right now?" "What have you accomplished today?" Even if you only get short answers, you can exploit them in short actuality cuts. And you can record some voicers and voice-alities on the scene—quoting the short answers, and emphasizing the mood and personalities of the people involved in the story.

Legalities of On-Scene Tape

You have the right to record (or broadcast live) from any *public* place that doesn't have a specific ban (such as a courtroom). Generally, any speech open to the public is also open to broadcast coverage. You do *not* need permission to record or broadcast somebody's voice—providing your microphone is visible and you're at a public event or on public property.

The Tape-on-the-Run section suggests you identify yourself as being from a radio station—when interviewing people who are not *themselves* in the news. This would include random reaction and eyewitness interviews. The line "(Hi) I'm from W----News" opens conversation and protects you against later claims that somebody wasn't aware who you were—or that they were going to be on the radio.

Court rulings leave it unclear whether someone may demand later that tape of them *not* be aired. If you run into this situation, check with your station attorney. It may be covered under state or provincial law, or court cases after this book went to print.

On *private* property you are a guest, and may be ordered off. If you expect a confrontation interview—make sure you have permission to be there (and taping or broadcasting live). Try for confrontation material in a public place—such as a sidewalk outside.

Covert newsgathering with *hidden microphones* is beyond the scope of this book. In a word—"don't"—without first consulting your station attorney.

Tape in Court

For the first half-century of radio "tape in court" was like "jumbo shrimp"—a term that contradicted itself. With very few exceptions, all recording and broadcasting equipment was banned from courts. The first broadcast coverage of an entire trial, from jury selection to verdict, wasn't until Miami's Zamora case in 1977.

Even today, many courts require broadcast reporters to surrender equipment before entering. Only notepads are allowed. Coverage typically consists of voicers and Q&A done on a nearby pay phone. Depending on the court and the level of security involved, reporters may not be able to leave freely and may have to wait until a recess to file.

Gradually, more courts are joining the trend toward allowing unobtrusive pool recording equipment. Only the mikes (and perhaps a camera) are visible in court. If both audio and video are available in a press room, it may be better to cover the trial from there. You'll see and hear everything and won't have to leave to file reports.

A September 1986 ruling from the 9th U.S. Circuit Court of Appeals in San Francisco allows us to use audio and videotape *evidence* from trials. It found radio and TV have constitutional and common-law rights to record and broadcast this material. But it gave trial judges discretion on protecting evidence against erasure. It also decided broadcasters would have to pay any costs involved, plus provide the equipment and personnel to make copies.

Whether or not you have access to trial testimony and evidence, key figures often can be interviewed going to or from court. In cases with a great deal of news coverage, the best option is to persuade them to hold impromptu news conferences. These are likely to produce far better questions and answers, with far less noise and clamor, than tape-on-the-run.

Tape from Other Sources

Reports from Amateur (Ham) and Citizens Band (CB) stations may be rebroadcast *without* their permission, under a 1985 FCC ruling.*

Ham operators are licensed and many have thousands of dollars invested in their "rigs." Many can relay phone calls over the air (or patch radio signals down the phone to your station). They are free to cooperate as much as they want with radio news organizations during and after emergencies—providing they're not paid for it. Ham signals can span the globe, and may be the only communications link when phone lines are down because of hurricanes, tornadoes, earthquakes and the like,

CB is a local service suitable for road reports, etc. Operators are unlicensed. Channel 9 is the emergency frequency routinely monitored by police; Channel 19 is the favorite of truckers. In many areas a volunteer group called "REACT" helps in monitoring frequencies. CB is also known as the "Children's Band" and anything other than routine road and weather information should be regarded as an unverified and possibly phony tip.

Your newsroom can monitor both groups on a commercial shortwave receiver capable of 3-30 MHz. That covers most Ham bands, CB channels and—in addition— the international broadcasters. To be truly useful, receivers must have "sideband" capability for Ham signals and a digital frequency readout. Prices begin near $200.

No permission is necessary to use tape cuts from international broadcasters such as the BBC (British Broadcasting Corporation) or Radio Moscow, providing the source is identified. Permission should be obtained from Canadian or Latin American stations. Material from the government's VOA (Voice of America) and AFRTS (Armed Forces Radio and Television Service) may *not* be rebroadcast on U.S. stations.

---

* The 1986 edition of a widely-used broadcast news textbook is wrong in stating the FCC "specifically prohibits rebroadcast" of Ham and CB transmissions. A 1985 change to Section 97.113 of the FCC Rules allows rebroadcast of Ham and CB operators without permission and without record-keeping. FCC Report and Order 85-302 explains this in detail.

The National Weather Service, part of the U.S. government, has transmitters in 372 cities/regions. NOAA Weather Radio includes key elements of the "weather wire" read aloud. It may be rebroadcast within one-hour and must be credited to the National Weather Service. Full information is in FCC Public Notice 70-1108.

Seven frequencies in the 162 MHz range are used, and special receivers begin near $20. Some models like the Radio Shack 12-140 ($40) will go on automatically when forecasters trigger a special alert tone to warn of severe weather.

NOAA Weather Radio is in the VHF-High band and can be added to virtually any newsroom "scanner" used to monitor police and fire frequencies. Maximum cost would be a $5 crystal in non-programmable models. The channel would be locked out of scanning.

Taping (and/or rebroadcasting) police and fire frequencies is *not* legal. Technically, even the information from "scanners" cannot be used without calling a dispatcher or interviewing someone at the scene to confirm it. Generally, this also holds true for most other forms of radio communications. If in doubt, consult your station attorney.

The air-signal of another AM or FM station may be rebroadcast, providing you have permission. This is normally done in writing. But for breaking news it could be handled in a phone call to the station's management. Both stations should, within a week, confirm the arrangement in writing.

Canned Tape

Not all radio news is, or needs to be, fast-breaking. Many of the best stories explore problems that have vegetated for months or years. These stories are the best to "can"—to put aside for the slow news period, from Saturday through Monday morning. Your Monday-morning-drive audience is as large as on any other weekday morning. But unless some tape has been "canned", they will hear only weekend news. Even in large cities, weekend news generally isn't much.

A phone call during the previous week to someone at a local college can produce a relevant story on one of the social problems in your area. You can get informed reaction on national issues, as well. Your City Hall staffer can do a "look-ahead" story on what will be happening the coming week. An undated City Hall story on a continuing issue can go all weekend. A check of your futures file for the upcoming week can lead to an advance story. Some local churches regularly have newsworthy weekend events and speakers.

And when you do an interview, or attend a news conference, you can be getting side-bar stories that can be saved for the slow period. When all the tape is in, things may still be a little skimpy. If that's the case, leave more than enough tape of the stories you *do* have, so newscasters can double-cut them—using two pieces of short tape on one story. A little extra effort the week before, by your staff, can produce enough news to carry through the weekend, and into Monday morning. It can make the difference between a newscast filled with irrelevant foreign news and some interesting close-to-home tape. If you run out of story ideas, get some random-reaction to a top story or issue of the day. It certainly doesn't hurt to have a montage running Monday morning.

In short, the key word on canned tape is: "Enterprise." Use imagination, and don't wait until Friday afternoon to work on weekend news. A little bit of tape squirreled away over the entire week will give you enough to last through the slow period.

11 | Writing for Tape

Vigorous writing is concise. A sentence should contain no unnecessary words, a paragraph no unnecessary sentences, for the same reason that a drawing should have no unnecessary lines and a machine no unnecessary parts. This requires not that the writer make all his sentences short, or that he avoid all detail and treat his subjects only in outline, but that every word tell.

—William Strunk, Jr.
The Elements of Style

A newscast is far more than a string of tape cuts. No matter how much tape a station is using, the newscast must be well-conceived and well-written to come across. If your tape is recorded and edited well, you're halfway there. Now comes the challenge of making the tape, scripts, and wire source copy into a finished news product.

Ideally, the lead story of every newscast should include tape. This consideration should be in the back of your mind as you prepare for airtime. Additionally, the tape in the first story should be as close to the beginning of the newscast itself as you can reasonably get it. This will give the newscast momentum, and establish the "eyewitness" or "first-person" aspect of your news without any need for additional hype. (Listen to some casts that use good tape near the beginning, you'll sense the momentum.) If you just don't *have* tape on the obvious lead story, okay. Try, instead, to make that first story a short one. And get tape into the second story in your cast—for sure.

After that, you're faced with the problem of keeping listener interest. Use a couple of short items, one or two-sentence things, to balance a longer story. Create a varied pattern of long story, tape, and short story items. Mix your ingredients well. Don't run successive long copy stories, if you can avoid it.

THIS:	NOT THIS:
Tape (Actuality)	Long Copy
Short Copy	Long Copy
Tape (Voicer)	Tape (Voicer)
Long Copy	Long Copy
Short Copy	Tape (Voicer)
Tape (Montage)	Short Copy
Short Copy	Long Copy
Short Copy	Long Copy
Tape (Actuality)	Tape (Actuality)
etc.	etc.

Also, tape-wise, shuffle things as best you can. Don't rely on one particular form of tape in a newscast. Use a mix of voicers, actualities, Q&A, voice-alities, montages, and sound. The combinations (assuming a good supply of tape) are endless. Integrate tape logically in your stories. Don't start out to tell the story by script alone, then shove in a tape cut as an after-thought. Get to the tape cut in a story quickly. Avoid using seven or eight sentences of copy before the tape and tag. But don't make it sound like you're the foreman in a tape factory. Every story should *not* contain tape—that only makes things drag.

Three work stations in main newsroom. —*Courtesy KPRC/Houston*

Writing for Tape

The same piece of tape should not run on consecutive newscasts unless those newscasts are several hours apart. Also, a piece of tape used in "morning drive-time" should not be used in "afternoon drive." Tape used in the afternoon should not be used the following morning. The story itself can be run, using different cuts.

All tape cuts should be uniformly "tight." The pause (if any) between newscaster and tape should be consistent.

When referring to your reporters, try to avoid sexism. A male is a "newsman," "reporter," or "correspondent." A female is a "newswoman," "reporter," or "correspondent." Mixed groups of males and females are "newspeople" or "reporters." Avoid use of the genderless term "newsperson" when you refer to an individual.

Many of the techniques can be combined with one another. And, of course, there are a great many ways of writing any of them.

Here are the different "leads" for tape cuts. The descriptive names originate with this book: 1. Traditional. 2. Paraphrase. 3. Surprise. 4. Question. 5. Conversational. 6. Hype. 7. Kinky. 8. Cold.

Actuality Leads

1. **Traditional**—SCRIPT: "President Smith has just delivered a speech on welfare. During the speech, Smith said:" TAPE: "I want all Americans to enjoy a decent standard . . ."

Other phrases include: "Smith told newspeople", "Smith told reporters", and so on.

2. **Paraphrase** (used to paraphrase *content*)—SCRIPT: "President Smith has just delivered a speech on welfare. In it, he's called for more aid for the poor." TAPE: "I want all Americans to enjoy a decent standard . . ."

2A. **Paraphrase** (used to paraphrase *mood*)—SCRIPT: "President Smith has just delivered a speech on welfare. About half-way through, the President got choked up." TAPE: "I want all Americans to enjoy a decent standard . . ."

2B. **Paraphrase** (used to paraphrase *mood* and *content*)—SCRIPT: "President Smith has just delivered a speech on welfare. His voice choked with emotion, as he called for more aid for the poor." TAPE: "I want all Americans to enjoy a decent standard . . ."

If a cart refuses to fire after a Paraphrase lead, you may be able to cover yourself by going to the scripted tag. Done smoothly enough, casual listeners won't notice anything was wrong.

3. **Surprise**—SCRIPT: "President Smith has just delivered a speech on welfare." TAPE: "I want all Americans to enjoy a decent standard . . ." or: SCRIPT: "A Gotham scientist has just won the Nobel Prize for Chemistry. He's Dr. John Jones." TAPE: "I'm very pleased to receive this award . . ."

There are several other ways of writing Surprise Leads. In all of them, the tape cut comes unexpectedly, after a *very* short copy introduction. One of the things that adds a great deal of impact to news is a sudden, unexpected difference in sound quality and location. This is one of the beauties of the Surprise Lead. When the tape is activated, it comes without warning to the listener. It has a different quality than studio sound. It provides a dramatic, "you are there" feeling, which adds authenticity to your news. It forces the listener to think, to link the tape to the story. And it jars him or her back to reality, if they've been mentally napping. This characteristic of the Surprise Lead applies to all types of tape.

4. **Question**—SCRIPT: "President Smith has just delivered a speech on welfare. What was the highlight of the message?" TAPE: "I want all Americans to enjoy a decent standard . . ."

This type of lead can sound very corny if it's not handled right. It doesn't lend itself to use often. The Question Lead can also be phrased other ways. One is the past tense: "President Smith *was asked* the highlight of his message." That's not very imaginative but not very corny either.

Another is a personal-interview style: "I (or we) talked to Joe Newsmaker, and asked him if the story was true." Or . . . "Just a few moments ago, I (we) asked Joe Newsmaker about that."

You can also be direct: SCRIPT: "The question is—does the local union president believe members are ready to strike?" TAPE: "You bet . . ."

5. **Conversational**—SCRIPT: "President Smith has just delivered a speech on welfare. What is it you want, Mr. Smith?" TAPE: "I want all Americans to enjoy a decent standard . . ."

This actuality lead is totally artificial, and insulting to your audience. It's mentioned here because it has only one limited use. It adds a beautiful touch to a humorous story.

6. **Hype**—SCRIPT: "President Smith has just delivered a speech on welfare. W--- microphones were there, as the President said . . ." TAPE: "I want all Americans to enjoy a decent standard . . ."

In some other circumstances the Hype Lead would be something like: "Joe Newsmaker tells W--- News . . ." This should only be used if the newsmaker was speaking into *your* microphones, or talking to *you* over the phone. As self-promotion it's okay . . . but it shouldn't be used routinely.

7. **Kinky**—SCRIPT: "President Smith is in favor of a new welfare bill because . . ." TAPE: "I want all Americans to enjoy a decent standard . . ."

Inflection is crucial on this type of lead, with a definite lift in the voice required on the word "because". The tape cut is used to complete the sentence; it must be absolutely "tight" with no pause at all. This is a flashy technique that should be used very sparingly.

8. **Cold**—TAPE: "I want all Americans to enjoy a decent standard of living." SCRIPT: "That's President Smith, making a speech on welfare."

Writing for Tape

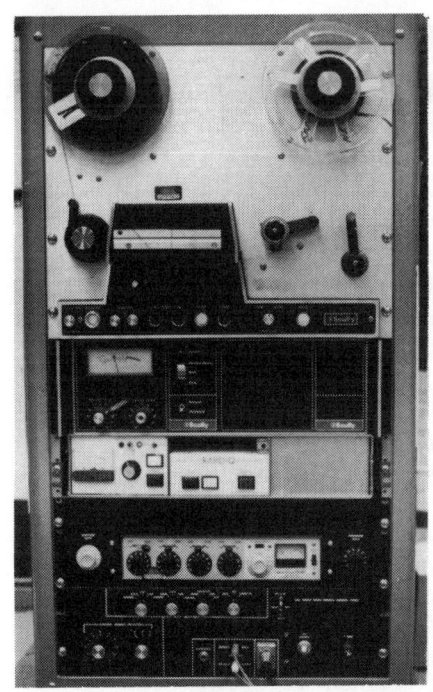

Custom newsroom work station used for routine dubbing, phone interviews, etc. From top: reel recorder; cart machine; mixer; input selectors; remote inputs from cassette/mike.

—*Courtesy KSL/Salt Lake City*

This type of lead works best when the actuality is extremely short, and a real attention-getter: TAPE: "I'm not a crook!" SCRIPT: "That's President Nixon, defending himself on Watergate charges. During a Florida appearance . . ."

Some people in this business think all leads should be complete sentences. They believe leads like "During his speech, Smith said . . ." are simply lazy writing. The Traditional Lead *is* greatly over-used, and perhaps should be saved only for special occasions (like Question or Hype leads). The best type of actuality lead for constant use is the Paraphrase. In most cases, it takes only one listen to a tape cut to paraphrase it. And this type of lead doesn't grow tiring to hear (if it's written with some flair). Nor does it have the "show biz" qualities of the Question, Hype and Kinky leads. It's possible to lead into a tape cut paraphrasing content, mood, or both.

Extremely short actuality cuts need special treatment. You must let your audience know, *in advance*, the tape will be short: SCRIPT: "It took only two seconds for the union boss to reply." TAPE: "The offer is no damn good!"

Or . . . SCRIPT: "The Mayor sums up the conference in three words." TAPE: "It wasn't much."

Voicer and Wraparound Leads

1. **Traditional**—SCRIPT: "A noisy demonstration is underway downtown. Reporter Tom Tape has the story from the Federal Building." TAPE: "Three-thousand people have gathered here . . ."

Other phrases include: "Tom Tape has more", "Tom Tape reports", "Tom Tape has details", "Here's Tom Tape" and so on.

2. **Paraphrase**—SCRIPT: "A demonstration is underway at the Federal Building downtown. Reporter Tom Tape says it's noisy and becoming violent." TAPE: "Three-thousand people have gathered here . . ."

3. **Surprise**—SCRIPT: "A noisy demonstration is underway in front of the Federal Building downtown." TAPE: "Three-thousand people have gathered here . . ."

This is basically the same as the Traditional Lead, minus the identification of the reporter before the tape. The first-hand aspect of the tape cut must be included, to make this type of lead effective.

4. **Question**—SCRIPT: "Reporter Tom Tape is covering a growing demonstration outside the Federal Building downtown. Are there any problems?" TAPE: "None so far. Police are watching the three-thousand . . ."

5. **Conversational**—SCRIPT: "A noisy demonstration is underway in front of the Federal Building downtown. On the scene is W---'s Tom Tape . . . Tom?" TAPE: "Three-thousand people have gathered . . ."

A well-equipped and well-marked working area for news.

—*Courtesy WBNS/Columbus, OH*

Or even more effective: SCRIPT: "A noisy demonstration is underway in front of the Federal Building downtown. On the scene is W---'s Tom Tape . . . Tom?" TAPE: "Joe, there are three-thousand people . . ." This lead is especially useful with live reports. It also can make a taped voicer/wraparound *sound* live.

6. **Hype**—SCRIPT: "W--- is on the scene of a noisy demonstration downtown at the Federal Building. Reporter Tom Tape was the first newsman there." TAPE: "So far, three-thousand people. . ."

7. **Kinky**—SCRIPT: "A noisy demonstration is underway downtown . . ." TAPE: "And police are massing now just across the street . . ."

Just as in the Kinky *actuality* Lead, the tape is used to complete a sentence. Inflection by the newscaster is all-important.

8. **Cold**—TAPE: "Three-thousand people have gathered here, outside the Federal Building downtown, for a demonstration."

The entire story can be included in one piece of tape. Or you can use a short tape cut, followed by a brief script, then the rest of the tape.

Q&A and Voice-ality Leads

1. **Traditional**—SCRIPT: "The 4th of July Parade is underway through downtown streets. Reporter Tom Tape is on the scene." TAPE: "The Air Force Band is marching . . ."

2. **Paraphrase**—SCRIPT: "The 4th of July Parade is underway through downtown streets. Reporter Tom Tape says it's a hot and colorful spectacle . . ." TAPE: "The Air Force Band is marching . . ."

3. **Surprise**—SCRIPT: "There's a lot of music in the downtown air." TAPE: "The Air Force Band is marching in front of me now, playing "America" for this Fourth of July crowd . . ."

The Surprise Lead just doesn't work in many situations. The reason is that a voice-ality tells only part of a story, frequently an unfolding one. The Surprise Lead can't generally be used on a late-breaking fire, or riot except in special circumstances. At times, it's possible to use a short voice-ality as an attention-getter, followed by a scripted story, or script and another piece of tape.

4. **Question**—SCRIPT: "The 4th of July Parade is underway through downtown streets. What does it look like?" TAPE: "The Air Force Band is marching . . ."

5. **Conversational**—SCRIPT: "The 4th of July Parade is underway through downtown streets. Reporter Tom Tape is there. Tom . . . what do you see?" TAPE: "Well, the Air Force Band . . ."

To use this technique, the tape cut must have an ad-lib quality at the start. All that's needed is the beginning word "well". This lead is also improved when the reporter inserts the first name of the newscaster, giving it a further "conversational" quality.

6. **Hype**—SCRIPT: "The 4th of July Parade is underway downtown, but W--- has been tipped on plans to disrupt it. Reporter Tom Tape says protestors plan to throw water on the marching bands." TAPE: "I've learned that . . ."

7. **Kinky**—SCRIPT: "The 4th of July Parade is underway downtown." TAPE: "And people seem to be enjoying it."

8. **Cold**—TAPE: "The Air Force Band is marching in front of me now, as part of the downtown 4th of July Parade." SCRIPT: "That's reporter Tom Tape . . ."

Sound Leads

1. **Traditional**—SCRIPT: "Police are breaking up a picket line around Capitalist Corporation right now. When officers arrived a few minutes ago, the strikers were chanting:" TAPE: "We deserve 30 percent more.!"

2. **Paraphrase**—SCRIPT: "Police are breaking up a picket line around Capitalist Corporation right now. When officers arrived, a few minutes ago, the strikers were loudly demanding a raise." TAPE: "We deserve 30 percent more!"

3. **Surprise**—SCRIPT: "Police are breaking up a picket line around Capitalist Corporation right now. Those strikers are loudly demanding a raise." TAPE: "We deserve 30 percent more!"

4. **Question**—SCRIPT: "Police are breaking up a picket line around Capitalist Corporation right now. Why are the workers striking?" TAPE: "We deserve 30 percent more!"

5. **Conversational**—SCRIPT: "Police are breaking up a picket line around Capitalist Corporation right now. The workers claim they deserve more money. In their words . . ." TAPE: "We deserve 30 percent more!"

6. **Hype**—SCRIPT: "Police are breaking up a picket line around Capitalist Corporation right now. When W--- arrived, minutes ago, the strikers started chanting." TAPE: "We deserve 30 percent more!"

7. **Kinky**—TAPE: "Police are breaking up a picket line around Capitalist Corporation right now. Workers are striking because:" TAPE: "We deserve 30 percent more!"

8. **Cold**—TAPE: "We deserve 30 percent more!" SCRIPT: "That's the sound of striking Capitalist Corporation workers, on a picket line. Their chanting has led police to break-up . . ."

Different Leads and Dangers

One way to vary your leads is to identify the newsmaker or reporter a couple of sentences before the tape.

> SCRIPT: "A noisy demonstration is underway downtown. Newsman Tom Tape is covering it from the Federal Building. He reports protestors are converging across the street. And their numbers are growing.
> TAPE: "Three-thousand people have gathered here . . ."

When you use this technique, be careful not to identify your tape *too* far back in the script.

The big pitfall in writing tape-stories is the "parroting" or "echo chamber" type of lead. It goes something like this:

> SCRIPT: "President Smith wants all Americans to enjoy a decent standard of living."
> TAPE: (Smith) "I want all Americans to enjoy a decent standard . . ."

Only our eternal vigilance will keep the airwaves free of this sort of abomination!

Hard and Throwaway Leads

These very general terms have been subdivided into the eight types just mentioned. But, so there's no confusion, a "Hard" lead is one that must be used because a voicer doesn't tell the complete story, and needs some specific introduction. For example:

> HARD LEAD: "A City Council meeting this afternoon has turned into a brawl. Reporter Tom Tape says, at latest count, half-a-dozen people have been hospitalized."
> TAPE: "It all started when the Police Chief called the Mayor a liar, and. . . ."

A "Hard" lead can also be required on an actuality, or any other type of tape:

> HARD LEAD: "The city says Acme Industries hasn't paid its property taxes, but Chief Tax Assessor Bill Collect doesn't plan a lawsuit."
> TAPE: "At least not at this time. . . ."

Again, the tape just doesn't make sense without the specific "Hard" lead. The other type is the "Throwaway" lead, sometimes known as a "teaser" or "soft" lead. This is just the opposite of the "Hard" lead. It's used to whet the interest of the audience, to get listeners prepared for the tape to follow:

> THROWAWAY LEAD: "There's a noisy demonstration underway downtown."
> TAPE: "Three-thousand people are. . . ."

Again, the "Throwaway" lead has been subdivided into several types.

Multiple Cuts

Sometimes, it's very effective to use two tape cuts in a story. The pro and con of an issue—a political charge and denial—the Arab side contrasted with the Israeli version. Generally, two cuts of tape is maximum in nearly all stories. Three (or more) only seem to slow down the pace, unless the story is so big it will make the history books. In some isolated cases, using the cuts of two people—back to back—can be effective:

> SCRIPT: "Two west side homeowners disagree whether that new freeway should be built through their backyards."
> TAPE: (Voice one) "Mr. Mayor, the freeway is utterly unthinkable. It would destroy our peaceful life in the suburbs." (Voice two) "Nonsense, Mr. Mayor, the freeway would mean we could get downtown without all those traffic jams."

This technique is best suited to short, terse cuts, where the two people are directly interacting with one another. Where actualities are involved, the two voices combined should run no longer than 20 or 25 seconds. Double-cutting can also be done with voicers and voice-alities. It's most effective when you plan things ahead of time, getting the reporters to bring up the same points in their stories.

Tags

We've dealt with ways to get *into* tape cuts. But getting out of them is just as important. Perhaps the worst technique for closing out a tape story goes like this:

> SCRIPT: "President Smith has just called for more help to the needy."
> TAPE: "I want all Americans . . .
>   14
>   . . . and the home of the brave."
> SCRIPT: *President Smith.*

Writing for Tape

A compact two-person newsroom at WIRK/W. Palm Beach, FL. Newscasts are done from the stand-up position at left with carts played from control room (through glass). —*Courtesy Mort Kaye Studios*

Or, how about this way of handling a voice-ality?

SCRIPT: "The 4th of July Parade is underway downtown. Reporter Tom Tape is on the scene."
TAPE: "In front of me now . . .
    18
    . . . crowd is enjoying the parade."
SCRIPT: *Reporter Tom Tape, watching the downtown festivities.*

The problem is, both those tags are stilted. A much better technique is to save a fact or two for use after the tape cut. Thus, you re-identify the tape (or sometimes identify it for the first time) and provide an additional fact or two.

Here's how the first example could be treated:

SCRIPT: "President Smith has just called for more help to the needy."
TAPE: "I want all Americans . . .
    14
    . . . and the home of the brave."
SCRIPT: *President Smith was speaking to the V-F-W post in Walla Walla. He's also been telling welfare recipients to be grateful for their handouts.*

The second story could be brought to a logical close, with a good tag:

SCRIPT: "The 4th of July Parade is underway downtown. Reporter Tom Tape is on the scene."
TAPE: "In front of me now . . .
    18
. . . crowd is enjoying the parade."
SCRIPT: *And reporter Tom Tape says soft drinks and ice cream are selling like mad downtown.*

The close to a tape cut should round off the story, and flow to a logical conclusion. You aren't likely to get much flow by saying "President Smith," or "Reporter Tom Tape."

Not everything needs to be tagged. If you end voicers with a sign-off, the tag is unnecessary. Many stations don't use tags after *any* form of tape. But, that means *all* the information you want to use on that particular story has to be run before the tape cut (or left out). And that reduces the possibilities for Surprise or Kinky leads.

Tape cuts that end with "neutral" and "up" inflections require special treatment. Here are two ways to handle them:

TAPE: ". . . that's what I think." (ends up)
SCRIPT: "The Police Chief goes on to say. . . ."

or:

TAPE: ". . . in my Administration." (ends neutral)
SCRIPT: "And President Smith also says. . . ."

You'll have to jump in immediately, on the end of the cut, as the last word is ending. And you'll have to punch the opening words of your tag, beginning on an "up" inflection yourself, to make it effective. Because of the unnatural ending to the cut, it's obvious to listeners that you've edited out of context. So a tag is mandatory, whether or not your station normally uses them on actualities.

A tag underscores the importance of tape cuts. Leaving it off can give the impression the story was a dud, and you're in a hurry to get on to something else. It also gives the subject the *last word* on the story. Eliminating the tag *does* produce a more rapid-paced newscast. It complements a rock-'n-roll format, but very little else.

Tape Quality

Tape, by itself, won't necessarily improve your story. If the cut was poorly recorded and/or transmitted over bad telephone lines, you're probably better off without it. A good rule-of-thumb is: "If you can't understand

Writing for Tape

the cut on the first hearing, your audience won't be able to understand it either."

Very little radio listening takes place under ideal, noise-free conditions. So, marginal tape should not be used except under unusual circumstances. If the story warrants the use of bad tape, the cut *must* be short—no more than 10 or 15 seconds.

You must also alert your listeners that a poor piece of tape is coming up: SCRIPT: "Officer Jones was calling for help over the police radio, as his partner was being shot to death. Listen closely."

Another technique is to justify the quality, letting your audience know *why* the tape is faulty: SCRIPT: "The armed bodyguard knocked our microphone to the ground, as his boss started swearing at W----News."

This way, even if your audience isn't able to understand the words in the cut, they'll get a feeling of what it was like to be on the scene. And the cut won't drag on long enough to become a tune-out.

Tape quality is especially a problem at stations with poor signals. If people in your area already have to contend with interference and static, you can literally make it *impossible* for them to listen, by using marginal tape-cuts.

If you have a lengthy marginal-quality cut that is mostly noise, you may want to run it *under* your script. Lead into the cut quickly, run the tape at 100% modulation for a few seconds, then fade it down under the rest of your story.

Voicers of marginal quality should not be used under any circumstances. If the story is important, you may want to lift two sentences from the cut to use as a Q&A. But, again, you'll have to set up your audience: SCRIPT: "Newsman Tom Tape is on the coast, watching the 110-mile-an-hour winds of the hurricane blow on shore." There is never any justification for running an entire marginal quality voicer.

12 | Tape Labelling, Handling and Morgue Systems

Set thine house in order . . .
2 Kings 20 (King James Version)

A chapter on "how to label carts" may seem ridiculous. But a tape-handling system that is not suited for your particular operation will cause problems every hour. A good system will speed up and simplify your tape handling, and actually encourage staffers to produce. Nearly every radio news operation puts its tape cuts onto cart, for reasons already explained. Basically, there are two cart-labelling systems and six tape-handling systems.

Numbered Labels

Labelling can be "numbered" or "informational." You can "number" carts on the front, in two ways: 1) *Permanently* with a Dymo-brand plastic

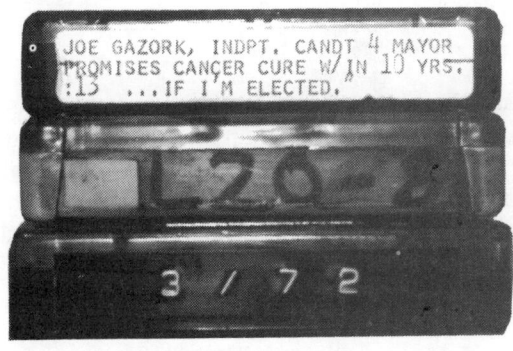

Three types of cart labels. Top: Informational. Middle: Daily Numbering. Bottom: Permanent Numbering.

label, or with a gummed file folder label. 2) *Daily* with a grease pencil. The Dymo-brand plastic label (or an equivalent) is the best way. You can buy a label-marker and enough plastic tape for several hundred carts for around $15. The labels will withstand years of daily use.

The best way is to label by cart length. One color of labelling tape for 20-second carts, another for 40s, a third for 70s, and so on. The colors make them easy to sort, and to spot in the rack. The labels might read: 20-19, 40-38—or just 2-19, 4-38, and so on. This way, carts are labelled consecutively, but are used at random. On the newscast script, carts are referred to by number only, which means newscasters have to double-check their accuracy in copying down numbers as they write.

Numbered carts can be stored in random order. But if you have a rack with enough space, you can set up designated slots for each cart. This may take up a lot of room, but will make finding a particular cart much easier.

Gummed file-folder labels can be used instead of the plastic ones. But they're not as durable, and have a tendency to fade. In the end, the plastic labels are both cheaper and more convenient because they don't need to be replaced as often.

The other cart-numbering system runs a poor second. Daily numbering, with a grease pencil, can lead to last-minute problems. If two people are processing tape at the same time, you can get two cuts with the same number. And you've got to devise a method for separating *today's* cart number 26 from *yesterday's* 26, which may still be in the rack. That may require using different colored grease pencils every day. Another method involves assigning a series of numbers to a certain reporter. But marking and erasing grease pencil numbers every day is a needless waste of time and effort.

Permanent numbered labels are far superior in convenience, legibility, and time saved. They also mean that, even in a last-minute situation, you don't have to deal with an un-numbered cart. The number is already on front for reference.

Informational Labels

These labels, naturally, change with every recording. Ordinary file-folder labels do the job, though you may want to shop around for a brand that's easy to remove from the cart. You can also put Scotch 'invisible' tape on the edge of the cart to prevent sticking.

Another possibility is using masking-tape (as strange as it sounds). The tape can be slapped onto the typewriter platen (or "wringer"), and used just like any other label for typing. It also removes easily from the cart.

Tape Labelling, Handling and Morgue Systems 171

Any informational label should include several pieces of compacted information:

1. Who.
2. Title.
3. Where.
4. Story lead.
5. Time of cut.
6. Out-cue of cut.

Here's one example:

```
Jim Hype, Spksm, Capitalist Corp
Chicago. No truth to Justice Dept
charges. :14 ...we are innocent."
```

The problem with the informational label is its size. There's just no room to explain a complicated or unfamiliar story. By itself, it's inadequate for a station using a lot of tape gathered independently of the wires and newspapers.

If there's no written material from which to write a complicated story, you might get something like this:

```
Dr. Argo Binufnook, Johns-Hopkins
Med Sch Balt MD. Exp cancer trtmt
helps some :14 "malignt melanoma"
```

One solution is to type up a fact sheet, from which the newscaster can write the story.

Handling Systems

Half-a-dozen basic tape handling systems are in common use. Some are best suited to small operations, others to large stations that originate many of their own stories, and re-write everything for each newscast. It's possible, of course, to do some modifying and combining of these systems. Some of the deficiencies are easily cured, simply by adding a fact sheet, with background information for the newscaster.

And computerization of radio newsrooms offers a chance to simplify tape handling by cutting down on paperwork, perhaps eliminating it altogether, by having tape information appear on a computer screen.

1. **Write the story itself when you process the tape.**

    Advantages: Quickest, most basic way of handling tape cuts. Story is all ready to go for air-use—no further work necessary. Works with either numbered or informational labels.

    Disadvantages: Copy grows stale, becomes tune-out if used repeatedly. Only background information on cut, is what's on the script, and possibly the label. System does not lend itself to further re-writes. Awkward for tape morgue system.

    Conclusion: Basic system—requires only minimal work. Ideal for a small news operation, workable for staffs producing a large amount of news, who may re-write the story later.

2. **Stick an informational label on the cart.**

    Advantages: Least complicated system for re-writing tape stories. All information is in one place—on the cart label.

    Disadvantages: Little room on label for story information, thus many cuts are difficult for newscaster to write. No room to indicate when cart was used on air, except by adding another label on top of cart. Label(s) must be pulled off when cart is erased. Awkward for tape morgue system.

    Conclusion: Works well in small operations, where there's rarely an unfamiliar story, and where there's no need for extensive tape morgue. Not suitable for unfamiliar stories, complicated stories, or stories that need extensive backgrounding—except by addition of separate "fact sheet."

3. **File folder label on top, numbered label on front.**

    Advantages: File folder labels available up to 3" x 5", big enough to hold necessary story information. Everything is on cart, nothing to misplace. Numbered label on front makes cart easy to spot in rack, compared with informational label.

    Disadvantages: Newscasters must sort through carts themselves to find out what's on them. Cart may be in machine when newscaster needs some label information. Awkward for tape morgue system.

    Conclusion: A workable basic system for re-writing tape cuts. It's an improvement over system #2, but not as good for larger operations as #5 and #6.

Tape Labelling, Handling and Morgue Systems

4. **Numbered cart label and multiple-cut log sheet.**

    Advantages: Numbers make cart easy to spot in rack. Log sheets mean more room for information on tape cut and story. Room on log to indicate when cart was used. Sheets can be put on inexpensive clipboard.

    DATE: _____

    WFAA/KZEW TAPE LOG

Cart #	TIME	WHO AND WHERE	V	A	V/A	DESCRIPTION	TIME USED

    A typical multiple-cut log sheet.   —*Courtesy WFAA-KZEW/Dallas*

    Disadvantages: Several cuts on one log sheet mean trouble. If one cut is killed, it must be crossed off. Reporter may be trying to finish logging cuts on sheet, when newscaster wants to use it for cuts already logged. Newscaster must wade through sheets on clipboard to find out what's available. Two items—cart and log sheet—necessary for each piece of tape. Morgue operations are complicated by having several cuts to a sheet, when only one is being saved.

    Conclusion: It works . . . and it's widely used. But the inherent problems make it the worst system of the six in common use. Many of the drawbacks have been corrected in the following two systems.

5. **Numbered cart and individual tape log sheets (1 cut to a sheet).**

    Advantages: Carts easy to spot in rack. Good-sized log sheet has plenty of room for all necessary information. Inexpensive clipboard can be used. Cuts easily killed and morgued, since only one to a sheet. Different color sheets can be used, one for actualities, another for voice-alities, and so on.

Disadvantages: Requires re-typing basic information onto each sheet (rather than once on a multiple-cut log system). Unless sheets are kept together, they can become lost. Two items—cart and log sheet—necessary for each piece of tape.

Conclusion: One of best systems for rewriting tape cuts. Initial time expended in filling out sheet is worth it. Complete story information is there for newscaster, along with a convenient morgue system.

6. **Numbered cart and individual tape log cards (1 cut to a card).**

Advantages: Carts easy to spot in rack. Cards (preferably 4" x 6") can be either blank, or with printed form. They have plenty of room for necessary story information, and can be color-coded (as in system #5). Cuts easily killed and morgued, since only one to a card. Cards more durable than paper sheets.

```
WDEE - NEWS TAPE LOG     USED:  145
         ⊙                       745
CART #    2/26
WHO       John Carter
TITLE     VicePres--UAW Local 653
LOCATION  Pontiac (Pontiac Motor Plant)
PHONE #   1-334-9917
FED/PROC  fg
DATE      19 Nov 76
TIME      1p

STORY     (lead with GM contract settlmt)
8         The big question now...is
7         whether skilled trades people
6         will be able to muster enough
5         votes...to reject this pact.
4         The Vice-president of one UAW
3         local admits...there is some
2         strong opposition.
1

IN CUE    We have some...
RUN TIME  :13
OUT CUE   ...will be ratified."

TAG       (dated tag:) UAW locals are
4         just now getting the official
3         word from their higherups. Some
2         still don't have any idea what
1         the pact contains.

DATED?
F/UP?
SAVE?
```

Here's one form, devised for system 6. The small circle next to the call letters is for typewriter alignment. "Fed/Proc" indicates who gathered and spliced the tape. "F/Up?" is used to indicate whether another angle on the story is available. "Save" can be used to hold this cut for the morgue. When in the card file, the top 4 or 5 lines are visible.

Disadvantages: Requires special card file (like that used for time cards) which is an extra expense. Requires re-typing basic information onto each card (rather than once on a multiple-cut log sheet). Cards can become misplaced, but not as much a problem as in system 5. Two items involved for each cut—cart and card.

A portable storage unit for both carts and cards, suitable for systems 5 and 6. Horizontal cart storage would be even better.

Conclusion: Slightly better than system #5, except in cost. Special card file means all cuts are visible at once. Newscaster can tell at a glance what's available, can build newscast around tape, knowing what kinds of tape are on hand. File(s) can be mounted next to cart rack for quick correlation of cart and card. Morgue operation is easily arranged, cards don't age like regular paper.

Elements of a Tape Morgue

The logical extension of a tape system for current cuts, is a system for "dead" cuts. A good, efficiently-organized tape morgue is invaluable.

It can give you necessary background cuts for information, legal troubles, contests, special events, and so on. If a public official makes a 180-degree turn in policy, you can use the new statement, with the old one dug up from the morgue in a matter of minutes.

Unless you're blessed with an abundance of carts, you'll want to dub the cuts onto a reel, or cassette. Tape systems #5 and #6 make saving and organizing cuts easy. Just save the card, or sheet, along with the cut. You can keep the cuts organized by speaker, by subject, or by the date they were gathered. The amount of material you save, and the way you save it, will vary with your station's needs.

As a general rule, you should save tape that fits into one or more of these three categories: 1) Major event that may have repercussions later; 2) Good tape for contest entries; 3) Controversial tape that could involve legal challenge.

Especially in the last category, you may want to save the *entire* raw tape, rather than just what was broadcast. Ideally, your tape morgue will become what a conventional morgue is to a newspaper. It will be an idea file for future stories, and also an unbeatable reference tool.

Appendix

Addresses of Specialty Equipment Manufacturers

(Products of these companies are included in the text and/or pictures. Some are the only source for a particular item.)

Atlas Sound
10 Pomeroy Rd.
Parsiappany, NJ 07054
(mike stands, etc.)

Beyer
5-05 Burns Ave.
Hicksville, NY 11801
(mikes)

Comrex
65 Nonset Path
Acton, MA 01720
(phone extenders)

Electro-Voice
600 Cecil St.
Buchanan, MI 49107
(mikes)

Elgin Electronics
5533 New Perry Hwy.
Erie, PA 16509
(phone couplers)

47th Street Photo
36 E. 19th St.
New York, NY 10036
(EQ; recorders)

Gentner Engineering
540 W. 3560 South
Salt Lake City, UT 84115
(Microtel, phone equip.)

J-ngineering
20811 Parthenia
Canoga Park, CA 91306
(two-way modifications)

Marantz
20525 Nordhoff St.
Chatsworth, CA 91311
(cassette recorders)

Marti Electronics
P.O. Box 661
Cleburne, TX 76031
(RPUs)

Moseley Electronics
111 Castilian Dr.
Goleta, CA 93017
(RPUs)

Nortronics
8101 Tenth Ave., N.
Minneapolis, MN 55427
(recorder equipment)

Olympus
Crossways Park
Woodbury, NY 11797
(Microcassettes)

Op-Amp Labs
1033 N. Sycamore
Los Angeles, CA 90038
(mult boxes)

Radio Shack
One Tandy Center
Ft. Worth, TX 76102

Sennheiser
48 W. 38th St.
New York, NY 10018
(mikes)

Shure
222 Hartrey Ave.
Evanston, IL 60204
(mikes)

Sony
Sony Drive
Park Ridge, NJ 07656
(cassette recorders)

Switchcraft
5555 N. Elston
Chicago, IL 60630
(plugs, jacks, cords)

3M
St. Paul, MN 55144

Voice Act
P.O. Box 572
Ridgefield, CT 06877

Walker
P.O. Box M
Ringgold, GA 30736
(phone equipment)

Glossary of Terms

This glossary lists nearly 500 commonly-used tape terms, as well as some basic radio terms ("spot", "drive-time", "housecleaning") that should help people just getting into the business.

A word of caution—some terms have different meanings in radio and in television. In addition, some radio terms vary in different parts of the U.S. and Canada.

Technical terms have been deliberately over-simplified, since this book is not intended to deal with the intricacies of electrical engineering.

Terms that originate with this book are marked with an asterisk * next to the entry.

AC — alternating current flow of electricity. Found in standard wall sockets. Standard source of power for nearly every electronic device, including tape machines. Nearly all sockets in North America supply 110 volts of power, while in Europe, 220 is typical. (Different from "DC" or "Direct Current").

Account — version, or report, of a particular news story.

AC/DC — alternating current/direct current. Usually designates equipment that can run off regular wall sockets (AC current), as well as batteries (DC current). Some of this equipment can also be powered by a car, through a special adapter plugged into the cigarette lighter.

Acetate Base — a type of plastic film no longer in common use for recording tape. Acetate tends to become brittle and crack under even moderate use, it has been replaced by new tape bases, most commonly, Polyester.

Acoustics — sound characteristics of a particular room or area. Ranges from "dead" with no sound reverberation, to "live" where sound bounces off walls and ceiling.

Action Central — old radio term for newsroom. Generally used in 50's and early 60's along with sound effects, bombastic writing style, and blatantly ridiculous promotion.

Actuality ("Ack") — the "actual" voice of someone in the news. First-person tape. One of the basic tape forms.

Adapter — small attachment that fits on jacks, plugs, or sockets. It allows different connectors to be used than those originally intended. Commonly used in radio news to match patch cords to available jacks on tape recorders or sound systems.

Ad-lib — supposedly unplanned, unwritten, report. Voice-alities and Q&A are ad-libbed, or should be written to sound unplanned.

Afternoon-Drive — time period when most radio stations have their second-highest Monday through Friday audience (behind Morning Drive). Hours vary, but coincide with a particular city's afternoon traffic rush hours sometime between 3 and 7 PM.

Aircheck — tape recording of material broadcast on the air. Used when applying for jobs, to demonstrate ability and sound. (*Also see* Resume).

Air Name — phony name used on the air, in place of "legal name". Allows person with awkward, funny, or otherwise unsuitable legal name to choose a different one. Sometimes also known as a "professional name".

Air Time — broadcast time of a newscast, or length it is supposed to run.

Alignment — proper adjustment of electronic components. Usually used to refer to the "heads" of tape machines, which must periodically be moved a tiny distance to make proper contact with the tape. Heads that are not properly adjusted are called "out of alignment." This is delicate work requiring a skilled person and proper technical equipment.

Alligator Clip — metal clip with spring action used to make temporary electronic connections. Long, narrow clip resembles jaws of an alligator. Used in pairs of two mostly to make connections to telephones and sound systems for feeding and recording tape.

AM — abbreviation for "Amplitude Modulation".

Amplify — to increase electronically. Usually refers to an increase in "volume" or "loudness". A device used to accomplish this is called an "amplifier".

Amplitude Modulation — one method of transmitting a broadcast signal. Usually used to denote standard "AM band" of stations between 540 and 1600 on the dial. Differs from "Frequency Modulation" or "FM" in both method of producing signal and quality of sound.

* **Amputated Wraparound** — tape form that consists of reporter's voice followed by an actuality, or vice-versa. Traditional close to report is left off. This form should be concluded by the newscaster, with a sentence or two of tag material.

Analog Recording — conventional technology of recording magnetic impulses based directly on audio source. (*See also* Digital Recording).

Analysis — report that explores the "whys" of a particular story.

Angle — one way of approaching a news story. Refers to a story beginning that will attract listener interest. Involves highlighting of one fact, or set of facts, which are sometimes known as a "news peg".

Antenna — device used to receive or transmit radio or television signals. "Receiving antennas" pick up signals and feed them into a radio or television set. "Transmitting antennas" radiate the signals into the air, after they're produced by a transmitter.

Attenuate — to turn down or decrease, usually done with a volume control or potentiometer.

Attribution — mention of the source for a particular fact or quotation.

Audio — sound. Can refer to all material broadcast on radio, or sound portion of a television broadcast. Sometimes also used in radio news, instead of "tape cuts".

Audio Frequency — sound range that can be heard by normal human ears. Roughly 15 Hz to 20,000 Hz at a maximum, with some people having a much more restricted range.

Audio Service — news organization that feeds tape, and sometimes "live" news material, to subscribers. There's

Glossary of Terms

no real dividing line between this term and "network".

Automatic Gain Control (*also* AGC, ALC, AVC *or* compression) — circuitry commonly found in cassette recorders that raises low volume levels. Net effect is to increase background noise when no voice material present. Compresses overly soft, and overly loud material into almost identical volume range on tape.

Automatic Shut-Off — safety and convenience device on some tape machines that stops tape motion when tape runs out, or breaks. Found on most professional-quality reel-to-reel and cassette recorders.

Average Peak — repeated high sound levels, as recorded on a "VU Meter". Term refers to modulation produced in typically loud passages. Should run between 80 and 100%, with occasional peaks higher.

Background Noise (room noise) — extraneous sound present in an area that is picked up on tape. It ranges from air-conditioner hum to sound of people talking in background. Can be a problem with "AGC" circuitry on cassette tape recorders, because this noise is amplified when no speech is present. Also refers to unwanted noise produced by tape equipment, such as hum or hiss.

Backing (base) — the actual "tape" itself, the material to which the magnetic oxide particles are attached. Most modern-day backings are made out of Polyester. Older backings were commonly Acetate.

Balance — 1. Fairness to all sides in a story. An accurate presentation of all viewpoints. 2. Engineering term sometimes used to describe relationship between bass and treble, or between left-and-right channels of a stereo system.

Ballsy — type of sound produced by deep, masculine voice, through microphone or telephone. Can also be achieved through proper equalization.

Banana Plug — connector used mainly for testing applications.

Bass (*pronounced:* BASE) — lower frequency range of spoken or musical sound. Generally below middle-"C" on a piano (256 Hz).

Bassy (*pronounced:* BASEY) — sound quality characterized by excessive bassiness, and lack of high-pitched material. Often distinct and boring to listen to. Can be corrected by proper equalization to add "crispness" to sound, eliminating some low-pitched material. (*Also called* Muddy)

Battery — electric storage device that generates "direct current" or "DC". Used to provide power to many pieces of equipment, including tape recorders and microphones. Some battery types are rechargeable, others can be used only once.

Battery Charger — electrical unit that restores power to used batteries. Used commonly with Ni-Cad (Nickel Cadmium) batteries which are designed for recharging. Of little use for common Zinc-Carbon or most Alkaline batteries, since tape recorders require a good deal of power, and most of these types are designed for one-time use.

Beat — area of routine news coverage. Usually a governmental agency or building, such as City Hall, Police Station, or Court House. Frequently, one reporter will be assigned to devote full or part time to cover these areas.

Beep Tone — distracting and annoying signal produced by some telephone equipment used to warn people their conversation is being recorded. Commonly found in one type of broadcast coupler that connects a telephone line to a tape recorder. No longer necessary under FCC (or Canadian CRTC) regulations.

Beeper — old term for "Voicer". Report from a newsperson done down telephone, recorded with "beep tone" on line. Term is no longer in general use.

Bias — 1. Slanting of a news story, usually unfavorable to the person or group involved in it. 2. High-frequency current that is added to tape recorded signal, eliminating distortion caused by magnetism. Bias signal is far above range of hearing.

Blank Tape — recording tape with no recorded material on it. Can be new, or old tape that has been bulk-erased. Also sometimes referred to as "empty" or "clean".

Block Programming — frequent changes in program material, typical of radio before the 50's. Broadcast day was divided into separate "shows". Still in use at some stations today, mostly in smaller markets. Television is "block programmed" with a different show typically coming on every hour or half-hour.

Blurb — one term for a news release.

Board — short for "control board". Mixing device that controls what sounds go on air, and at what level. Commonly contains several "pots" that are used to regulate sound levels on different "channels". Also contains a "VU meter" to indicate relative loudness of program material.

Boomy — sound characteristic produced by acoustically "live" room, improper microphone placement, or a combination. "Boomy" sound picked up on tape has bounced off hard surfaces, as well as come directly from the speaker's mouth. The same sound is, thus, recorded several times at split-second intervals.

Breaking Story — news event that is developing at the present time. Late breaking nature may outdate information you put on the air.

Breath Filter — (*See* Pop Filter)

Broadcast Band — standard AM (Amplitude Modulation) frequency span assigned to commercial stations. Stretches from 535 to 1605 KHz. Includes all stations from 540 to 1600 on the AM dial.

Broadcast Journalism — a fancy term for radio news, or television news. Practitioners are called "Broadcast Journalists".

Broadcast Quality — 1. Equipment designed for broadcast use. 2. Tape that is suitable for broadcast, and will be understandable even with unavoidable loss in transmission and reception.

Bulk Eraser — strong electromagnet used to remove all recorded signals from tape in a few seconds, when they are passed over the device. Some are desk-top models, others are hand-held during the erasing procedure.

Bulletin — originally a wire service term for news that is both unexpected and highly significant. Originally, below only a "flash" in importance. Usage has now been changed to include all news developments that warrant interrupting normal program material to broadcast.

Burp — (*See* Upcut).

Call Letters — federally-assigned sets of three or four (in Canada sometimes five) letters used to designate a particular radio or television station. American call letters, under international treaty, run from KAA to KZZZ, and WAA to WZZZ. Letters NAA to NZZZ are also available but not yet assigned. (Broadcast stations in Canada are assigned CBA to CBZZ, and CFA to CKZZ.)

Can — a verb meaning "save" or "hold". Used to denote tape that is gathered for use at a later time, especially on weekends or Monday morning. This material is called "canned tape".

Canned Tape — news material gathered in advance of its intended use. Used frequently on weekends, and Monday mornings, to provide "fresh" stories during a slow news period. Also referred to as "Hold for Release" tape, or abbreviated "HFR".

Cans — radio slang for "earphones" or "headphones". (*See* "Earphones")

Glossary of Terms

Capstan — rotating metal shaft of a tape recorder that determines tape speed. Used with a freely-rotating rubber wheel, known as a "pinch roller" or "pressure roller" to pull tape past the heads at a constant speed.

Capstan Idler — (*See* Pinch Roller).

Carbon Microphone — inexpensive, rugged unit used in telephones, aircraft, and two-way radios. Sound strikes carbon granules, changing electrical current that flows through them. Carbon miocrophones have frequency range of roughly 400 to 4,000 Hz, suitable only for basic voice transmissions.

Cardioid — common microphone pick-up pattern. Provides "heart-shaped" response. Area directly in back of microphone is "nulled". Areas in front and to sides of microphone are picked up. Widely used in both studio and outside news work. (*Also see* Super Cardioid.)

Cartridge (cart) — one of three commonly used types of recording tape. Contains a single spool of tape, which automatically recycles to beginning through use of "cue-tones". Carts are used in broadcasting for final tape product that is played on the air, by a "cart machine".

Casing — plastic outer housing of a cassette or cart. Usually contains two parts which are joined together by screws or sonically welded.

Cassette — one of the three commonly used types, or forms, of recording tape. Contains miniature feed and take-up reel of tape, all completely enclosed in a protective plastic housing. Used to record news outside the station, with a "cassette recorder". Standard cassette speed is 1⅞ ips, a few models offer an additional speed.

Cassette Quality — tape recorded on a cassette.

Cast — abbreviation for "newscast".

C-Clamp — adjustable clamp used to affix microphone stand to edges of desks, podiums, etc. Also known as "bracket clamp".

Cellular Telephone — hand-held or in-car telephone operating over radio waves instead of wires. This new technology splits major cities into "cells" each capable of handling many calls and automatically transferring them into adjoining cells as users drive or walk.

Channel — complete sound or signal path. Monaural (monophonic) tape has one output channel. Stereo has two. Quadraphonic has four. (Not to be confused with "tracks" which refer to the number of things that can be recorded on a piece of tape.)

Chassis — frame or box on which parts of an electronic device are located. Generally, a metal housing, but not the outside cabinet.

Chromium-Dioxide Tape — special tape formulation used in some cassettes to provide increased "frequency response", and better "signal-to-noise ratio". Requires special circuitry, and switch, on cassette recorder. Is not compatible with other standard cassette tapes. Also known as "CrO_2".

Clips — 1. Another term for tape "cuts". 2. Alligator clips, used to make temporary electrical connections to phones and sound systems.

Close-Talking Microphone — microphone designed to cancel extraneous noise. Requires user to practically "kiss" microphone when talking. Used mainly in paging systems, also has some limited broadcast use.

Coating — magnetic layer on tape. The actual magnetic oxide particles are held together by a glue-like "binder", which is stuck to the "backing" or "base".

* **Cold Lead** — really, not a lead to a tape cut at all. Short cut is run cold, then newscaster tags it with story information . . . putting the tape cut in context.

Commitment — prior to deregulation in U.S., promise made by station as a condition of its license, to broadcast a certain amount of news and public affairs programming per week. Living up to commitment was known as "fulfilling" it.

Compatible — able to be used together. Refers to equipment with characteristics allowing it to be electronically linked to another piece of equipment.

* **Compound Wraparound** — wraparound tape story that does not include the traditional voice/actuality/voice construction. May start with voice, actuality or sound, contain any number of segments and end with any type of tape.

Compression — (*See* Automatic Gain Control.)

Condenser Microphone — high-quality, generally high-cost mike commonly used in studios. Requires its own power supply, which may involve separate unit, or just a small battery in some newer models. Also known as "electrostatic microphone" or "capacitor microphone".

Consultant — expert, or psuedo-expert, paid to advise radio stations. Usually works for several stations in different markets, making suggestions on format, programming, news, etc. Sometimes actually controls stations, has power to hire and fire.

* **Contact Point** — point on tape where it is in contact with playback head of tape machine.

Control Board — (*See* Board)

Converter — device that changes one form of electricity to another. Commonly used to run tape recorder through cigarette lighter in cars. Also can power battery-operated recorders through wall current. (Also known as "inverter".)

Copy — written news material (as opposed to tape). Can also refer to written story that includes tape. (*See also* Script.)

Countdown — verbal indication that a reporter is starting a voicer or wraparound. Used when feeding material from outside the station. Reporter feeds suggested "lead" to story, then the countdown of "3-2-1" before starting story. Makes editing and producing of tape cut easier at station. (Sometimes countdown contains a "3-2-1-*punch*", which is unnecessary.)

Counter — digital indicator, used to find passages on cassette and reel-to-reel tape recorders. Digital counter shows number of revolutions in the take-up reel. Notation made of counter numbers when recording, can aid in finding passages on tape later, during playback. Counter accuracy varies widely from machine to machine. (Also known as "digital counter", "tape counter" or "index counter".)

Coupler — general term for two types of telephone devices that link a telephone line to a recorder.

CPS — abbreviation for "cycles per second". Under fairly new terminology . . . one cycle is the same as one "Hertz".

Crap-Out — technical malfunction in equipment.

Crisp — inclusion of high-pitched audio material in sound. Refers to ideal equalization of tape, so both high and low sounds are included. Opposite of "crisp" is "muddy" or "bassy".

Cross-fade — smooth transition between two program elements. Usually a mixing of music. Can also be applied to mixing of news material, and blending of one sound with another. (*See also* Segue)

Cross-talk — extraneous sound caused by accidental leaking of signals from one channel or track to another. Can also refer to unwanted signal on a "dirty" piece of tape.

Cruise for News — practice, discredited since energy shortage, of driving around in news cars, monitoring police and fire radios, while looking for stories. The term "News Cruiser" grew out of this.

Cue — 1. Hand or electronic signal used to indicate radio or television performer is "on". Also used by on-air newspeople to tell engineer or disc-jockey that pre-determined tape cut or commercial should be run. 2. Electronic tone used by cart machines to perform stopping, and other functions. Consists of "primary cue", which tells machine to stop, "secondary" and "tertiary" cues which can be hooked up for various functions, including electronic editing, and warning lights. (*Also see* False Cue). 3. Dead-end audio circuit on boards used to audition material.

Cueing — physical moving of tape to a particular point.

Cue Tone — tone placed on cart during recording, that activates machine functions, such as stopping. Tone is on a separate "track" from the program material, and is not heard.

Cut — 1. Verb meaning physical process of editing or "cutting" tape. 2. Noun meaning a "tape cut" which is edited and ready for use.

Cycle — change or vibration of an alternating wave from zero to its positive peak, back through zero to its negative peak, and back to zero. Used to measure frequency of sound and electrical waves, as in "cycles per second". Range of hearing, for example, is 15 cycles to 20,000 cycles per second. At frequencies high above this, the actual "transmission" of radio signals takes place. Cycle is now replaced by the term "Hertz" which means exactly the same thing. It honors German scientist Heinrich Hertz.

Dated — tape that cannot be used in its present form, because it refers to a time element already past. A tape cut from Friday with the words "this afternoon" is no good the following morning. This can be avoided by choosing other phrases to indicate time. (Also known as "outdated".)

Dateline — city or place where a story originates. Term is used by wire services, which usually include a dateline before the story itself.

Daybook — listing of news stories for a particular day. Used to make "assignments" and keep track of events. Other forms include: listings on a blackboard, on a separate "assignment sheet", or just making assignments verbally.

dB — (*See* Decibel)

DC — abbreviation for "Direct Current".

Dead — acoustically quiet. Refers to room or area where sound does not bounce to cause echo or hollow sound. Usually a room with plenty of sound-absorbing material, like carpeting, draperies, acoustical tile, etc. The opposite of a "live" room.

Dead Air — an accidental halt in program material for one reason or another, resulting in no sound on the air.

Decibel — (pronounced: DESS-ah-bull) — measure of relative sound power or intensity. One decibel is smallest difference in sound normal human ear can detect. Also abbreviated "dB".

Deck — tape recorder stripped of case, amplifiers, and speakers. Can record, but cannot play back tape, without other "components". Usually used as part of sound system, and usually mounted in a rack or cabinet.

Degausser — another term for "bulk-eraser".

Delivery — style of news presentation. Involves use of tape, reading speed, writing, and voice quality. Some common types are loosely known as "up-tempo", "authoritative", "personality", "conversational", and "laid-back"—all of which are self-descriptive.

Demagnetizer — small device that removes built-up magnetism in record and playback heads of tape recorders.

Deregulation — process under which U.S. broadcast industry in early 1980's was released from many government (FCC) controls, including news commitments.

Diaphragm — flexible part of a microphone used to produce vibrations. Sound striking diaphragm is passed to other parts of mike to generate small electrical current.

Digital Counter — (*See* Counter)

Digital Recording — developing technology of rapidly sampling audio material and translating this into a series of "1" and "0" instead of recording magnetic impulses directly from audio as in older "Analog" process. Digital allows better sound reproduction and signal-to-noise ratio.

Direct Current — power supplied by a battery. Differs from "alternating current" or "AC" which is supplied by commercial power companies, and obtained through a wall socket. Car batteries also produce direct current.

Directional Microphone — general term for microphones that do not pick up sound from all sides (known as "omni-directional"). Directional mikes may have "pickup pattern" that "nulls" or cancels sound from many different angles, or from just one angle.

Dirty Tape — tape that has been improperly erased, or not erased at all.

Disc Jockey — one of many terms for host of music programs on radio. At most stations, Disc Jockey (or "DJ") plays own records (or carts). At others, an engineer handles the technical end, and the disc jockey does little more than talk.

Distortion — error in recording or playback that caused changes in original sound. Seriously affected material that sounds strange on playback, for one reason or another, is called "distorted".

Documentary — in-depth examination of a particular issue, problem, or other news event. Frequently takes weeks or months to research and prepare. (*See also* Horizontal Documentary *and* Vertical Documentary.)

Dolby System — trade name for cassette sound system invented by Dr. Ray Dolby. Involves electronic coding on tape to widen "dynamic range" while lessening tape and equipment noise.

Double-cut — use of two pieces of tape in a particular news story. Cuts can be of the same type, even the same person. Used to give "in-depth" treatment to story and sometimes to surprise the audience.

Double Out-cue — ending words on a tape cut appear twice. Cut must be marked so newscaster realizes not to use the scripted tag after the first time the words appear. Cut can be logged with words: "Double Out-cue" or "Second Time".

Double Play — reel tape of twice the usual length. Extra length achieved by using thinner tape, often one-third the normal thickness. Not recommended except for special recording applications, because this tape is notoriously fragile.

Drain — electrical energy taken from a battery. Refers to how much power the battery will lose under certain uses.

Drive-Time — periods of time when most radio stations have their largest audience. "Morning drive" lasts anywhere from 5-9 AM Monday through Saturday. "Afternoon drive" runs anywhere from 3-7 PM, Monday through Friday. Term is derived from large number of listeners who are driving to or from work.

Drop-out — sudden loss of all or part of signal on tape. Usually due to too little oxide coating on tape at that point. Can also be due to stretching of tape, or improper splice.

Glossary of Terms

Dual-Track — (*See* Two-track.)

Dual-Track Recorder — one term for a machine that can record two "monophonic" programs on one tape. Also called "half-track" or "two-track". (*See* Two-track.)

Dub — 1. Copy of a tape. 2. Electronic process of duplicating a tape. Involves playing the first or "master" tape, and recording one or more "dubs" from it.

Duty Cycle — period of time an electric device (usually "bulk-eraser") can be continuously operated without internal damage. Usually not more than a few minutes.

Dynamic Microphone — generally good-quality microphone widely used in both studio and outside applications. Sound strikes diaphragm, which is attached to coil, generating electric current. Generally very rugged mikes, most suitable for outside news coverage.

Dynamic Range — difference between the softest and loudest sounds a piece of equipment (tape or tape machine) can produce without noticeable distortion.

Earphones — small speaker(s) worn over the ear(s). Used in studios to monitor sound while it is being produced. Also known as "headphones", "headsets" or "cans".

Echo — reverberating effect caused by "live" rooms or areas, that don't contain sound-absorbing material, such as curtains or rugs. Sound bounces off these surfaces, and is picked up on tape several times. This effect can also be created electronically and is sometimes used to add fullness to a radio station's sound.

EdiTall — trade name for metal bar used to splice tape. Tape fits into recessed slot in bar, grooves provide cutting angle for razor blade. Good way to splice tape, easier and quicker than with mechanical cutting devices.

Editing — (*See* Splicing.)

Editorial — official "feeling" or "position" voiced by station management on a particular issue. Theoretically, an editorial also states facts in support of the opinion.

Electret Condenser Microphone — good-quality mike that contains its own power supply from a built-in battery. Provides high-quality at a moderate-to-high cost.

Electrical Noise — unwanted discharges picked up on tape. Generally involves "static", possibly ignition noise from a car, or truck, or noise from a large motor.

Electronic Splicing — actually a process of dubbing tape cuts onto cart. Various fragments are then electronically joined. Not recommended except in critical, last-minute situations.

Enterprise Story — news item developed independently of other news media. Involves digging and investigation to uncover what may be hidden facts. Also known, in some cases, as an "investigative story". The exact opposite of "handout".

Equalization — process of changing blend of sound frequencies. Usually done as final step before tape cut is "dubbed" onto a cart. Through use of an "equalizer" it's possible to add low-frequency sounds to an otherwise "tinny" tape, or the other way around.

Erase Head — tape recorder head that removes previously recorded sound. This head is inactive during "playback" functions, and operates only when machine is in "record". Will remove old sound a split-second before new material is recorded.

Erasure — magnetic removal of sounds from tape. Can be done by the "erase head" of a tape machine, by a small magnet, or by a "bulk-eraser" which lifts all recorded sounds from a reel, cart, or cassette passed over its surface.

Evergreen — a story that will not become dated, quickly. Generally refers to a story that can be saved for use later.

Exclusive — important story that is being reported by only one radio station, or other news medium.

Eyewitness Actuality — tape of someone who actually saw a "spot news" development. One type of actuality.

Fact Sheet — background story information designed to help newscasters write tape stories. Also known as "poop sheet".

Fade — gradual lowering of volume.

Fader — (See Sliding Pot.)

False Cue — unwanted stop (or "Primary") cue put on cart. Can be left over from poorly-erased previous recording, or put on accidentally. Carts with a false cue must be re-done to prevent mistakes on the air.

Fast Forward — tape machine function that rapidly moves the tape ahead, in the same direction it runs while in "record" or "play". Used to locate appropriate section of tape. Rapid movement in the other direction is called "rewind".

F.C.C. — abbreviation for Federal Communications Commission.

Federal Communications Commission — U.S. governmental agency that regulates, among other things, broadcasting.

Feed Reel — (See Supply Reel.)

Feed Through — (See Cross Talk.)

Feedback — high-pitched howling or whine caused when signal rapidly recirculates through board, speaker, headphones or on-air signal.

Feeding — Process of transmitting a tape cut, or live report, to a newsroom. Term can also be applied to material going "live" on the air, however.

Female — one part of an electronic connection. Usually a "jack" or "socket". The male connector, usually a "plug" will fit inside.

Fidelity — quality and accuracy with which sound is recorded or reproduced by certain equipment.

flack — (usually not capitalized) one term for a public relations man or woman.

Flag — 1. Paper inserted within reel of tape, indicating location of cut(s). 2. Microphone attachment advertising call letters, etc.

Flash — highest priority wire-service news material. Usually a story that can be told in two or three words: "Kennedy shot." "Nixon resigns."

Flat Response — sound reproduction that is equal in level throughout the entire range of human hearing. No parts of the "audio frequency" spectrum are increased or reduced in level.

Flutter — short, quick variations in tape speed. Causes annoying distortion in sound "pitch" and sometimes "volume". Similar to another speed variation called "Wow".

FM — abbreviation for "Frequency Modulation."

Foot Switch — mechanical pedal that stops and starts tape recorder. Now generally replaced by hand-held remote-control switches, commonly used with cassette recorders.

Format — overall concept of a radio station's sound. Includes factors like music, news, personalities, along with number and placement of "spots" and "jingles". May be only a broad overall idea. Can also be highly detailed, rigid set of slogans and top songs that are endlessly repeated. When a station changes formats, something else may change too. (See Housecleaning.)

Four-track Recording — recording over one-quarter of tape-width, which leaves room for four separate "tracks" or "recordings". Found only on some reel-to-reel machines. Not generally used for news purposes. Cannot be edited without affecting all tracks.

Freebie — story that involves something free for person covering it. Can be luncheon speech which will be genuinely newsworthy, and also includes free lunch. Can also be

Glossary of Terms

ethically-questionable free trip and expenses, for reporting of story in which trip-provider has a vested interest. (*Also see* Junket.)

Frequency — measure of vibrations per second. We hear between 15 and 20,000 Hertz (or vibrations) per second. Radio stations transmit their signals at a much higher range, expressed in Kilohertz (1,000 Hertz) and megahertz (1,000,000 Hertz) for AM and FM respectively.

Frequency Modulation — method of transmitting broadcast signal, by changing (modulating) frequency. Used to denote "FM band" of stations between 88 and 108 MHz.

Frequency Response — upper and lower limits of sounds that can be produced, without unacceptable "distortion", by certain equipment. Also known as "frequency range".

Full-track Recording — recording using the entire width of the tape. Means only one thing can be recorded at any one point on the tape. Found on most reel-to-reel machines designed for broadcast use.

Futures File — system for keeping track of stories before they occur. Uses folder for each day, advance word on upcoming stories is filed accordingly.

Gain — 1. Technical term for the increase in a signal between its "input" and "output". 2. The same thing as "level" or "volume". 3. The same as "pot" or "volume control" as in: "Turn up the gain".

Gap — incredibly tiny distance between the positive and negative poles of a tape recorder "head". Generally runs between 1/10,000 and 1/20,000 of an inch. At this point, all recording and playing of the tape actually takes place.

Generation — relationship of a particular tape to the original recording, known as a "master." Tape dubbed directly from a "master" is first-generation." Tape dubbed from a "first generation copy" is "second generation" and so on.

Ground — point in an electrical system that has no voltage. Usually the "chassis" or sometimes an actual wire link to the soil, or a cold-water pipe.

Half-track — (*See* Two-track.)

Handout — story provided by someone involved in it, who wants publicity. Ranges from routine news releases cranked out by PR departments, all the way to the "Pentagon Papers", given to the *New York Times* for publication. Tape can be handed out, too, by phone or through the mail.

"Hard" Lead — general term for some scripted introductions to tape cuts. These specifically-worded leads are required because tape cut doesn't tell whole story and otherwise wouldn't make sense. This category is subdivided in this book.

"Hard" News — story that is newsworthy as judged by traditional standards. Usually an action, occurence, or statement. The opposite of "soft" or "feature" news, which may deal more with human conditions, feelings, and emotions.

Harmonics — middle and high-frequency vibrations present in all speaking and music (except that produced by some electronic instruments). These multiples of the basic frequency of speech or music are not consciously heard, but add an important brilliance and clarity to listening. (*Also see* Crisp.)

Head — electro-magnetic device upon which everything else in a tape recorder depends. Erase head removes previously-recorded magnetic impulses from tape. Record head imprints magnetic impulses onto oxide layer of tape. Playback head scans the tape, sensing the impulses, which are then translated into sound.

Head Alignment — (*See* Alignment.)

Head Demagnetizer — device that removes built-up magnetism from tape

machine heads. Similar in principle to "bulk-tape eraser" but much smaller, magnetic field is concentrated in small tip. (Also known as "head degausser".)
Head Lifter — (*See* Tape Lifter.)
Hertz — (abbreviated Hz) new term for "cycle". One-thousand Hertz is one "kilohertz". One-million Hertz is one "megahertz". (*Also see* Cycle.)
HFR — (*See* Hold-for-Release.)
Hiss — high-pitched "S" sound resulting from background noise on tape. Especially a problem on cassettes.
Hold-for-Release — story that is done in advance of actual intended use. "Hold" can be ordered by news source (as is frequently the case on "handout" material) or by reporter, who wants undated story saved for later use. (*See also* Canned Tape.)
Horizontal Documentary — documentary produced in traditional form, running continuously, from beginning to end. (*See also* Vertical Documentary.)
Hotline — direct telephone connection to a newsroom. Frequently used to receive news tips from listeners, in return for incentive of some sort.
Housecleaning — sudden and often total replacement of station air-staff (sometimes involving other departments as well). Usually accompanied by a change in management, change in format, hiring of a consultant, bad ratings, or a combination. Usually done in person, accompanied by an apology, and two-weeks severance pay. But sometimes done through a brief phone call, informing you that you're unemployed.
Hum — droning, low-pitched noise, produced by electrical malfunction, or leakage onto tape.
Hz — (*See* Hertz.)
ID — term meaning "station identification". Consists of station call letters and location (in Canada, just call letters) announced on or near the top of the hour. Also referred to as a "legal ID" since it's required by government regulations.
IFB — Interruptable Foldback (or Feedback). Method of combining program material and cue information on one circuit. Commonly used for live reports.
Impedance — resistance (measured in ohms) to AC electric current in a circuit. Commonly referred to as "high" and "low" impedance in tape recorders and microphones. Hookups between different pieces of equipment must match in impedance, otherwise distortion or low-level recording results. Impedance is also abbreviated: "Z". (*See also* Mismatch.)
Inches per Second — (abbreviated "ips") measure of tape speed as it passes "capstan" of machine. Reel-to-reel and carts for broadcast commonly operate at 7½ ips, cassettes at 1⅞ ips. Tape speed is determined by number of revolutions in capstan, which pulls tape past heads of machine.
In-cue — beginning few words of a tape cut.
Index counter — (*See* Counter.)
Inflection — natural raising or lowering of voice pitch and volume. Used to give emphasis to speech, and provide vocal punctuation. Generally, spoken sentences end with a "down" inflection. Sometimes, for editing purposes, cuts must be ended with a "neutral" or "up" inflection, which must be compensated for by newscaster.
In-line Heads — stereo head arrangement. Two head gaps (and thus recording tracks) are located one directly above the other. (Also called "stacked heads".)
Input — signal fed into a tape recorder through a microphone, patch cord, or some other source. Also used to mean "input jack" which is the female receptacle for an incoming signal.
Interference — general term for all unwanted sounds on a radio signal.

Glossary of Terms

Includes "static" and all other distractions.

Interview — a conversation between one or more reporters, and one or more news sources. Usually thought of as a "question-and-answer session".

Inverter — (See Converter.)

ips — (abbreviation for "Inches per Second".) Usually in lower-case letters, with no periods between.

Jack — female connector, commonly used to transfer electrical sound current. Used with male connector, a "plug", which fits inside the "jack".

Jingle — recorded singing, usually of station call letters or slogan. Can run from less than a second to over a minute, depending on "format" of station.

Junket — news story that includes trip for reporter covering it. Sometimes trip is provided, free, by group involved in story. Thus, reporter is used as vehicle for free publicity. Term "junket" itself connotes ethically-questionable practice. (Also see Freebie.)

kcs — abbreviation meaning "kilocycles". Now generally replaced by new term "kHz" for "kilohertz". (See Cycle and Hertz.)

Key — one term for multi-position switches. Used occasionally when referring to switches on a "board".

kHz — abbreviation meaning "kilohertz" or "thousand-cycles". (See Cycle and Hertz.)

Kicker — humorous or light-hearted story sometimes used at end of newscast.

* **Kinky Lead** — introduction that uses tape cut to complete a scripted sentence. Newscaster ends on "up" inflection in middle of sentence, tape cut completes it. This flashy technique should not be used routinely.

Knob — actually the piece of metal or plastic that is turned to change an internal equipment function. More commonly referred to in radio as a "pot", short for "potentiometer".

* **Lag Time** — difference between time a cart is started and when audio material begins. Ideally should be around one-half second, allowing cart enough space to re-cue without "burping". Lag time should be completely silent, with tape cut starting cleanly.

Lead (pronounced: LEED) — 1. Scripted story of one or more sentences that introduces a tape cut. Used with a scripted "tag" that follows tape cut. 2. Short for "lead story" which is first, and usually most important, story in newscast.

Lead Story — (See Lead, definition two.)

Leader Tape — non-magnetic plastic (or sometimes paper) tape. Several feet are commonly spliced to both ends of magnetic reel-to-reel tape, to get full use of it. Can also be used to separate cuts within tape. Cassettes have this tape built-in at both ends, carts never use it. (Also called "timing tape".)

Legman — obsolete (and somewhat chauvinistic) term for an outside newsman. Now generally replaced by "reporter" which includes both male and female.

Level — strength or loudness of material being recorded or played back. (Also see Gain.)

Level Indicator — small meter on tape recorder that gives rough approximation of recording input volume. Generally has only a "black" and "red" area, with no other markings. Actually a small "VU meter". This indicator generally can also be used to check battery condition.

Line Cord — (See Power Cord.)

Line-Level Mike — microphone-amplifier combination that boosts low mike-level signal to higher line-level. Allows mike to feed phone line directly.

Line Noise — noise and/or distortion caused by telephone, network, or local broadcast line. Normally includes limiting of the frequency response.

Live — 1. Material that is not recorded and is thus broadcast as it is spoken. 2. Acoustical quality of a room or area that causes a great deal of reverberation. Lack of sound-absorbing material means sound will be picked up by recorder directly, and as it bounces off walls, floors, etc., leading to "echo" on tape.

Lockout — (*See* Sign-off.)

Log — legal record of radio station operations. Usually two types. "Station" or "program" log indicates placement and length of required program material, plus commercials. "Transmitter" log indicates required technical readings and changes. Both are subject to government inspection at any time.

Logo — (pronouced: LOW-go) 1. Small piece of advertising that fits onto microphone or microphone stand, and contains station call-letters, etc. Used when covering news events to get free publicity in television videotape, and newspaper pictures. 2. Musical theme to open radio newscast or other show, similar to singing "jingle". This is also known as a "news sig".

Look-Ahead Story — report done in advance of actual news event. Used to give background and significance to upcoming story. Sometimes includes speculation on what will occur. (Also known as "preview story".)

Loudness — relative strength of sound, measured by human ear. This roughly corresponds with VU meter scale, in most cases.

Low-Noise Tape — improvement over standard tapes, reduces "hiss" and other background noise. However, term has become overused as an advertising gimmick. Not all "low-noise tape" deserves to be called that.

Magnetic Field — force generated by recording heads in transferring impulses onto tape. Also generated by bulk-eraser in removing them.

Major Market — generally, cities with over one-million in total population. Includes all radio stations in those cities, as well as strong ones licensed to nearby cities that capture a significant part of the audience. (No commonly-accepted definition of this term exists. Some limit it to the ten largest American and two largest Canadian cities.)

Male — one part of an electronic connection. Usually a "plug" which fits into a female "jack" or "socket".

Marginal Quality — tape that is barely useable on air. Content, however, may justify use of a short cut of this tape.

Master Tape — actual recording of a news program or event. Any number of "masters" can be recorded at one time, directly from the source. From these, "dubs" are made. (*See also* Generation.)

Medium Market — generally, cities between 100,000 and one-million in total population. Includes all radio stations in those cities as well as strong ones licensed to other nearby cities that capture a significant part of the audience. (No commonly-accepted definition of this term exists.)

Microcassette — miniature recording device similar to, but ¼ the size of a "cassette". Contains a feed and take-up reel of tape, completely enclosed in a protective plastic housing. Used in broadcasting to record news outside the station with a "Microcassette recorder".

Microphone — device that converts sound waves into electrical energy by various means. (Also known as "mike" or "mic".)

Mid-days — period from 9 AM to 3 PM Monday through Friday.

Mike — radio term for "microphone".

Mike Fright — fear of talking into a microphone. Very common, not only among people being interviewed, but among radio people early in careers, or on new jobs.

Mike Stand — base, usually metal or plastic, that supports a microphone.

Glossary of Terms

Term includes "desk stand" and "floor stand".

Mil — measure of, among other things, thickness of recording tape. A mil is 1/1,000 of an inch. Recording tapes generally vary from 0.5 to 1.5 mils.

Mismatch — improper impedance hookup. Happens when output of one piece of equipment is fed into another piece of equipment which has different electrical resistance. Result is distortion or low-level recording. (*See also* Impedance.)

Mixer — device used to combine sounds from different sources. Contains two or more "pots" which regulate sound levels from each source, into a common output.

Mixing — the actual combining of sound from different sources. Usually done through a "mixer".

Mobile Telephone — phone receiver and transmitter that broadcasts over airwaves, to point where signal is fed into telephone lines. Used at some stations for communications between a newsroom and reporters in mobile units.

Modular — telephones with standardized connector cords, plugs, and jacks, allowing easy removal. A phone with nothing but modular connectors linking the handset, base and phone wall jack is said to be "fully modular".

Modulation — electrical strength of a signal, measured on a VU meter. Close to, but not always the same as "loudness" measured by the human ear. (*Also see* Over-modulation.)

Monaural — (*See* Monophonic.)

Monitor — 1. Verb meaning "to listen". 2. Marking sometimes used instead of "output" or "speaker". Indicates jack on tape recorder where patch cord can be connected to transfer recorded tape to another piece of equipment. 3. Police or fire monitor, used to listen to their communications.

Monitor Head — also known as "playback head". Allows checking of tape as it is being recorded.

Monophonic — tape recorder that plays back one complete channel of sound at a time. Differs from "stereophonic" (2 channels) and "quadraphonic" (4 channels). Also refers to tape which has been recorded with "monophonic" signal. Tape can actually contain up to four "tracks" of material, but only one is played back at any one time.

Montage — originally a French term for a picture made up of several parts. In news, an actuality made up of several voices. Usually used to present public opinion and thinking on a story. Sometimes known by Latin term "Vox Populi" meaning "voice of the people".

Morgue — file of old tape stories. Used to maintain important tape cuts for reference, legal trouble, contests, year-end reviews, or continuing-interest stories.

Morning Drive — period of time from Monday through Saturday when a radio station characteristically has its highest audience. Lasts anywhere from 5 to 9 AM depending on the city. Name derived from great number of people listening in cars while going to work.

Muddy — (*See* Bassy.)

Mult-Box — audio distribution center commonly used on major pre-planned news stories, especially those involving national news coverage. Allows one or two microphones to feed all recorders and live broadcast equipment.

Natural Sound — (*See* Sound.)

Nemo — obsolete term for "remote".

Net — abbreviation for "network".

Network — news organization that feeds tape, and sometimes "live" news material, to subscribers. There's no real dividing line between term and "audio service".

News Block — extended news programming. Usually thought of as being over 15 minutes in length. At some stations, may include several hours of news, or continuous news, broken up into segments.

Newscast — capsule summary of news stories. Usually lasts no more than 15 minutes. (Longer continuous newscasts are frequently called "news blocks".)

Newscaster — person who reads news on the air, and frequently writes his or her own material.

News Cruiser — one term for "news car" or "mobile unit". Originated in days when reporters would "cruise" around the city, looking for news.

News Director — person responsible for overseeing and managing operation of news department. Usually has powers of hiring and firing, and is responsible for day-to-day decisions.

News Peg — (See Angle.)

News Release — (See Handout.)

News Sig — (See Logo, definition two.)

Nicad — (See Nickel-Cadmium.)

Nickel-Cadmium — a rechargeable battery made of these two elements.

Noise — general category for any unwanted sound that is picked up on tape. Sometimes due to tape, machine, or recording conditions. (Also see Background Noise, Hum and Hiss.)

Null — area(s) in which a microphone will not pick up sound. Can range from null in one direction from microphone, to a mike "pickup pattern" that rejects sound from all areas except one.

O&O — abbreviation for network owned-and-operated station(s).

* **Octopus** — patch cord device allowing phone feeding through modular handset plug, modular line cord plug, and alligator clips.

Off-mike — acoustic characteristic where sound is picked up at a distance from microphone, or outside of normal microphone pattern. Tape will sound "boomy".

Ohm — measurement of electrical resistance or "impedance". (See also Impedance and Mismatch.)

One-on-one — personal interview involving one reporter and one newsmaker.

Open Reel — another term for "reel-to-reel" or "reel" tape. Refers to any size reel which must be manually threaded through tape recorder.

Out-cue — final words on a tape cut. Sometimes also used to indicate "sign-off" . . . the name and location of the reporter doing the story.

Out-dated — (See Dated.)

Output — signal or power coming out of a piece of equipment. Refers to sound from speaker, or electric voltage delivered to output jack(s) in tape recorder.

Outtakes — taped material that is not used on the air for one reason or another. Can be either erased, or discarded.

Over-modulation — recording or playback of signal that is too strong. Can be corrected by carefully watching VU meter, and listening to sound. (See also Distortion.)

Oxide — coating of microscopic magnetic particles on tape. The needle-like pieces are stuck together in a "binder" and coated on the plastic "base" of the tape. They are magnetized during recording, and maintain their magnetic force until erased.

* **Paraphrase Lead** — introduction to tape cut that summarizes it in different words. Lead actually paraphrases content. One of the most basic and useful leads.

Patch — temporary electronic connection between two pieces of equipment, usually accomplished by joining them with a "patch cord".

Patch Bay — (See Patch Panel.)

Patch Cord — cord used to make temporary electronic contact between two pieces of equipment. Most have a "plug" at both ends, some have a

Glossary of Terms

"jack" or set of "alligator clips" at one or both ends. This general term is modified by describing the connectors at both ends: "mini-plug-to-alligator-clip patch cord".

Patch Panel — piece of equipment used to make temporary electronic connections. Contains row(s) of "jacks" which have been internally wired to connect with other equipment.

Pause Control — useful feature on some reel and cassette machines that allows tape to be stopped temporarily. In most cases, "pinch roller" simply disengages, stopping tape travel, while other machine functions remain on. Helpful in cueing and editing.

Peak — maximum level of sound produced by a piece of equipment. Term usually refers to modulation as recorded on a "VU meter." (See also Average Peak).

Peg — (See Angle).

* **Permission Sentence** — words needed for legal permission to record, or broadcast live, a phone conversation. Under FCC rules, this must come before a phone interview.

Pickup Pattern — directions or areas surrounding microphone where sound can be received. Refers to "lobe(s)" which are in pickup area, and "null(s)" which are not. There are many types of pickup patterns, such as "cardioid," "figure 8" etc.

Pinch Roller — freely rotating rubber wheel that holds tape tightly against "capstan." Permits tape to be drawn, by capstan, at constant speed, and turns itself, as tape moves. (Also called "pressure roller," and occasionally "capstan idler" or "puck").

Pipes — resonance in a voice. (See also Ballsy).

Pitch — frequency of spoken or musical tone. (See also Audio Frequency, Ballsy, Bassy, and Crisp).

Playback — reproduction of already-recorded magnetic signals on tape. In this function, only the "playback head" of a tape machine is in use.

Playback Head — magnetic head that reproduces already-recorded sound. Located at the far right in any head assembly. Sometimes combined with the "record" head.

Plosive — sound like letters "B" and "P" that involves lip noise and forcing air out of mouth. Can, in some circumstances, cause explosive "popping" noise as air-blast hits microphone.

Plug — male connector, commonly used to transfer electrical sound current. Fits inside a female connector, known as a "jack" or "socket".

Polyester Base — recording tape base. Does not break easily, but tends to stretch under extreme force.

Poop Sheet — (See Fact Sheet).

Pop Filter — provision, built into microphone, to limit breath noises. Often confused with external "windscreen".

Popping — noise caused by air-blast into microphone. Usually comes when speaking letter "P," or in some cases, "B." Due to an improper microphone technique, microphone placement, or a combination. (Sometimes referred to as "popping your P's").

Post-Equalization — changing of frequency composition of tape after it has been recorded, to preserve fidelity. Commonly done in unit connected from output of reel-machine to input of cart-machine. Also known a "post emphasis." (See also Equalization).

Pot — (abbreviation for "potentiometer"). Rotary volume control device. Raises or lowers sound levels. Also known as "rotary pot." (See also Sliding Pot).

Potentiometer — (See Pot).

Power Amplifier — device that increases tape recorded signal so it can be played through a speaker.

Power Cord — cord that supplies electrical current to equipment. Runs from wall socket to jack on equipment. Also known as "line cord."

Pre-Amplifier — device that increases extremely weak signal from playback head of tape recorder. Usually raises signal level to where it can be further amplified by a "power amplifier."

Pre-Equalization — changing of frequency composition of material before it is recorded, to preserve fidelity. Commonly done in unit that connects to input of tape recorder. Also known as "pre-emphasis." (*See also* Equalization).

Pre-Recorded Tape — tape of any type, recorded commercially. Usually contains music or educational material.

Presence — intimacy of sound. Tape with this quality will have illusion of being very close by, distinct, and natural. Due to proper balance of frequencies in tape, or correct equalization.

Press Card — identification card issued by a radio or TV station, government, or law-enforcement agency. Frequently required when covering stories where security is involved, such as Presidential trips, disaster scenes, or riots. As a general rule, you should apply for any local or state press card you might possibly need. If none are available, make one yourself, and coat it with plastic laminate.

Press Release — (*See* Handout).

Pressure Pad — pad of foam rubber, felt, or lubricated plastic that pushes tape against head(s). Found inside all cassettes and carts. Also found on many reel-to-reel machines.

Pressure Roller — (*See* Pinch Roller).

Preview Story — (*See* Look-Ahead Story).

Print Journalism — news reporting that relies on written, rather than spoken words. Includes all reporting for "print media" such as newspapers, magazines, books, etc.

Print-through — leakage of magnetic signals from one layer to another when tape is stored. Results in "echo" effect, as sound is heard in several places. Can be minimized by use of special tape.

Professionalism — ability and dedication of a particular news person or organization. Refers to a combination of on-air, reporting, writing and interviewing skills, as well as ethical practices, to produce a top-notch news product. No real standards of "professionalism" exist, this elusive quality is judged, subjectively, by others in the profession.

PSA — (Abbreviation for "Public Service Announcement"). Mention on air of worthwhile event or service. PSA time is donated by station to advertise worthy causes, free of charge.

Puck — (*See* Pinch Roller).

Push-to-talk Switch — switch that disconnects microphone in telephone mouthpiece. Used when gathering tape over phone, to eliminate background noises.

Q-and-A — abbreviation for "Question-and-Answer." Another term for "interview."

Quad — (*See* Quadraphonic).

Quadraphonic — recording employing four channels at once. Reproduced with speakers at left and right in front, and left and right in back of listening position. Used only for music, has no news applications.

Quarter-Track — (*See* Four Track).

* **Question Lead** — introduction to tape cut that poses a question. Tape is used as an answer, sometimes in direct response.

Radio Wire — AP or UPI (in Canada, BN) wire designed for broadcast use. Supposedly, material transmitted on this wire is written for broadcast. However, this is frequently not the case.

Random-Reaction Actuality — tape of someone reacting to a news story. One type of actuality.

Ratings — periodic measurement of a radio station's audience size and

Glossary of Terms

composition. Can be done by telephone survey, in-home diary-keeping, or a combination. Many radio people regularly live and die by this audience estimation. When ratings are bad, changes may occur. (*See* Housecleaning).

Raw Tape — recorded material that has not been spliced or edited. Also known as "raw sound" or "uncut tape."

Record Head — magnetic head that translates sound material into magnetic waves. Head transfers magnetic force onto tape in process known as "recording."

Recording — 1. Tape used to store sound material. 2. Process of applying magnetic force to tape, thus placing sound material on it.

Record-playback Head — combination head that performs both recording and playback functions. Found in cassette recorders, and some reel-to-reel units.

Reel-to-reel Tape — recording tape wound on plastic or metal reels. Reel tape must be threaded over heads and guides of a reel machine, and onto a "take-up reel." This tape is used for most recording in the newsroom, and all splicing.

Remote Pickup — radio communications device that links newsroom with reporters in mobile units. Provides superior quality, allowing reporters to feed material with almost no loss in sound.

RENG — acronym for "Radio Electronic News Gathering". Actually, radio never had any other kind (except for pencil and notepad). This meaningless term grew from ENG ("Electronic News Gathering") which replaced film in TV news during the 1970s.

Reporter — general term for someone who gathers and reports news. Usually refers to someone working outside, but can also apply to a newsperson gathering material over the phone.

Reproduce Head — (*See* Playback Head).

Response — output characteristics of a particular piece of equipment. Usually "frequency response," the range between the lowest and highest sounds the equipment will record and/or reproduce.

Resume — written listing of job experience, personal background, education, and references. Used when applying for jobs. (*See also* Aircheck).

Rewind — tape machine function that rapidly moves tape backward, in the opposite direction it runs while in record, play, or fast forward. Used to back-up tape for editing, or to replace it onto "feed reel" for storage.

Re-write — the opposite of "rip-n-read." Involves writing stories for air use, using wire copy as source material only. Generally, there's a direct relationsip between the "professionalism" of a news operation, and the amount of rewriting it does.

RF — (abbreviation for "radio frequency"). Portion of frequency spectrum used to transmit radio and television signals.

Ribbon Microphone — extremely sensitive, high-quality microphone suitable only for studio work. Thin strip of metal is suspended in magnetic field inside microphone, and moves when sound waves strike, creating electrical current.

Ride Gain — process of continually adjusting level(s) in recording, or actual broadcasting of material over the air. Sometimes necessary because of faulty recording, or sounds from different sources.

Rip-n-read — practice of using wire copy on air. Frequently used as derogatory term, referring to "rip-n-read operations" that have incompetent, lazy, or limited news staffs. (*Also see the opposite term:* Re-write).

Room Noise — (*See* Background Noise).

ROS — abbreviation for: "Reporter on scene." Occasionally used instead of "ROSR."

ROSR — (pronounced: ROSE-rrr) Abbreviation for "Radio On-Scene Report." Tape of reporter recorded at story location. Also sometimes known as a "scener."

Rotary Pot — (See Pot.)

Routing Switcher — electronic patch panel used to make temporary audio connections inside a station. Functions through a push-button or dial-up control.

RPU — (abbreviation for "Remote Pick-Up").

RTNDA — abbreviation for "Radio Television News Directors Association." Professional organization to which many broadcast News Directors and other employees belong.

Scanner — radio monitoring device that "scans" a number of frequencies, and locks into one when it is transmitting. Commonly used to monitor police and fire departments. Since only one channel can be on speaker at a time, frequently much is missed.

Scener — one term for "on-scene report." Also known as "ROSR" or "Radio On-Scene Report."

Schematic — electronic diagram of a piece of equipment, showing the parts, or "components," and their electrical connections.

Screening Plate — metal plate that blocks out extraneous magnetic impulses from head. Commonly found on cassette machines.

Script — written material that is used in a newscast. Can contain a particular story in its entirety, or be used along with tape cut to tell a story. "Wire copy" can also be considered as a type of script. (See also Copy.)

Segue — (pronounced: SEG-way) A smooth transition between program elements. Used sometimes when referring to blending of music or of different sounds in a newscast. (Also see Crossfade.)

Self-threading Reel — tape reel that eliminates most manual-threading problems. Provided with some reel-to-reel machines to simplify tape handling.

Set — one label for a "record" button on a cart machine.

Shotgun Mike — highly-directional, usually highly expensive microphone. Used to pick up sounds from long distances away.

Sibilant — (pronounced: SIBB-ah-lint) A hissing "S" sound. Commonly found in words that have the letters "C," "S," "X" and "Z." Presence of some hissing from these sounds in play-back indicates correct "equalization" of tape. These usually are the highest-pitched sounds produced by the human voice.

Sidebar — secondary story related to a major one. In flood disaster, for example, one sidebar could be on relief operations, another on National Guard activation. Main story remains the flood and damage.

Signal-to-Noise Ratio — ratio, expressed in "dB," between sound output of equipment and noise caused by equipment.

Sign-off — 1) Traditional closing words of voicer or wraparound. Usually consists of reporter's name, station call letters, and location. 2) Announcement that a station is leaving the air temporarily.

Single-track Recording — (See Full-track Recording.)

Slaved — method of rebroadcasting signal of walkie-talkie unit through another radio unit. Commonly used to link walkie-talkie to mobile unit, where signal is received, and broadcast back to newsroom. Provides better quality and stronger signal than walkie-talkie alone.

Sliding Pot — volume control device that moves in a straight, instead of a circular, path. Raises or lowers sound levels when moved up or down. Also known as a "fader." Performs same function as a "rotary pot" (*See also* Pot.)

Slow News Day — day in which not much is happening. Saturday and Sunday traditionally fall into this category. As a result, news departments must generate their own stories.

Small Market — generally, cities under 100,000 in total population. Commonly, lowest levels of pay and professional standards exist in these markets. (No commonly-accepted definition of this term exists.)

"Soft" Lead — general term for some scripted introductions to tape cuts, generally voicers and wraparounds. These are nothing more than "teasers" used to introduce tape stories that are complete, or nearly complete, in themselves. This category is subdivided in this book.

Sound — one of the six basic "tape forms." Non-spoken recorded material, such as airplane roar, cows mooing, and rushing water, fall into category. Used to bring realism to scripted stories.

Source — 1) Sound source, such as a microphone, speaker, or another tape recorder. 2) News source, who provides material to a particular reporter or news organization.

Speaker Tap — temporary electronic connection used to record material from speaker. Involves hooking "alligator clips" to speaker "leads."

Speed — quickness with which tape passes by heads. Depends on speed of capstan, which controls tape movement. Broadcast reel-to-reel machines commonly operate at 15 and 7½ inches per second (ips). Carts run at 7½ ips, and cassettes at 1⅞ ips.

Splice — physical joining of two tape parts with "splicing tape."

Splicing — process of physically or electronically improving tape quality. Involves eliminating stumbles, pauses, and other imperfections in a particular cut of tape.

Splicing Block — grooved metal or plastic device that holds tape during splicing process. Commonly contains recessed area that secures tape, and two indented grooves to guide razor blade in cutting tape.. (*See also* EdiTall.)

Splicing Tape — special tape used for joining magnetic tape pieces together. Specially formulated to avoid being sticky, which could damage recorder heads and tape, itself.

Spot — radio term for "commercial" or "advertisement." Commonly sold in 10, 30, and 60-second lengths.

Spot-News — suddenly-breaking unexpected events. Usually involves happenings that fall under police or fire department jurisdiction, such as murders, robberies, accidents, explosions and so on.

Squawk Box — one term for a police or fire communications monitor.

Squeal — 1. High-frequency noise produced by "acoustic feedback." 2. Noise caused by friction between tape and recorder mechanism. Can be corrected by cleaning, or replacement of worn tape.

Static — pulsating interference with a radio signal. Commonly caused by electrical currents, and friction from cars and trucks, picked up on car radios. Static level on a given radio signal increases with the distance from the transmitter.

Stereo — sound recording and reproduction using two tracks simultaneously. Same sound is recorded from different angles, using two microphones (or one stereo microphone) and reproduced by two speakers placed at different locations.

Stringer — person who covers news, but is not actually on full-time payroll at a station. Usually paid a fee for each story used, or a small weekly or monthly salary. Utilized to cover news from the outlying areas where a full-time reporter is not necessary, or to beef-up in-town staff at key times.

Studio — enclosed room that shuts out most outside sound. Used for actual broadcasting. Some stations, however, do news from the newsroom itself.

Studio Quality — tape recorded in a studio.

Super Cardioid — fairly common microphone pickup pattern. Provides "heart-shaped" response. Most areas to back and sides of microphone are nulled. Areas in front and somewhat to sides are picked-up. A more concentrated pattern than the normal "cardioid."

Supply Reel — plastic or metal reel that supplies tape, usually located on left side of tape recorder. Also known as "feed reel." Used in combination with a "take-up reel" which collects tape passed over heads of machine.

** **Surprise Lead** — introduction to tape cut that gives no hint tape is actually upcoming. Tape is a surprise, has a different sound quality, and can jar daydreaming listeners back into consciousness.

Tag — scripted close to a tape story. Can consist of just speaker's name. But should include at least one complete sentence, presenting additional information along with a re-identification of the speaker.

Take-up Reel — plastic or metal reel that gathers tape after it passes over heads. Usually located on right side of tape recorder. Used in combination with a "supply reel" which normally stores the tape.

Talent — 1) Person who performs on the air. Includes newscasters, but does not include reporters and others in the newsroom. 2) Ability and/or potential. (*See also* Professionalism.)

Talk-Through — ability of cassette, Microcassette recorders to function as amplifier without actually recording.

Used to do live reports on telephone, bypassing mike in phone handset.

Tap — (*See* Speaker Tap.)

Tape — flexible plastic ribbon coated on one side with magnetic particles. Sometmes called "recording tape."

Tape Coil — magnetic tape that is wound together. Can refer to reel-tape, carts, or cassettes.

Tape Counter — (*See* Counter.)

Tape Deck — (*See* Deck.)

Tape Forms — six basic types of recorded news material. Includes "actuality," "Q&A," "voicer," "wrap-around," "voice-ality" and "sound."

Tape Guides — grooved posts, pins, or rollers located on either side of head assembly. Used to keep tape moving in proper place across heads.

Tape Lifter(s) — device(s) that remove tape from contact with heads during "rewind" and "fast forward." This prevents rapid loss of delicate head surface.

Tape Loop — 1) Short length of tape spliced together to form circle. Used with reel-to-reel recorder for tape "delay" system. 2) Tape length in a cart that extends from the hub, over the heads, and back.

Tape Mass — (*See* Tape Coil.)

Tape Player — unit that will only playback already-recorded tapes. Device is not able to record material. Usually refers to a cassette or cart machine that is strictly designed for public, rather than broadcast use.

Tape Speed — (*See* Speed.)

Teaser — (*See* Throwaway Lead.)

Telegraphone — original wire recorder, invented before turn of the century, that started magnetic recording.

Telephone Pickup — general term for devices that transfer phone conversations onto tape. Can be an "induction coil," "suction cup" or other similar device. Direct wiring of patch cord to phone, and equipment installed by the phone company itself do not fall into this category.

Glossary of Terms

Telephone Quality — tape recorded over a telephone.
Terminal — general term for several types of connection points.
Think-Piece — (*See* Analysis).
Throwaway Lead — introduction to tape cut that merely teases the audience, and does not, in itself, present any information. This is a general category which has been subdivided in this book.
Tightness — little or no separation between live and taped segments of a newscast. What is ideal for one station may sound awkward for another because of the "format."
Timing Tape — (*See* Leader Tape).
Tinny — sound that has little or no low-frequency material included, and is thus unpleasant to listen to.
Tip — piece of inside information which can be followed up into useable story.
Tipline — (*See* Hotline).
Toilet Break — what a newscast means to many disc jockeys.
Tone Control — pot, sometimes a switch, that controls quality of sound output from a tape recorder. On many units, this control will simply increase or decrease the amount of "treble." But on others, it can greatly change sound quality.
Tower(s) — metal structure(s) used to support broadcasting antennas located near the top. However, in AM radio, the tower itself forms part of the antenna, and radiates electrical energy into the air.
Track — sound path a "recording head" makes along a tape. Can involve entire tape width, or just a part of it. (*See also* Full Track, Two Track *and* Four Track *recording*.)
* **Traditional Lead** — introduction to tape cut that clearly mentions name and identification of speaker. May be used in combination with a time-worn phrase like: "The Governor tells reporters . . ." right before the cut.

Transmitter — piece of equipment that combines audible sound material, produced by a radio station, with a carrier signal. Both are then sent into an antenna, which radiates the combination into the air. The power of the transmitter is one of the key factors in determining the distance a signal will travel.
Transport — mechanical and magnetic parts of a tape recorder. Includes heads, controls, motor(s), etc. Does not include case, pre-amplifiers, or speakers.
Treble — higher frequency range of spoken or musical sound. Generally above middle-"C" on piano (256 Hertz).
Trickle Charge — gradual rejuvenation of batteries for portable equipment. Usually involves leaving unit plugged into wall socket overnight.
Tune-out — subjective term for any radio programming that does not interest listeners, and causes them to tune to another station, or mentally ignore the radio.
Tuner — electrical device that receives radio signals. Does not contain amplifier or speakers.
Turntable — mechanism for playing records. Includes revolving platform, along with "tone arm" and "needle." Used in combination with other equipment to amplify sound and put it on air.
Tweeter — speaker that produces high-frequency sounds. Usually used in combination with a "woofer" in a speaker system to reproduce entire sound range.
Two-track — recording over one-half of tape width, leaving room for two "tracks" or "recordings," one in each direction. Found on all cassette machines, as well as many reel-to-reel machines. Cannot be edited without affecting both tracks.
Two-way — a type of radio unit designed for basic communications. Has

quality approximately the same as a telephone. Used for communications between a newsroom and reporters in mobile units.

Uncut Tape — (*See* Raw Tape.)

Uni-directional microphone — mike that picks up sound from only one direction. Usually has a highly-concentrated "pickup pattern" that is designed to receive sound over long distances. (*see also* Shotgun Mike.)

Upcut — cart incorrectly produced so it recues during first word. First syllable is lost when cart is played on air. It then appears as a "burp" on air, when cart recues.

Urgent — news material of more than routine importance. Ranks below "bulletin" and the highest-priority material, slugged "flash" on wire service machines.

Velocity Microphone — (*See* Ribbon Microphone.)

Verbatim — tape handling system used at some networks that includes transcripts of tape cut.

Vertical Documentary — documentary produced into several "segments" not broadcast all at once. This type is commonly spread out over several days, with one segment running each day, in the same time period. (*See also* Horizontal Documentary.)

Virgin Tape — tape that has never been used for recording.

Voice-Act — telephone device, intended for radio news use, that amplifies and improves sound. Used for outside applications, screws onto phone, in place of regular "mouthpiece."

Voice-Actuality — (*See* Wraparound.)

Voice-ality — one of the six basic "tape forms." This is a tape of a news reporter ad-libbing, or seeming to ad lib. It is used frequently to cover stories where mood, color, and emotion play a large part.

Voicer — one of the six basic "tape forms." This consists of a reporter doing a written, prepared, story, frequently "signing off" with his or her name and location.

Volume — measurement of sound waves, rather than electricity. Refers to sound intensity, heard by the ear.

Volume Control — (*See* Pot.)

Vox Populi — (*See* Montage.)

VU Meter — meter that shows sound intensity in "Volume Units." Levels roughly correspond to normal human hearing. These meters actually indicate electronic strength of sound material being fed into or out of a tape recorder.

Walkie-talkie — battery-powered two-way radio device. Allows communications with other units on the same frequency. Used to report events "live" from areas where telephones are unavailable, or where their use is impractical. Also called "Handie-Talkie."

Wild Sound — (*See* Sound.)

Wind Noise — distortion caused by wind striking microphone, can result in explosion-like sound on tape. Limited by use of a "wind screen."

Wind Screen — protective cover for microphone that limits "wind noise." Usually made of foam rubber, sometimes fabric, to deflect force of wind from striking mike directly and causing noise on tape. (Often confused with "pop filter").

Wire Copy — news material written by the wire services (AP, UPI, etc.). (*See also* Rip-n-read.)

Wire Recorder — original type of magnetic recorder, from which conventional tape recorders were developed. First wire recorder, developed before 1900, actually used piano wire wound around a brass drum.

Woofer — speaker that produces low-frequency sounds. Usually used in combination with a "tweeter" in speaker system to reproduce entire sound range.

Wow — long, gradual variations in tape speed. Causes annoying distortion in sound "pitch." Similar to another speed variation called "flutter."

Wrap — 1) An abbreviation for "wraparound." 2) Technical term for contact between tape and heads of recorder. Sometimes angle of contact is measured.

Wraparound — one of the six basic tape forms. Consists of reporter introducing an "actuality" then closing off with perhaps more information, along with name and location. This form can be varied greatly. But all wraparounds, by definition, include one or more inserts of actuality or sound material.

Wrapper — abbreviation for "wraparound."

Z — abbreviation for "impedance." Usually used as "low-Z" or "high-Z" to indicate low or high impedance.

Index

A

actualities, 51, 52-54
   leads, 157-159
AGC (Automatic Gain Control), 110, 121
alligator clip feeds, 88, *89*
alligator clips, 107
all-news (stations), 6
Ampex, *2,* 3
audio connectors, 104-106, *105*

B

banana plug, 106, *107*
bare wire lead, 107
base station, 126
batteries, 122-123
   alkaline, 123
   carbon-zinc, 123
   mercury, 123
   nickel-cadmium (nicad), 123
block programmed, 6
Brady, John, 67
broadcasting (live), 125-138
   equipment, 126-133
   format, 136-137
   monitoring, 135-136
   problems, 133-135
   satellites, 137-138
broadcasting (tape), 51-66
Broadcasting Yearbook, 78

C

canned tape, 153-154
Cannon connector, 105, *106*
carbon microphone, 89, 97, 117
cardioid-pattern mike, 115
cart (cartridge), 15, *16,* 48-50
   cleaning, 19
   erasing, 23
   recording time, 18
   splice-finding, 50
   winder, 49
Cassette Housing, 114
cassette recorder, 110-112
   features, 110-112
cassettes, 13, 112-113
   cleaning, 19
   erasing, 23
   recording time, 18
   repairs, 113-114
cellular telephone, 128-129
   hand-held, 131-132, *131*
ceramic mike, 118
Churchill, Sir Winston, 103
Citizens Band (CB), 152
Comrex, 98-99, *98*
condenser microphone, 118
confrontation situation, 150
contact point, 26
content (of tape), 51-66
control board, 9-11
   splicing, 25
cordless telephone, 133
corner post, 49
court, 151-152
Cox, Merrilee, 125
crispness, 74
Crosby, Bing, 3
cross-fade, 73

crystal mike, 117
cue, 44

D

dead cuts, 175
demagnetization, 19, *19*, 20
deregulation, 7
dial position, 10
DIN connectors, 106, *106*
distortion, 11
documentaries, 63
dual jack adapter, 86, 94-95
dubbing, 41-50
    carts, 48-50
    generations of, 47
    quality, 44-46
    seven steps of, 41-44
duty cycle, 23
dynamic microphone, 118

E

Edison, Thomas, 2
Edit button, 24
editing (*see also* splicing), 31-33
    internal, 35
    marking tape, 33
electret condenser mike, 97
equalizer, 74, *75*
equalizing (EQ), 73-75, *75*
    guidelines, 74
    telephone feeding, 83-84
equipment, 103-124, 126-135
    audio connectors, 104-107, *105*
    batteries, 122-123
    cassette recorder, 110-112
    cassettes, 112-114
    human, 103-104
    in-car radio systems, 126-130
    kits, 84-86, 107-110
    microcassette recorders, 114-116
    microcassettes, 116-117
    microphones (mikes), 117-122
    mixers, 123-124
    portable radio systems, 130-133
erasers (bulk)
    hand-held, 23, *23*
    heavy-duty, 21
    medium-duty, 22
erasing (tape), 21-23
eyewitness actuality, 149-150

F

faders, 10
Federal Communications Commission (FCC), 7
feedback, 12
feeding (telephone), 83-101
    alligator clip, 89, *89*
    equalizing, 84
    equipment & devices, 84-86, 92-93, 97-98
    frequency extenders, 98-99
    mixing, 94-95
    modular handset, 87
    modular line cord, 87-88
    networks, 99-101
    octopus kit, 85-86
    party lines, 92
    pay phone, 90-92
    problem phones, 92
    procedures, 86
    talk-through, 93-94
    voice act, 96-97, *96*
Fidelipac, 3, 48-49, *48*
forms (of tape), 51-66
    actuality, 51, 52-54
    montages, 64-65
    Q & A, 51, 54
    sound, 52, 64
    voice-ality, 52, 63-64
    voicer, 51, 54-61
    wraparound, 52, 61-63
feed tape, 140-142
frequency extenders, 98-99
frequency response, 10
fundamental frequency, 103

G

gain control, 10
Gibson Girl, 37-38, *37*
Graphic Equalizer, 74, 83

H

ham operators, 152
handling systems (for tape), 171-175
handset cord, 84
hard lead, 163
Hargett, Glenn, 136
harmonics, 103
heads, 13
    cleaning, 19
    demagnetizing, 19

Index

Hemingway, Ernest, 51
Hertz, 103
hotlines, 80-81

I

idler reel, 44
impedance (Z), 118-119
incue, 94
international broadcasters, 152
Interruptable Foldback (IFB), 136
interviews (personal), 145-147

J

jack, 104
Johnson, Nicholas, 9
jumping in, 44

K

Kendrick, Alexander, 1
kits,
    Cassette Editing & Repair, 113
    Level I, *107*, 108
    Level II, 108
    octopus, 84-86

L

labelling (tape), 169-176
    informational, 170-171
    numbered, 169-170
lag time, 45
late tape, 144-145
leads, 157-164
    actuality, 157-159
    dangers, 163
    hard, 163-164
    Q & A, 161-162
    sound, 162
    throwaway, 163-166
    voice-ality, 161-162
    voicer, 160-161
    wraparound, 160-161
LEDs (Light Emitting Diodes), 11
legalities,
    on-scene tape, 150-151
    telephone, 70-72
Lindsay, Harold, *2*
line cord, 84
lobe, 119
lollypop, 44

M

Magic of Radio, 8
magnetophone, 2
McLendon, Gordon, 6
microcassette recorders, 114-116
microcassettes, 13, 116-117
microphones (mikes), 117-122
    impedance, 118-119
    line-level, 119
    patterns, 119-120
    problems, 121-122
    systems, 121
    types, 117-118
    wireless, 133
Microtel, 97, *98*
mini-cassette, 116
mini-jacks, 84
mini-plugs, 84, 105, *105*
mixers, 123-124
mixing, 94-95
mobile telephone, 127-128
    hand-held, 131
mobile unit, 126
modular,
    duplex jack, 87
    handset feeds, 87, *87*
    jack, 84
    line cord feeds, 87-88, *88*
    mike system, 121
modulation, 11
montages, 65-66
morgue (tape), 175-176
mult box, 144, *144*
multiple cuts, 164
Murrow, Edward R., 1, 5

N

network (feeding), 99-101
news conferences, 78-79, 142-143
new (definition of), 7
newsgathering,
    on-scene, 68-70
    telephone, 67-82
noise reduction, 110
null, 119

O

octopus kit, 84-86
    building kit, 85
on-spec, 100
on-the-air, 10

opinion lines, 81-82
outcue, 94
over-modulation, 11
overtones, 103
oxide, 12, *13*, 15

P

patch cords, 84
patch panel, 11, *12*
patterns (pick-up),
   bi-directional (figure-eight), 120, *120*
   cardioid, 119, *120*
   omni-directional, 119, *120*
   super-cardioid, 119
   uni-directional (shotgun), 120, *120*
pay phone (feeds), 90-92
peak, 11
permission sentences, 70-71
personal interviews, 146-148
phone patch, 127
phone plug, 105, *105*
pick-up patterns (*see* patterns)
Picocassette, 116
Pillow Speaker, 90, *91*
playback, 13
plug, 104
Polillo, Pat, 83
pop-filters, 121
portable recorders (*see also* recorders (portable))
   history of, 3
pot (potentiometer), 10
Poulsen, Valdemar, 1
press conference, 142
press emergency, 79
proximity effect, 115
public relations (PR), 139
pulse dialing, 93
push-to-talk switch, 72-73

Q

Q & A, 54
   leads, 161-162
QKT coupler, 72
quarter modular, 93
quick tape, 145

R

radio,
   frequency (RF), 111
   in-car systems, 126-130

portable systems, 130-133
   station set-up, 9-10
random-reaction cut, 149
RCA plug (phone plug), 105, *105*
RCZ (recorder-connector), 72
recorders (portable), 110-119
   care & feeding, 117
   cassette, 110-112
   microcassette, 114-116
   mini-cassette, 116
   Picocassette, 116
reel-to-reel (tape), 13, *14*
   cleaning, 19
   erasing, 22
   splicing, 24-25
   table of recording times, 18
   thickness, 36
remote control jack, 111
remote pickups (RPU), 129-130, *129*
   hand-held, 132-133, *132*
RENG (Radio Electronic News Gathering), 125
repeaters, 127
reporting (live) (*see also* broadcasting (live)),
   history of, 4
reporting (situations), 139-154
   canned tape, 153-154
   confrontation, 150
   court, 151-152
   eyewitness actuality, 149-150
   free tape, 140-142
   late tape, 145-146
   legalities, 150-151
   news conferences, 142-143
   personal interviews, 146-148
   public relations (PR), 139
   quick tape, 145
   random-reaction cut, 149
   speeches, 143-145
   sources, 152-153
   tough tape, 148
ribbon microphone, 118
Rogers, Mike, 99, 101
ROSR (Radio On-Scene Report), 63
routing switchers, 11

S

satellites, 137
scanner, 153
scener, 63
scrambler, 127

sideband, 152
skimmer reel, 137
slave, 127, 129
slide pots, 10
Smyth, Dick, 41
soft lead (*see* throwaway lead)
sound, 65
   leads, 162
speech range, 126
speeches, 143-145
splice-finders, 50
splicing, 21-39, 113-114
   block, 3, 24, 37
   contact point, 26
   definition of, 23
   devices, 37
   electronic, 47-48
   ethics of, 39
   internal editing, 35
   marking tape, 33
   materials, 36, 38
   speeds & angles, 36
   tab, 38
   tape thickness, 36
   tips & shortcuts, 30-33
   twelve-steps of, 25-29
   undoing, 29
spot, 140
spot-news, 77-78
Squelch Tail, 136
SRDS, 78
stringers, 99
Strunk, William, Jr., 155
sub-mini plug, 105, *105*

T

tags, 164-166
talk-through, 93-94, 111
tape,
   cartridge, 15
   cassette, 13
   cleaning, 19
   coil, 49
   composition of, 12, 36-37
   dubbing, 41-50
   equalizing, 73-75
   erasing, 21
   forms & content, 51-66
   handling systems, 171-175
   labelling, 169-176
   philosophy of, 7
   recorder (definition), 13

   reel-to-reel, 13, *15*
   speeds, 16
   splicing, 21-39, 47-48
   tracks, 16
   types, 111
   when to not use, 66
taped-handout, 140
teaser (*see* throwaway lead)
technology,
   German, 2
telegraphone, 1, *1*
telephone,
   callbacks, 79-80
   cellular, 128-129, 131-132
   cordless, 133
   equalizing tape, 73-75
   equipment (for gathering), 72-73
   feeding, 83-101
   hotlines & Tipsters, 80-81
   legalities, 70-72
   mobile, 127-128, 131
   news conference, 78-79
   newsgathering, 67-82
   opinion lines, 81-82
   overseas calling, 79
   spot-news, 77-78
   tips, 76-77
   vs. on-scene, 68-70
throwaway lead, 163-166
   multiple cuts, 164
   tags, 164-166
thumbwheel, 11
tip, ring & sleeve connector, 106, *107*
tipsters, 80-81
top wire, 49
tough tape, 147
tracks,
   full-track (single-track), 16, 17
   two-track (half-track), 17
transmitter, 10
Turner, Ted, 6
tweaking, 91
two-way radios, 126-127, *126*

U

under-modulation, 11
uplinks, 137

V

velocity mike, 118
voice-act, 96-97, *96*

voice-alities, 63-65
  leads, 161-162
voicers, 54-61
  feeding, 59-61
  future tense, 59
  guidelines, 54-55
  leads, 160-161
  past tense, 58
  present tense, 58-59
  variety, 57-59
VU meter (Volume Units), 11

W

walkie-talkie, 130, *130*
Weather Radio (NOAA), 153

weather wire, 153
Welles, Orson, 139
wire guide, 49
wraparounds, 61-63
  amputated, 62-63
  compound, 63
  double, 61
  leads, 160-161
  standard, 61-62
writing (for tape), 155-167

X

XLR connector, 105, *106*

Z

Zappa, Frank, 21